THE

NEW ENGLAND THEOCRACY.

A HISTORY

OF THE

CONGREGATIONALISTS IN NEW ENGLAND

TO THE REVIVALS OF 1740

BY H. F. UHDEN.

WITH

A PREFACE BY THE LATE DR. NEANDER.

Translated from the Second German Edition

BY

H. C. CONANT,

AUTHOR OF "THE ENGLISH BIBLE," ETC. ETC.

BOSTON:

GOULD AND LINCOLN,

59 WASHINGTON STREET.

NEW YORK: SHELDON, BLAKEMAN & CO.

CINCINNATI: GEORGE S. BLANCHARD.

1858.

ELECTROTYPED AND PRINTED BY
W. F. DRAPER, ANDOVER, MASS.

TRANSLATOR'S PREFACE.

It is a singular fact, that the New England Theocracy has found no historian on our own shores. A subject so rich in interest, so intimately connected with our history as a people, it would seem should long since have busied some master-hand among ourselves. The record of this great experiment of our Puritan fathers, among the most unique and instructive in ecclesiastical history, is here for the first time presented for our study, as a connected whole, by a foreign scholar. This circumstance is, however, a ground rather of congratulation than regret; for the conflicting interests, germinated in the stormy infancy of New England, have still too much vitality, and have spread their roots too widely, to allow a native historian, of whatever creed, to escape the suspicion of partiality.

In the influences which originated and directed the present work, we have special cause of satisfaction. From the Preface by the late Dr. Neander, we learn that it was prepared under his own eye, by one whom he had selected as peculiarly fitted for the task; and that he gave his unqualified approval to its publication, —thus pledging his own name for its thoroughness, ability, and candor.

The work itself fully justifies this endorsement. From the list of authorities, at the end of the volume, it will be seen that the author had access to the original sources necessary for forming an independent and comprehensive judgment. The materials, thus obtained from a wide range of works, have been so thoroughly sifted and arranged as to present, within these moderate limits, a philosophical-religious sketch of the Congregationalist Theocracy, in which all the determining features of its character and career are clearly exhibited, in their inward relation to the system, and in their bearings on the final result. Thus viewed as a whole, the subject offers a study so instructive to all who are concerned for the progress of true religion and of human rights, that it seems strange that Uhden's work was not long since translated into English. This delay is the less to be regretted, as recent indications of change, in the policy of some of the religious bodies interested in the working of the principles here exhibited, will give it a fresh practical significance for the present time.

The closing chapter has a two-fold value. From Dr. Neander's Preface we learn, that the deep interest felt by that great man in the Revivals, which form so striking a feature in the religious life of this country, gave occasion to the present volume. The delineation and analysis of their peculiar characteristics, as exhibited in that earliest and purest type, the Awakening at Northampton under Jonathan Edwards, occupies the last forty pages; and the manner leaves us no room to doubt, that Uhden has here faithfully mirrored the views of his illustrious teacher and friend. His philosophic genius, and all-embracing christian heart, glow through every page. At the present moment, when our land is the scene of one of the most extensive and striking of these religious movements ever witnessed, the suggestions of a man like Neander cannot but have a deep interest for all thoughtful Christians. For those to whom, as preachers and pastors, is committed the guidance of these crises in the life of a great christian community, they possess a special value.

The translator has carefully verified the author's dates and statements of fact, and has given the extracts in their original English form. The liberty which has been taken of breaking the long chapters into sections, according to the subjects, will render the work more clear and convenient to the reader. The leading title, "The New England Theocracy," has been prefixed by the translator, as being the term constantly applied by the author himself to the peculiar politico-religious institution of which he treats, and as suggesting at the first glance the precise subject of the work.

H. C. C.

SEPTEMBER, 1858.

DR. NEANDER'S PREFACE

TO THE

FIRST EDITION.

The investigations, of which the results are here given to the public, received their first impulse from myself. Having been deeply interested, through a volume on the subject by the Rev. Dr. Sprague of Albany, in the Revivals of religion in North America, I solicited my highly valued young friend Uhden, (already honorably known by his biography of the great Wilberforce) to present in German these instructive details of occurrences so important, both in a psychological view, and in their relation to the history of the christian life. He acceded to my wish; but soon became convinced that a true understanding and correct judgment of these phenomena required a more thorough research into the ecclesiastical and religious condition of a country whose entire social state differs so widely from our own. Thus there grew up in his mind the plan of a more comprehensive historical development. From what he communicated to me of the plan and progress of his work, I was led to encourage him to complete it, and to give to the world the fruits of his extensive original investigations in this field. In this way arose the present work, as a necessary preliminary to the history of those religious awakenings, the delineation of which was at first his sole object.

The present can, indeed, in no case, be rightly

apprehended except in connection with what preceded and contributed to produce it. Hence, this Monograph will serve as preparatory to a correct view of the present ecclesiastical and religious state of that interesting land, so important in the world's commerce, and consequently in the world's history. It will show how the reäction from the one-sided principle of a Church-Theocracy, derived rather from the Old than from the New Testament, helped to bring about the subsequent total separation of Church and State. The more we suffer from the evils most strongly in contrast with the state of things in North America, — those, namely, proceeding from an intermingling of the Ecclesiastical and the Political, — the more all among us, to whom the highest interests of humanity are dear, long for an emancipation of the Church from the State, (not, however, that this absolutely requires that total separation of the two witnessed in North America); so much the greater interest, with reference to the present time, will attach to the development-course here portrayed by my friend. To desire and to labor for this, viz., that all the interests of humanity be allowed each its rights, and a free development according to its own peculiar laws; that no one of them be sacrificed to another, — this is the genuine, this is CHRISTIAN LIBERALISM.

* * * * * * *

DR. NEANDER.

CONTENTS.

CHAPTER I.

CHAPTER II.

CHAPTER III.

CHAPTER IV.

CHAPTER V.

CHAPTER VI.

DISSOLUTION OF THE THEOCRATIC RELATION, FROM THE ECCLESIASTICAL AND THE POLITICAL SIDE.

CHAPTER VII.

REACTIONARY INFLUENCES PROCEEDING FROM THE THEOCRACY AFTER ITS ABROGATION.

CHAPTER VIII.

DECLINE OF CONGREGATIONALISM.

CHAPTER IX.

THE REVIVALS.

THE

NEW ENGLAND THEOCRACY.

CHAPTER I.

RISE OF THE INDEPENDENTS IN ENGLAND—THEIR EMIGRATION TO HOLLAND.

REFORMATION IN ENGLAND UNDER HENRY VIII.

THE Independents, or Congregationalists, came forth from the bosom of the English Church under the reign of Queen Elizabeth. But to comprehend the distinctive form of these communities requires not only a consideration of the state of the English Church at that period, but a general survey of the circumstances which marked the origin and progress of the Reformation in England.

Henry Eighth had not commenced his struggle against the Papacy from a feeling of inadequacy in the existing condition of things to meet the religious wants of himself, or of the English people. It was solely from personal aims that he espoused a cause which, in the beginning of his reign, he had opposed with vehement denunciation and bloody persecution.

After a union of almost twenty years with Katherine of Arragon, he had become desirous of a divorce. His disquieted conscience, so he declared, was not appeased by the dispensation granted in 1503 by Pope Julius II.; such a union being contrary to the word of God, which forbids marriage with a deceased brother's wife.[1] These scruples of the king, which he began to express as early as 1526, were listened to with favor by Clement VII., and compliance was promised with his wishes. But through fear of the Emperor Charles V., nephew of the queen, this was deferred on one pretext after another, through a long course of years. By the advice of Cranmer, afterwards Archbishop of Canterbury, Henry at length solicited the opinions of the chief universities of Europe. Their answer was the same as had already been given at a convocation of the English clergy, viz., that it was neither according to the law of God that one should marry his brother's wife, nor had the pope power to grant a dispensation from the law of God. The pope, however, declared Katherine's appeal to the See of Rome valid, and cited the king to answer before him in person. Henry now resolved not only to break off connection with Rome, but to abolish the pope's authority altogether. This authority he transferred to his own hands. But a large portion of the clergy were at first disinclined to recognize the king as "sole and supreme head of the Church of England." Hence the clause was added, "so far as may be agreeable to the laws of Christ;" which was acceded to by the king; but on the subsequent confirmation of that title by Parliament and by another convocation of the clergy, it was stricken out. On the 23d of May, 1533, the king's marriage was declared void. The following year, an act of Parliament deprived the pope of all his revenues from England, and prohibited appeals to Rome, as also the papal confirmation of bishops.

[1] Levit. 18: 16. Comp. 20: 21.

The severe laws against heretics, enacted in former reigns, were now repealed, and license was granted for the translation of the Bible, which had hitherto been opposed with bloody persecution. Parliament, by the Act of 1534, in connection with the above-named title, conferred on the king, in express terms, the right of final decision in matters of doctrine. Thereupon followed a visitation of the monasteries, occasioned, in part, by the open resistance of the monks to the king's proceedings. This business was committed to Thomas, Lord Cromwell, vicar-general to the king in spiritual affairs, who as secretary to Wolsey, had already been made acquainted with a similar plan, and initiated into the methods for carrying it into effect. The cause of church reform was, moreover, one which lay near his own heart. Anne Boleyn, who had shown herself a zealous promoter of the Reformation, had, indeed, fallen not long after under the displeasure of the king, and was executed on the 19th of May 1536. But the Reformation was not thereby arrested; on the contrary, there now appeared the first indications that it was something more than a mere external work which was in progress, and the influence of those who were using Henry VIII. as an instrument for the attainment of higher objects, became clearly manifest. About Michaelmas, 1536, were set forth the first Articles of Faith; these having been approved by the king, were confirmed by the convocation of the clergy and by both houses of Parliament. The doctrine of Transubstantiation was taught in these articles; auricular confession and the worship of saints and images were retained, and the doctrine of purgatory was left doubtful. But with all this, they recognized the Holy Scriptures and the primitive confessions of the church as the standard of appeal, without reference to tradition or the papal decrees; and even admitted, though under somewhat vague terms, the doctrine of Justification by Faith.

These measures found a hearty response in England. Not indeed that the assent of Parliament is to be taken in proof; that body being always ready, not merely to gratify, but even to anticipate every arbitrary caprice of the king. But hardly would the pope's bull of excommunication have proved so impotent, hardly would the disturbances it created have been so easily quelled, had there not existed among the people themselves a disaffection towards their former relations to the Romish See. That direction of the popular mind, which owed its first impulse to the labors of Wickliffe, had not yet expended its force. Not merely had attention been turned to the crying abuses in the lives of the clergy and in the condition of the monasteries, but to that which was the source of all these evils, departure from the Holy Scriptures and from the fundamental doctrines of the Church. The movement thus originated within England itself had been still farther developed by the influence of the Reformation in Germany, whose traces we see in the martyrs of the earlier part of Henry's reign, and in Tyndale's English translation of the New Testament, (printed in Antwerp, so early as 1527.[1]) This connection manifested itself most decidedly in Cranmer. The king's wish for a divorce he had used for promoting reforms in the constitution and doctrines of the church; and in respect to the former, so much of a change had indeed been effected, as to transfer to the king the power hitherto exercised by the pope.

But because just this was effected and no more, the work came to a stand. True, the Holy Scriptures were trans-

1 In 1525, as shown by Anderson in his "Annals of the English Bible."—Tr.

lated into English, the monasteries were curtailed, visitations were instituted; but no farther steps could the king be induced to take. True, he had rejected the reconciliation proffered by the pope after the execution of Anne Boleyn; true, also, that her successor, Jane Seymour, was zealously devoted to the Reformation. But the death of the latter, in 1537, and the sundering of the king's subsequent marriage with Anne of Cleves, were followed by the fall of Cromwell, that active and skilful promoter of the Reformation. The influence of a powerful catholic party at court, to whose secret intrigues the favorite had fallen a victim during Henry's temporary displeasure, Cranmer was in no condition to counteract. Scarcely did the reverence with which his upright and irreproachable character had inspired the king suffice for securing his personal safety. The Six Articles, promulgated in June 1539, retained the doctrine of Transubstantiation, declared communion in both kinds to be unnecessary, the marriage of priests unlawful, vows of chastity of binding obligation, and required the continuance of private masses and auricular confession. In no Catholic country has been witnessed greater rigor against heretics than marked the treatment of such as dissented from this royal Confession of Faith. In vain did Melancthon and the German princes urge the correction of abuses and false doctrines.[1] The king's answer was dictated wholly by the counsels of Bishop Gardiner,[2] whose sentiments came fully to light at a later period, under the reign of Mary the Catholic. It was of no avail, that one

[1] Burnet's History of the Reformation contains, in the Appendix to the Collections of Records, a letter from Melancthon, of April 1st, 1539, one from the German Ambassadors of Aug. 5, 1538, and an answer to the latter from the king.

[2] Burnet, I., p. 367, Addenda to the Hist. of the Reformation.

bishopric after another became occupied by men at heart devoted to the Reformation; Henry and his advisers would hear of no farther progress. So far from this, steps were taken in a retrograde direction. Not only was all opposition to the Six Articles punished with the utmost rigor; not only were the writings of the Reformers and Tyndale's translation of the Bible prohibited; but in 1543 even the reading of the version, once approved and earnestly recommended by the king himself, was forbidden to the common people.[1]

Thus had the English Church assumed a new form, by acquiring, through the influence of personal interest and self-will, a different head. How much the Spirit of God, through the agency of His word, had contributed to this change, and what part He would hereafter take in it could not be seen till, on the death of Henry, January 28th, 1547, the reins of government passed into other hands.

PROGRESS OF THE REFORMATION UNDER EDWARD VI. — FIRST DEVELOPMENT OF THE PURITAN ELEMENT.

The accession of Edward VI., in his tenth year, under a regency, was adapted to awaken the most cheering hopes. The young king and his advisers were disposed to carry forward the work already begun; or rather, of that which originated in self-will, to make a genuine reformation. With the existing church constitution, of the highest moment must have been the Parliament Act of 1539,[2] empowering the councillors of the king's successor, during his minority, to issue proclamations in his name, which were to be obeyed in the same manner with those set forth by the king himself. Numbers of the clergy, who,

1 Burnet, I., p. 321. 2 Burnet, Part I., Book III.

during the former reign, had been driven away by the harsh enforcement of the Six Articles, now returned to England. With them came many foreign reformers of distinction. Parliament repealed the rigorous enactments against heretics. Private masses, denial of the cup, and celibacy were done away with. With these abuses ceased also the hostile attitude which the German princes had been constrained to take during the preceding reign. The visitation of the cloisters no longer had for its object the plunder of their property for the benefit of the Head of the Church, but the diffusion of the word of God, and of the knowledge of its doctrines among both clergy and laity.

We must here mention a controversy, afterwards renewed with the first secession of the Independents, which if not the immediate occasion of the subsequent resistance to the Episcopal church under Elizabeth, at least determined its form. Hooper, an English clergyman, who during the closing years of Henry's life resided in Zurich, had now returned to his native land. His preaching of the divine word was so favorably received, and produced so marked an impression, that he was at first commissioned to preach through certain counties, as a means of influencing the public mind in favor of the Reformation, and in July, 1550, he was nominated to the vacant bishopric of Gloucester. This he declined on two grounds. The clause "with the Saints," in the formula of the oath of office, seemed to him objectionable, since, as he explained, the appeal should be made to God alone, as the only searcher of hearts. Thereupon, the young king struck out the clause with his own hand. Hooper's scruples in regard to the Romish vestments it was not so easy to relieve. Yet, assuredly, this could not be reckoned a question of secondary importance; these vestments not only being regarded as a kind of symbol of that worship which had departed from the simplicity of the Scriptures and of the primitive church, but being associated in the popular mind with a multitude of superstitious notions. The king and his council seem to have been inclined to yield the point. But, in spite of the judgment expressed by distinguished foreign reformers in favor of Hooper's views, a majority of the Bishops were decidedly for retaining the vestments. Cranmer regarded the matter as an *adiaphoron*.[1] Hooper's resignation was declined, and every method, even that of sending him to prison for a time, was used to induce compliance. It was not till after nine months of such discipline that he yielded so far as to be consecrated in the robes; on the condition, however, of being dispensed from the farther use of them. Subsequent ordinations showed the increasing influence of his views. The spirit of genuine toleration was manifested, moreover, in the following ordinance respecting the German church, formed in London, under the superintendence of John a Lasco: "We command the Lord Mayor, the aldermen and magistrates of the city of London, that they permit the said superintendent and ministers to enjoy and exercise their own proper rites and ceremonies, and their proper and peculiar ecclesiastical discipline, without hindrance, let, or molestation, albeit they differ from the usages and ceremonies of our realm, any law, proclamation or ordinance, which may have been set forth, to the contrary notwithstanding."

[1] So likewise Calvin, who in a letter to Bullinger, March 10th, 1551, sympathizes indeed with Hooper in the rejection of the vestments, but adds, nevertheless: maluissem non usque adeo ipsum pugnare, idque nuper suadebam.

Still, with all their good intentions, their sagacity and zeal, the English Reformers had to contend against great difficulties. Among these, none is more worthy of notice than the one mentioned by Calvin, in a letter to Farel, in the year 1551; for it has reference to the inner condition of the church. He says: "The nobility, having seized on the revenues of the church, during the king's minority, caused the offices of the clergy to be exercised, or their places to be occupied by mercenary hirelings. The church is robbed of its faithful servants." In this we see the fruits of the policy by which the Reformation was urged forward under Henry VIII. Cranmer's efforts were zealously seconded by the Lord Protector, the Duke of Somerset, to whose own heart the interests of the Reformation lay very near, as appears from a letter addressed to him by Calvin; who also bears witness to what the Duke had to contend with. The bishops who made open resistance were indeed deposed; but the irresolution manifest in dealing with those who held themselves uncommitted, gives evidence that the former were strengthened in their position by members of the regency (for instance, Lord Chancellor Wriothsley), who were favorably inclined to the papacy, as well as by the prospect that a Catholic of the most rigid sort might be Edward's successor. At length, the king's privy council resolved to comply with the appeals made to them from various quarters,[1] by proceeding to a reformation of the church doctrines. Cranmer, and Ridley, bishop of Rochester, were charged with this undertaking. They drew up forty-two articles on the leading points of the Christian faith, copies of which were sent to the rest of the bishops, and other learned clergymen, for their suggestions; these being

[1] See also Calvin, in a letter to Cranmer, in the year 1551.

added, and the whole thoroughly revised by Cranmer, they were submitted to the Privy Council, and received the confirmation of the king. It is a noticeable circumstance, that the articles were neither laid before the clergy in Parliament, nor in the houses of convocation, although reference is made to the latter, in the title under which they appear. This omission is to be attributed, not merely to the purpose of establishing the king's ecclesiastical supremacy, but, in part, no doubt, to the fear of an opposition, which it would not have been easy to override. Cranmer had it in mind, moreover, to bring about a better representation of the clergy[1] in these assemblies. Soon after the publication of the Articles of Faith, the revision of the service was taken in hand, and a far simpler form of divine worship was set forth in the Book of Common Prayer, and most of the popish ceremonies were abrogated. While, however, it was merely reforms in existing usages and institutions, which were attempted in these proceedings, it was with the manifest design of extending them, step by step, into a thorough reformation. The Confession of Faith was the Augustine; through the foreign advisers, whose agency in the new measures is not to be mistaken, the English Reformation was placed in intimate connection with that of the Swiss Church. It was certain that, so soon as Edward VI. should come into the exercise of supreme power, all influences would be made to concur for the furtherance of the work thus begun. The brilliant qualities of the young king were acknowledged by the unanimous voice of his time, and Calvin extols in him the union of superior gifts with rare piety. But he

1 In the year 1558 an ordinance was passed making the Houses of Convocation entirely independent of the crown. — *Neal's History of the Puritans,* I. p. 132.

died in 1553, not having yet completed his sixteenth year. Calvin thus writes to Farel, in August of the same year: "What you say is true; that country has been deprived of an incomparable jewel, of which it was not worthy. I maintain that, in the death of this minor, the whole nation has lost its best father."

REIGN OF CATHOLIC MARY — THE PROTESTANT EXILES.

Mary, daughter of Henry VIII. and of Katherine of Arragon, now ascended the throne. Her devotion to the papacy finds its solution in the sufferings endured by herself, as well as by her mother, in consequence of her father's rupture with the Romish See. At first, indeed, she promised to make no change in the religion, and subsequently declared her resolution to constrain no one, except through the teachings of the Word. But, ere long, it became manifest that she was determined to use the ecclesiastical supremacy, now attached to the crown, for the complete restoration of the former relations to Rome. Her first step was, to release from prison the adherents of the papacy, and to put in their place the "leaders of the Reformation." The foreigners who had favored this work were notified to leave the kingdom. These exiles were accompanied by many English fugitives; among them, five bishops, as many deans, four archdeacons, and about fifty doctors of theology and distinguished preachers. By the beginning of November, 1553, all the ordinances issued under Edward VI., for the regulation of religion, were abolished. The bishops and ministers known to be hostile to the papacy were then deposed by a visitation; some on the ground that they were married, some simply "by the royal pleasure," that being, indeed, the sole tenure on which their offices were held. The number thus deposed is estimated at three thousand. At the same time, mass was everywhere reëstablished. A disputation with the leaders of the suppressed party, appointed to be held at Oxford, in April, failed of the desired result, through their steadfast confession of the truth, so far as they had attained it. In the summons for a parliament, in November of the same year, the title, "Supreme Head of the Church," was omitted. The sentence pronounced under Henry VIII. against Cardinal Pole, a kinsman of the royal family, for intriguing, from Italy, in favor of the Pope, was annulled. He then made his appearance, as legate of the Romish See; and Parliament, after having first received pardon for past offences, again subjected the kingdom to the dominion of the Pope. In January, 1555, Parliament repealed the laws, all and several, issued against the papal chair since the twentieth year of Henry's reign, and restored the former ordinances respecting the burning of heretics. The execution of the ordinances, in which Bishop Gardiner (the same who has been already mentioned) made himself especially conspicuous, gave character to Mary's reign. Two hundred and seventy-seven persons, of all ranks and ages, among them Cranmer, Ridley, and Hooper, sealed their faith with their blood: while not a less number, who were appointed to the same fate, were released from prison by Mary's successor. It must, by no means, be overlooked, that here, also, the blood of the martyrs became the seed of a spiritual Christianity; for a faith so sealed was a kind of preaching far more impressive and efficacious than any governmental statutes and ordinances.

Another result of the persecution, not less important, was the close and endearing connection into which the

English Reformation was brought, through the numerous body of exiles, with those foreign churches in which the great change had begun more within and below, and thence had worked outwards and upwards. In many places in Switzerland and western Germany, where the Calvinistic doctrines prevailed, there were formed English churches.

But now a question came up, which hitherto had been kept out of sight or glossed over, viz.: whether it were lawful, or, if so, whether it were expedient, for the exiles to extend the Reformation beyond the limits determined under Edward VI. The English theologians of Strasburg and Basle advocated a strict adherence to the liturgy prescribed in the Book of Common Prayer. The church in Frankfort, on the contrary, omitted in their public worship certain customary usages, as the litany and responses. To this it was objected, at Strasburg, that, "by deviating at this crisis from King Edward's Book, they seemed to cast reproach on those who were now sealing it with their blood, and gave occasion to their opposers to accuse them of instability." The Frankfort brethren replied, December 2d, 1554, that "they had set aside as few ceremonies as was possible, and were therefore in no danger of being charged with instability. They supposed the martyrs in England did not die in defence of changeable ceremonies; in reference to doctrine, there existed no difference."

Agreement on the disputed point not being secured, the Frankfort church solicited the advice of Calvin. In a letter dated January 18th, 1555, the Reformer expresses his deep regret, that, under the present circumstances, dissensions should have arisen from such causes. He adds: "In the English liturgy there are, I perceive, many weaknesses to be borne with. In these two words I would say, that while all the purity has not indeed been attained that could be desired, yet, since the defects cannot be remedied all in a moment, and contain nothing openly unscriptural, they should be borne with for a time. On this basis, there might be an accommodation. Still it were advisable that learned, upright, and zealous servants of Christ should make it an object to perfect the work into something more pure and edifying. If true religion is again to flourish in England, some things in it must be amended, and much done away with." He concedes to them the right to institute such changes, and very plainly charges those who oppose it with narrowness and obstinacy; while at the same time, he warns the Frankfort brethren not to be too rigid. Confirmed by this decision of Calvin, the Frankfort church adhered to the order which they had adopted, under the guidance of their pastor, John Knox, afterwards the celebrated Scotch Reformer. Not long after, Cox, former tutor to Edward VI., arrived in Frankfort with others of the same views, and attempted to introduce the liturgy unchanged. Being admitted, with his friends, to a voice in the church, he managed to secure a majority; and by an accusation against Knox before the magistrate, on the ground of a former writing in which the Reformer had indulged in some hard thrusts at the Emperor, obtained his removal. Neither the consciousnesss of their depressed state, nor the counsels of the Frankfort government, with all the confidence it had inspired by its protection of the church, could reëstablish peace. Equally unavailing was a letter from Calvin to Cox and his adherents, who had sought his countenance to their proceedings. He expressed his disapprobation of "burdening the church with corrupting and useless ceremonies, when liberty was enjoyed for introducing a pure and simple order. The measures against Knox were neither pious nor brotherly. It was their duty to make any sacrifice for appeasing the strife; but if it should be impossible to remain in the same place with their opponents, yet let unity in spirit be still maintained." The old church, however, was obliged to abandon Frankfort. Some of them went to Basle; but the greater part, of whom Knox was one, repaired to Geneva, where they adopted the church order there established. They published a liturgy on this model, and several distinguished ministers among them occupied themselves with a revision of Tyndale's translation of the Bible. The new church at Frankfort subsequently experienced still another division, which, though of less importance than the former, again terminated in the secession of a minority, in December, 1557. But soon after this, a total change of relations was brought about by the death of Queen Mary. She died on the 17th of November, 1558; and Elizabeth, daughter of Anne Boleyn, who had been subjected to harsh treatment, and even exposed to great danger under her sister's reign, ascended the English throne.

ELIZABETH—THE PRELATISTS AND PURITANS—CARTWRIGHT.

At the beginning of the year 1559, a Parliament assembled which was decidedly favorable to a reformation. After the repeal of certain laws passed during the previous reign, the ecclesiastical supremacy of the crown was reëstablished by an Act, whereby the queen was likewise authorized to constitute a High Commission Court, for the examination and punishment of all errors, heresies, divisions, abuses and contempts. These decisions respecting the supremacy, though not void of offence to some, and though a disappointment to many who had looked for progress in this respect, were nevertheless acceded to. But the Act, thereupon resolved on in Parliament, for uniformity in divine service, awakened the opposition of those who, on account of their efforts for the purification of divine service, were termed *Puritans*. It is worthy of note that the words: "From the tyranny of the Bishop of Rome and his abominable cruelties, deliver us," were struck out of the new Litany. Another deviation from the liturgy of Edward, was the omission of the words: "By the kneeling at the sacrament, no worship of a bodily presence of Christ is signified." Both these changes were manifestly made in favor of the Catholic party, which, however, refused to be propitiated. The papal bishops agreed on five Articles, which they submitted to Parliament, maintaining the bodily presence of Christ in the sacrament of the altar, transubstantiation, mass, and the supremacy of the Romish See; and that no authority in matters of faith and discipline is to be conceded to the laity. They were thereupon dismissed in a body. Towards the end of the year 1559, the archbishopric of Canterbury, having remained a year[1] vacant, was conferred on Matthew Parker. By his influence, the queen, who was naturally a lover of pomp, was instigated to such severities against the Puritans as could not fail to produce a breach. Still, Elizabeth might have consented to a simplification of the ceremonies, as she subsequently yielded her early prejudice against the marriage of the clergy, had not the question presented itself to her as an infringement of her ecclesiastical supremacy. In the year 1562, the former Confession of Faith under Edward,

1 Cardinal Pole, the successor of Cranmer, had died on the same day with Queen Mary.

the Thirty-nine Articles, so called, was reëstablished. The changes were unessential as far as the supplementary clause of the twentieth article: "The Church has power to institute rites and ceremonies, and authority in religious controversies." It is indeed doubtful whether these words were added at that time; but incontestably they stand in the Confession of Faith as confirmed by Parliament. But, general as was the subscription of the English clergy to these Articles, an antipathy to the prescribed ceremonies manifested itself on every side, which found support in the views of many bishops and distinguished clergymen of England, as well as in those of the most esteemed foreign theologians. The nation at large, also, and the leading statesmen, gave open signs of dissatisfaction with a ceremonial which reminded them of the preceding unhappy reign. But the queen, under date of 25th January, 1564, wrote to the archbishops of Canterbury and York that "they should take effectual means for bringing about an exact order and uniformity in all outward rites and ceremonies, established by law and good usage; and henceforth only such should be admitted to any spiritual office as were disposed to follow common order, and should formally promise to act in accordance thereto." As the result of this letter, a series of advertisements were issued by the commission in spiritual matters, consisting of the Archbishop of Canterbury, and the Bishops of London and Rochester, requiring that on the 1st of March, 1564, all licenses to clerical offices should be renewed, and the former canonical vestments be universally resumed. To these advertisements it was owing that the Puritan views, which had hitherto been merely a denial of, and an opposition to, the dominant views, now assumed a positive form. The requisitions were boldly and firmly protested against, both as the occasion of great offence to the people, and as an infringement of the christian liberty proper in such matters. Thirty-seven London ministers, at a conference on the 26th March, 1565, united in such a protest. Their deprivation, in consequence of this step, left many churches desolate; but this made as little impression as did an appeal to the queen and the commission. The dissenting clergymen then set forth a defence of their proceedings, through the press; but on the 29th June, 1566, a law forbade the printing and sale of all writings of this kind. During this time the deprived ministers had held assemblies in London, to which resorted great numbers of the laity, unintimidated by the severe penalties incurred by those who did not attend their parish churches. But on the 19th of June, 1567, one of these assemblies was discovered and broken up. Of those who were apprehended on this occasion, seven or eight were tried on the following day. On the charge of having "contemned the royal authority for settling things indifferent in respect to divine service," they were, after a bold and candid defence of their conduct, condemned to imprisonment, which they suffered for about a year.

Still, the proceedings against Puritans were as yet restrained within certain limits, since, in some of the remote districts of England, they found protectors even in the bishops themselves.

It was during this very period that the attention of the queen was especially directed towards the Catholics. The Catholic princes had concluded a league among themselves, against the Reformation; in the north, insurrections had broken out under distinguished leaders; and, in 1569, the pope excommunicated the queen and kingdom.

But, in spite of all this, the breach continually widened.

The vestments, though they gave the first impulse to the controversy, formed but one among many points, in which the Puritans dissented from the State Church. In 1570, these points, which had previously come singly under consideration, were exhibited in connection by Thomas Cartwright, the same who has been called the father of the Puritans, though his labor was rather that of apologist than founder. Cartwright was a Professor at Cambridge, and, in Beza's opinion, there was no more learned man under the sun. His main positions were these: "Everything in the church must be brought back to the apostolic form; hence the only offices should be those of bishop and deacon; not only the archbishops and archdeacons, but the bishops, chancellors and officials should be dispensed with; the sign of the cross at baptism, the fasts, and festivals, should be abrogated, and, on the other hand, an exact observance of the Sabbath be introduced. Bishops should not be appointed by civil authority, but be chosen by the church, and each congregation should have its own pastor. He protested also against the requirement of the liturgy, ordained by special command of the queen, that every person must kneel at the reception of the sacrament." For maintaining these opinions, Cartwright was expelled from the University. Leaving England, he officiated for two years as preacher to the English merchants in Holland. On his return to England, he was subjected to severe persecutions; but at length the favor of the Earl of Leicester obtained for him a quiet retreat.

In Parliament, the Puritans seem to have found a powerful support, voices of weight being there repeatedly raised in their favor. When, in 1571, an act was passed confirming the thirty-nine Articles, and requiring subscription to the same, the clause "which concerns only the confession of the true faith, and the doctrines of the sacrament," was added, to prevent the differences in reference to discipline and ceremonies being made a ground of removal from office. To this, however, the ecclesiastical commission paid no attention; while the queen sent to the tower those members who had ventured to speak their minds freely. On a subsequent occasion of this kind, she even went so far as to tell Parliament that "they might busy themselves with what was out of the way in their respective shires; but affairs of State they were to leave to herself and her privy council; and, in like manner, those of the Church to herself and the bishops." The persecutions were also continued against such of the laity as neglected their parish churches. Yet in 1572 there arose, in the immediate neighborhood of London, a presbytery wherein elders were elected whose members were so fortunate as to remain for a time undiscovered. The Puritans were not permitted to connect themselves with the foreign churches existing in London; nor were they allowed public disputations, whose results, or rather want of result, it was to be sure easy to foresee.

In the year 1575 Archbishop Parker died. Soon after, two Anabaptists perished at the stake, the first martyrs to their opinions under this reign. Grindal, Archbishop of York, having succeeded to the See of Canterbury, pushed on at first the persecution of the Puritans; but when the queen peremptorily required the cessation of those assemblies, in which clergymen had been accustomed to meet for their own edification and improvement, Grindal took these exercises under his protection. Nay, he even admonished the queen, "That she should not pronounce so absolutely and peremptorily in matters of faith and religion, where the will of God, and not of any earthly creature, is to take place." But the queen immediately deprived him of his archiepiscopal functions, in which he was not reïnstated till the year before his death, which happened in 1583. Still the persecutions did not cease. In 1582, two clergymen were executed for circulating anti-prelatical writings, though the author himself, Robert Brown, of whom we shall hear more particularly by and by, was released from prison.

On the accession of Whitgift, the personal enemy of Cartwright, to the See of Canterbury, the measures for the suppression of the Puritans became yet more rigorous. He petitioned the queen for the new organization of a High Commission, which should be clothed with the power of the former vicar general of the kingdom,[1] for applying all ways and means for the detection and punishment of dissent. Among these is particularly mentioned the oath, by which the accused was compelled to testify all he knew concerning himself and others.

How the articles of this Commission were regarded may be seen by a letter from Lord Treasurer Burleigh to the Archbishop, dated 15th July, 1584. After explaining that he had been solicited, not alone by sundry ministers, but by councillors and statesmen, to oppose the hard dealing of the archbishop, as affording encouragement to papists, and exposing the queen to great danger, he proceeds: "I find the articles so full of branches and circumstances, as I think the Inquisitors of Spain use not so many questions to comprehend and to trap their preys...... This sifting of poor ministers is not to edify or reform. I write with the testimony of a good conscience. I desire the peace of the church. I desire concord and unity in the

[1] Thomas Cromwell, under Henry VIII. See p. 23.

exercise of our religion. I favor no sensual and wilful recusants. But I conclude that, according to my simple judgment, this kind of proceeding is too much savoring of the Romish Inquisition, and is rather a device to seek for offenders than to reform any."

But this letter had as little effect as the opinion expressed this same year by the whole Privy Council, to the High Commission, "that the people ought not to be robbed of their faithful, learned and godly ministers on account of certain points respecting ceremonies, by which their consciences were disquieted." The clergy were deprived in great numbers, so that complaints of the want of ministers poured in from every quarter; and imprisonments of the severest kind were inflicted on both clergy and laity. It should not indeed be omitted that, in many cases, the demeanor of the Puritans in courts of justice, and the tone of their satirical writings, were not such as tended to promote a reconciliation. But in general they seem to have been constrained to resistance by the force of conscience. Nor had they as yet relinquished the hope of some modification of these rigorous positions, on the part of the Church leaders; for their dissent thus far had reference chiefly to single points, and no clearly defined principle, embracing all these, had distinctly confronted the teachings of the Church.

ORGANIZATION OF THE PURITAN PARTY THROUGH BROWN; SEPARATISTIC ELEMENTS.

A firmer organization was at length given to Puritanic dissent by a man whose headstrong and self-seeking temper certainly did not qualify him to be the founder of a new church-party, and who served in his labors merely as a transition to the Independents of a later period. It was in the year 1586, that Robert Brown, from whom his adherents derived the name of Brownists, propounded a more complete theory in reference to church government. Brown, who was born in 1549, was descended from a distinguished family, and was a relative of Lord Treasurer Burleigh. As early as 1517, when a preacher in London, he had been cited before Archbishop Parker for some departures from the prescribed cerémonies; but his position as chaplain to the Duke of Norfolk had then saved him from punishment. Subsequently, he assailed the discipline and ceremonies of the Church with great violence, and counselled his hearers on no conditions to submit to them. Having been thrown into prison on this account at Norwich, in 1580, and then brought to London at the instance of the Lord Treasurer, he confessed that he had erred, retracted, and was dismissed. Two years after appeared his book: "The Life and Manners of true Christians." Again cited to answer for the charges therein contained against the bishops, he confessed himself the author of the book, but declared that it had been published against his will. Again his powerful friends stepped in and saved him; though, as has been already mentioned, in 1583 two ministers were executed for circulating this very book. Brown now kept himself quiet for several years. But in the year 1586, he began to itinerate through the country, preaching against bishops, ceremonies, spiritual courts, and the forms used in ordaining the clergy. He afterwards boasted of having lain in thirty-two prisons. At length he succeeded in organizing a church on his own principles; but so vigilant was the persecution against him, that he saw himself compelled to leave England. Several of his friends accompanied him to Holland, where they obtained leave of the government to worship God after their own manner, and founded a church in Middleburg. Divisions soon succeeded which disclosed the arbitrary and imperious temper of Brown. In 1589, he returned to England, recanted his former opinions, and became rector of a church in Northamptonshire. At a later period, he neither exhibited the strictness of the Puritans in his domestic life, nor concerned himself about the duties of his office; while the rigor with which he enforced his personal claim to the tithes was in glaring contrast with the principles he had formerly expressed.

These principles, which were for a time adhered to by his followers in England, were, in respect to their negative as well as their positive side, separatistic in character. Though not dissenting from the Articles of Faith held by the English church, the Brownists declared it "to be no true church, and the ordination of the clergy in the same to be null; since its discipline was popish and antichristian, and it bore the sign of a false church in its persecution for matters of conscience." Hence all association with it in prayer, in attendance on preaching, or in any part of public worship whatever, was forbidden to their communities. Nay, they were not only to abstain from all fellowship with the church of England, but with all other reformed churches not modelled after their own pattern. Their doctrine was, that each church is to be bounded by the limits of the single congregation, and must be purely democratic in its government. At the formation of such a congregation or church, the members, all being present, agreed on a Confession of Faith, and subscribed a covenant by which they bound themselves to walk according to the ordinances of the gospel, and expressed their assent to certain stated laws and regulations. In respect to the admission or exclusion of members, and all matters of debate, the decision was in the hands of the collective body. The church officers both for preaching the word and caring for the poor, were chosen by themselves, and were set apart to their several offices by fasting, prayer, and the laying on of hands by certain of the brethren. The priests were neither to form a distinct class, nor, necessarily, to remain priests in perpetuity. As it was the voice of the body which gave to each his office, and permission to exercise it among them by preaching and the administration of the sacraments, so might the same power dismiss him from office, and reduce him again to the position of a common church member. In case the number of members became too great for one and the same place of assembly, they were to divide; forming, by the choice of new officers, sister churches in fellowship with each other. No church might exercise any judicial right or authority over another; but merely counsel and admonish, if it walked disorderly, or renounced the fundamental truths of religion; but if the offending church did not receive the admonition, the rest were to withdraw themselves from it, and publicly disown it as no true church of Christ. The exercise of the church offices was restricted within the narrow limits of the single society; a pastor being allowed to administer baptism and the Lord's Supper, only to the members of his own charge or to their immediate children. The Brownists were opposed to every prescribed form of prayer, and permitted the lay members to take part in preaching and exhortation in the congregations.

This rigid opposition to the state church, expressed not unfrequently with unbecoming heat and violence, as well as this more determinate form of the churches of the

Brownists, drew upon them the special attention of the bishops. Their number, in spite of the recantation of their leader, was now greatly multiplied in England. Several among them were executed; many of them lay long years in prison; some were banished, and others fled voluntarily to their brethren in Holland. Yet in 1592 their number was stated, by Sir Walter Raleigh in Parliament, to be about twenty thousand. Among the communities which they formed in Holland, that spirit of rigid exclusiveness in respect to other churches seems to have been soon moderated; in England it was still kept up by persecution. This suffered no interruption by the death of Elizabeth in 1603. James I, who had grown up in Scotland under Presbyterian influences, deceived the hopes of the Puritans. At the Conference at Hampton Court, in 1604, he himself took decided ground against them; and as the result of renewed ordinances, about three hundred ministers were, the same year, deprived, thrown into prison, or banished from the country. By these persecutions, that man also was driven from England who is to be regarded as the Father of the Independents; that is, of the Brownists, as purified from separatistic elements.

ROBINSON, THE FATHER OF THE INDEPENDENTS.

As early as 1602, a number of Brownists living in the north of England had subscribed a Confession of Faith, in which they renounced connection with the established church. Their residences being remote from each other, and being obliged therefore to assemble for worship in two different houses, they formed two churches, which chose for their Pastors John Smith and John Robinson. The former soon left England, however, and went to Amsterdam, where he found Brownists already settled. Divisions had arisen among them, whose effect had been to moderate their pastor, Ainsworth, in his opposition to other churches. But Smith[1], a man who had not hesitated to say that his present views must be looked for only in his last writings, could not unite with these Brownists. He connected himself with the Anabaptists, left Amsterdam, and settled in Ley, (perhaps Leeum, in Brabant), where, being unable to find any qualified administrator of the sacrament of baptism, he first baptized himself, whence he received the name Se-Baptist, and then performed the rite for others. Subsequently, he professed himself of the doctrine of Arminius, in whose defence he came out openly in 1611. At his death, soon after, the church itself became extinct. Robinson, in connection with Elder William Brewster, presided several years longer over the church in the north of England. In 1608[2] the continued persecutions, by the bishops and the spiritual courts, obliged them to leave England and follow their brethren in the faith to Holland. Finding, on his arrival in Amsterdam, that the controversies among them were still kept up, Robinson removed with his congregation, and settled in Leyden. Here they obtained from the magistracy permission to rent a house for their meetings, and established a form of public worship in accordance with their own principles.

At first, the views of Robinson in respect to other churches were strictly those of the Brownists. But after some interchange of opinions with the ministers of the churches previously established in Leyden, it seemed to him, that though right and necessary still to remain separated from the reformed churches among which he lived, yet this

1 Neal's History of the Puritans II. p. 49.

2 Neal's History of New England, I. p. 76.

should not be in the spirit of harsh antagonism. "We acknowledge," says he, in his Apology for the Brownists, "before God and man, that we harmonize so perfectly with the reformed churches of the Netherlands in matters of religion, as to be ready to subscribe their Articles of Faith, and every one of them, as they are set forth in their Confession. We recognize these reformed churches as true and genuine; we hold fellowship with them as far as we can; those among us who understand Dutch, attend their preaching; we offer the Supper to such of their members as are known to us, and may occasionally desire it." But, at the same time, he steadfastly maintained that each single church, or society of Christians, possesses within itself full ecclesiastical authority for choosing officers, for administering all the ordinances of the gospel, and for all exercise of authority and discipline over its members; that, consequently, it was independent of all synods, convocations, and councils. He granted that synods and councils might be useful for healing divisions between the churches, and imparting to them friendly advice; but not for exercising any judical right or authority whatever over them, or for imposing on them any canon, or any article of faith without the free assent of the church itself. He rejected, as national, the constitution of the church of England, her liturgy, her prescribed prayers and unrestricted communion. He held it necessary to exclude unworthy communicants, and that those who desired the privilege of christian fellowship should be able to give proofs of the operation of the grace of God in their hearts. This latter principle, opposition to unrestricted communion, was of the greatest moment in the development of the Independent churches, especially in America. While in a single congregation, isolated among a foreign people, it could be carried out without any special difficulty, it gave rise, when applied to a great community, to those disputes and conflicts amidst which the New England church unfolded into its peculiar form.

Before passing to the emigration of the Independents from Holland to America, we will mention some farther opinions and views of Robinson, which serve to indicate the stand-point of this remarkable man. Especially characteristic is his language respecting the Reformation, in his "Justification of separation from the Church of England," a work published in 1610 as an answer to the objections of an Episcopal clergyman. He says:[1]

"You speak much of the reformation of your church after popery. There was, indeed, a great reformation of things in your church, but very little of the church, to speak truly and properly. The people are the church; and to make a reformed church, there must first be a reformed people; and so they should have been with you, by the preaching of repentance from dead works, and faith in Christ; that the people, as the Lord should have vouchsafed grace, being first fitted for, and made capable of the sacraments and other ordinances, might afterwards have communicated in the pure use of them; for want of which, instead of a pure use, there hath been, and is at this day, a most profane abuse of them, to the great dishonor of Christ and his gospel, and to the hardening of thousands in their impenitency. Others also endeavoring yet a further reformation, have sued and do sue to kings, and to queens, and parliaments, for the rooting out of the prelacy, and with it of such other evil fruits as grow from that bitter root; and, on the contrary, to have the ministry, government, and discipline of Christ set over the parishes as they stand; the first fruit of which reformation, if it were

[1] Backus's History of New England, Boston, 1777. Vol. I. p. 25.

obtained, would be the profanation of the more of God's ordinances upon such as to whom they appertained not; and so to the further provocation of his majesty unto anger against all such as so practised, or consented thereunto. Is it not strange that men, in the reforming of a church, should almost, or altogether, forget the church, which is the people, or should labor to crown Christ a king over a people whose prophet he hath not first been? Or to set him to rule, by his laws and officers, over the professed subjects of antichrist and the devil? Is it possible that they should ever submit to the discipline of Christ, which have not been first prepared, in some measure, by his holy doctrine, and taught with meekness to stoop under his yoke?"

The following passage discusses one peculiarity in the working of the English Reformation, and points out the connection of the kingdom of Christ with the priesthood:[1]

"What sway authority hath in the Church of England, appeareth in the laws of the land, which make the government of the church ALTERABLE at the magistrate's pleasure; and so the clergy, in their submission to King Henry VIII., do derive, as they pretend, their ecclesiastical authority from him, and so execute it. Indeed many of the late bishops and their proctors, seeing how monstrous the ministration is of DIVINE things by an human authority and calling, and growing bold upon the present disposition of the magistrate, have disclaimed that former title, and do professedly hold their ecclesiastical power *de jure divino*, and so, consequently, by God's law unalterable. Of whom I would demand this one question: 'What if the king should discharge and expel the present ecclesiastical government, and plant instead of it the pres-

[1] Backus, I. p. 29.

bytery or eldership, would they submit unto the government of the elders, yea, or no?' If yea, then were they traitors to the Lord Jesus, submitting to a government overthrowing his government, as doth the Presbyterian government that which is Episcopal. If no, then how could they free themselves from such imputations of disloyalty to princes, and disturbance of states, as wherewith they load us and others opposing them. But to the question itself: as the kingdom of Christ is not of this world but spiritual, and he a spiritual king (John 18:36), so must the government of this spiritual kingdom under this spiritual king needs be spiritual, and all the laws of it. And as Christ Jesus hath, by the merits of his priesthood, redeemed as well the body as the soul (1 Cor., 6:20), so is he also by the sceptre of his kingdom to rule and reign over both. Unto which, christian magistrates, as well as meaner persons, ought to submit themselves, and the more christian they are, the more meekly to take the yoke of Christ upon them; and the greater authority they have, the more effectually to advance his sceptre over themselves and their people, by all good means. Neither can there be any reason given why the merits of saints may not as well be mingled with the merits of Christ, for the saving of the church, as the laws of men with his laws, for the ruling and guiding of it. He is as absolute and entire a king as he is a priest, and his people must be as careful to preserve the dignity of the one, as to enjoy the benefits of the other."

To these extracts we add some remarks of Robinson on the power of the keys, which exhibit also his style of interpreting Scripture:

"It is granted by all sides that Christ gave unto Peter the keys of the kingdom, that is, the power to remit and retain sins declaratively, as they speak; as also, that in what respect this power was given to Peter, in the same respect it was and is given to such as succeed Peter. But the question is, in what respect or consideration this power spoken of was delegated to him? The papist affirms it was given to Peter as the prince of the apostles, and so to the bishops of Rome, as Peter's successors, and thus they stablish the pope's primacy. The prelates say nay, but unto Peter, an apostle, that is, a chief officer of the church, and so to us, as chief officers succeeding him. Others affirm it to belong to Peter here as a minister of the word and sacraments, and the like, and so, consequently, to all ministers of the gospel equally, which succeed Peter in those and the like administrations. But we, for our parts, do believe and profess that this promise is not made to Peter in any of these respects, nor to any office, order, estate, dignity or degree in the church or world, but to the confession of faith which Peter made by way of answer to Christ's question: "Thou art Christ, the Son of the living God.' To this Christ replies: 'Blessed art thou; thou art Peter, and upon this rock will I build my church; I will give unto thee the keys,' etc. So that the building of the church is upon the rock of Peter's confession, that is, Christ whom he confessed. This faith is the foundation of the church; this faith hath the keys of the kingdom of heaven; what this faith shall bind or loose on earth is bound and loosed in heaven. Thus the Protestant divines, when they deal against the pope's supremacy, do generally expound this Scripture. Now it followeth, that whatsoever person hath received the same precious faith with Peter, as all the faithful have (2 Pet. 1: 1), that person hath a part in this gift of Christ. Whosoever doth confess, publish, manifest, or make known Jesus to be the

Christ, the Son of the living God, and Saviour of the world, that person opens heaven's gates, looseth sin, and partakes with Peter in the use of the keys; and hereupon it followeth necessarily, that one faithful man, yea, or woman either, may as truly and effectually bind, both in heaven and earth, as all the ministers in the world. But here, I know, the lordly clergy, like the bulls of Bashan, will roar loud upon me, as speaking things intolerably derogatory to the dignity of the priesthood; and it may be some others also, either through ignorance or superstition, will take offence at this speech, as confounding all things; but there is no such cause of exception. For howsoever the keys be one and the same in nature and efficacy, in what faithful man or men's hands soever, as not depending either on the number or excellency of any persons, but upon Christ alone; yet it is ever to be remembered that the order and manner of using them is very different. The keys, in doctrine, may be turned as well upon them which are without the church, as upon them which are within, and their sins either loosed or bound (Matt. 28: 19); but in discipline not so, but only upon them which are within (1 Cor. 12:13). Again, the apostles by their office had these keys to use in all churches, yea, in all nations upon earth; ordinary elders for their particular flocks, (Acts 14:23, and 20:28). Lastly, there is a use of the keys publicly to be had, and a use privately; a use of them by one person severally, and a use of them by the whole church jointly and together; a use of them ministerially or in office, and a use of them out of office. But the power of the gospel is still one and the same, notwithstanding the diverse manner of using it."

Having shown by these statements how the doctrine of the independence of each church was understood, supported and explained by Robinson, we will now add his defence of the opposition to unrestricted communion. In reference to this point, the parable of the tares among the wheat had been urged upon Robinson. He answers: "Since the Lord Jesus, who best knew his own meaning, calls the field the world and makes the harvest, which is the end of the field, the end of the world and not of the church, why should we admit of any other interpretation? Neither is it likely that Christ, in the expounding of one parable, would speak another, as he should have done, if in calling the field the world he had meant the church. As God there in the beginning made man good, and placed him in the field of the world, there to grow; whereby the envy of the serpent he was soon corrupted, so ever since hath the seed of the serpent, stirred up by their father the devil, snarled at the heel of the woman's seed, and like noisome tares vexed and pestered the good and holy seed; which, though the children of God both see and feel to their pain, yet must they not therefore, forgetting what spirit they are of, presently call for fire from heaven, nor prevent the Lord's hand, but wait his leisure, either for the converting of these tares into wheat, which in many is daily seen (and then how great pity had it been they should so untimely have been plucked up), or for their final perdition in the day of the Lord, when the church shall be no more offended by them. And that the Lord Jesus no way speaks of the toleration of profane persons in the church, doth appear by these reasons: 1. Because he doth not contradict himself, by forbidding the use of the keys in one place, which in another he hath turned upon impenitent offenders, Matt. 18. 2. In the excommunication of sinners apparently obstinate, with due circumspection, and in the spirit of wisdom, meekness, and long-suffering, with such other general christian virtues as with which all our special sacrifices ought to be seasoned, what danger can there be of any such disorder, as the plucking up of the wheat with the tares, which the husbandman feareth? 3. The Lord Jesus speaks of the utter ruinating and destruction of the tares — the plucking them up by the roots. But excommunication rightly administered is not for the ruin and destruction of any, but for the salvation of the party thereby humbled, 1 Cor. 5 : 5. The Lord's field is sown only with good seed — his church, saints beloved of God, all and every one of them, though by the malice of Satan and negligence of such as should keep this field, vineyard, and house of God, adulterated seed and abominable persons may be foisted in, yea, and suffered also."

In the year 1613,[1] Robinson was drawn by the solicitations of Polydorus, the opponent of Episcopius, into active participation in the Arminian controversy; for he was then regarded in Holland as a no less gifted than zealous defender of the fundamental truths of the gospel. It is worthy of note, that the Indifferentism in matters of faith, which was promoted by the adherents of Arminius, universally repelled the Puritans, who, nevertheless, claimed freedom in regard to discipline and rites; while on the contrary, it soon spread very generally through the Episcopal Church.

The Independents[2] continued to live in Leyden without any disturbance on the part of the Holland government, as without any dissensions among themselves. Under the care of their teacher, they remained free from those divisions to which their brethren had been exposed who came previously to Holland. But after some years, the appre-

1 Backus, I. 37. Mather's Magnalia Dei Americana I, II. p. 1.

2 Neal's History of New England.

hension awoke among them of becoming gradually extinct. Their older members were dying out; the accessions from England, which were at first numerous,[1] soon ceased, and so far from having a prospect of spreading their views among a people who did not understand their language, their younger members frequently married into Holland families. So vital, and so deeply stamped into their being, was the feeling of their church relations, that although left undisturbed to worship God according to their own convictions, that extinction, and the prospective disappearance of their distinctive church characteristics, seemed to them an evil, escape from which demanded the greatest personal sacrifices. A return to their native country was not to be thought of, if they wished still to maintain the free exercise of their religion. They now directed their eyes towards a newly discovered land.

1 Backus, I. p. 32.

CHAPTER II.

THE EMIGRATION TO AMERICA — FORMATION OF THE THEOCRATIC STATE IN NEW ENGLAND — A GLANCE AT THE POLITICAL HISTORY, THE MISSIONARY EFFORTS, AND FIRST UNIVERSITY OF NEW ENGLAND.

EARLY ATTEMPTS TO COLONIZE THE NORTH AMERICAN CONTINENT FROM ENGLAND. EMIGRATION OF THE LEYDEN CHURCH. NEW PLYMOUTH.

THE first discovery of the continent of North America, after the visits of the Normans several hundred years previous, was made by Sebastian Cabot, during the reign of Henry VII. of England. Yet almost a century had passed away, before the plan was formed of a settlement in the country. In 1584, Sir Walter Raleigh obtained a patent for that purpose; and in connection with certain merchants and other men of wealth, fitted out an expedition, which landed in what is now the State of North Carolina. In honor of Queen Elizabeth, the new territory, including the whole eastern coast of the present North American republics, was named Virginia. That first attempt had, however, as little permanence as those which followed. Most of the colonists perished either in expeditions against the Indians, or from excessive toils and privations; the remainder returned to England in ships which had been sent out for their assistance. In the year 1602, Captain Gosnold, by a direct course towards the more northerly regions of North America, reached what is now called

Massachusetts Bay. He entered into traffic with the natives, and on his return to England gave a very favorable description of the excellent harbors, the capacity of the soil, and of the natural facilities both for commerce and fisheries. This revived the desire for establishing settlements in the country, and in 1606, two companies received from James I. a patent for this purpose. They were destined for South and North Virginia, by which latter designation was understood the region north of the present State of Maryland. Both companies fitted out expeditions; the former founded Jamestown, in the State of Virginia; the latter, in 1608, effected a settlement on the river Sagadehoc in Maine, which, however, shared the fate of the earlier attempts, and was soon abandoned. A farther attempt was made in 1614, by Captain John Smith,[1] who gave the name of New England to the region around Massachusetts Bay, and brought a chart of the same to England. Still the Company for North Virginia, (called also Plymouth Company, on account of its members being mostly from the county of Devonshire), did not succeed in forming a permanent settlement till, after the lapse of several years, they connected themselves with the Independent churches in Leyden.

In the year 1617, the latter concluded decisively on emigration, and sent agents to the Virginia Company, to negotiate respecting an extensive tract in the northern part of the new continent. The proposition was favorably

1 John Smith, one of the boldest adventurers of that age, had been of great service also in the colonization and permanent settlement of South Virginia, where he was for a time governor. A description of his eventful life is found in The Library of American Biography, by Jared Sparks: Boston, 1834. He himself wrote a history of the colonies: The general history of Virginia and New England, by Capitaine John Smith, sometimes governour in those countrys, and Amirall of New England. London, 1627.

entertained, the more so, from the encouragement they had for believing that this settlement possessed the necessary elements of permanence.[1] The emigrants were sufficiently numerous; inured, by long separation from their native land, to privations; industrious and temperate; their peculiar organization tended to internal unity and firm mutual adherence; and as their object was simply the promotion of pure religion, so they doubted not of the blessing of Almighty God upon their undertaking. Application was made in their behalf to the Privy Council, setting forth the advantages to be derived by the crown of England from such a settlement, in regard to the promotion of commerce. But the King's hostility to the Puritans gave rise to serious difficulties. He promised not to molest them there, so long as they demeaned themselves peaceably, but refused them the warrant of his signature, as tolerated and recognized. They hesitated, without some such security, to emigrate to a land which was yet to be reduced to tillage. The negotiations were consequently broken off; but, two years after, the wishes of the church being seconded by the encouraging assurances of the company, they were again resumed. By unremitted efforts, a patent was at length obtained from government, under the seal of the Virginia Company, and they now resolved to put their plan in execution without delay. As all of their number were not fully prepared for the emigration, it was concluded that a part should go first, under the guidance of their Elder, William Brewster, while Robinson should, for a while, remain behind with the others; both divisions, however, still constituting one church, neither of them formally dismissing members to the other, nor requiring of them new evidence before admission. They pur-

1 Backus, I. 34.

chased, in England, two ships, in the larger of which, the "Mayflower," of one hundred and eighty tons, the emigrants embarked from Holland. All being now in readiness, Robinson and his church held, on the 2d of July, 1620, a day of solemn fasting and prayer, for supplicating the divine blessing on this bold adventure. We subjoin the closing part of Robinson's address to them on this occasion, as showing that the Independents regarded their organization as a necessary step in the progress of the Reformation; while, on the other hand, they expressly disclaimed the separatistic element, properly so called, which had proceeded from Brown:

"Brethren: we are now quickly to part from one another, and whether I may ever live to see your faces on earth any more, the God of heaven only knows; but, whether the Lord has appointed that or no, I charge you, before God and his blessed angels, that you follow me no farther than you have seen me follow the Lord Jesus Christ. If God reveal anything to you, by any other instrument of his, be as ready to receive it as ever you were to receive any truth by my ministry; for I am verily persuaded the Lord has more truth yet to break forth out of his holy word. For my part, I cannot sufficiently bewail the condition of the Reformed churches, who are come to a period in religion, and will go, at present, no farther than the instruments of their reformation. The Lutherans cannot be drawn to go beyond what Luther saw; whatever part of his will our God has revealed to Calvin, they will rather die than embrace it; and the Calvinists, you see, stick fast where they were left by that great man of God, who yet saw not all things. This is a misery much to be lamented, for though they were burning and shining lights in their times, yet they penetrated not into the whole counsel of God; but, were they now living, would be as willing to embrace farther light, as that which they first received. I beseech you remember — it is an article of your church covenant — that ye be ready to receive whatever truth shall be made known to you from the written word of God. Remember that, and every other article of your sacred covenant. But I must here, withal, exhort you to take heed what you receive as truth, — examine it, consider it, and compare it with other scriptures of truth before you receive it; for it is not possible the christian world should come so lately out of such thick, antichristian darkness, and that perfection of knowledge should break forth at once. I must also advise you to abandon, avoid, and shake off the name of Brownists; it is a mere nickname, and a brand for making religion and the professors of it odious to the christian world. Unto this end, I should be extremely glad if some godly minister would go with you, or come to you, before you can have any company; for there will be no difference between the unconformable ministers of England and you, when you come to the practice of evangelical ordinances out of the kingdom. And I would wish you, by all means, to close with the godly people of England; study union with them in all things wherein you can have it without sin, rather than in the least measure to effect a division or separation from them. Neither would I have you loth to take another pastor besides myself; inasmuch as a flock that hath two shepherds is not thereby endangered, but secured."

The emigrants left Leyden soon after, accompanied, as far as Delfthaven, by Robinson and the greater part of those who remained behind. On taking leave, they were commended by their pastor to the protection of Heaven, and amidst heartfelt demonstrations of mutual attachment the travellers departed, in order to set sail from Southampton in the county of Hampshire. Here they received a letter from Robinson,[1] in which he exhorted them to make sure their own peace with God, to avoid all offences among themselves, mutually to forbear each other, to subördinate their private interests to the common good, and after choosing their civil governors with wisdom, to submit to their authority as an ordinance established by God.

On the 5th of August, 1620, they set sail in their two ships from Southampton. Soon after their departure, the captain of the smaller vessel declared it unseaworthy. Although it was repaired in Dartmouth harbor, yet, after running out a second time, he repeated his apprehensions, and both ships were compelled to return again to Plymouth. The smaller one remained behind, and with it some of the voyagers; the remainder embarked in the Mayflower, which on the 6th of September again put out to sea, with one hundred and twenty passengers. After a very difficult voyage, they arrived on the 9th of November at Cape Cod, 42° north latitude, and between 52° and 53° west longitude. Their destination was not this region, but the mouth of the Hudson. But on again weighing anchor, the captain ran the ship among dangerous cliffs and breakers, and a storm drove them back to the Cape; and they now resolved, on account of the advanced season, to attempt a settlement where they were. It has been asserted that the captain was bribed by the Dutch, who wished themselves to take possession of the mouth of the Hudson. They did, indeed, found there the colony of New Amsterdam soon after, but subsequently were

1 Backus, I., p. 35, ff. Appendix I.

obliged to relinquish it to the English. Of our settlers, forty-one men, making with their families in all one hundred and one persons, reached America. On their arrival, they organized themselves by the following act:

"In the name of God, Amen. We whose names are underwritten, loyal subjects of our dread sovereign lord, King James, by the grace of God of Great Britain, France and Ireland King, Defender of the Faith, etc. Having undertaken, for the glory of God and advancement of the christian faith and honor of our king and country, a voyage to plant the first colony in the northern parts of Virginia, by these presents do solemnly and mutually, in the presence of God and of one another, covenant and combine ourselves into a civil body politic for our better ordering and preservation and furtherance of the ends aforesaid, and by virtue hereof to enact, constitute and frame such just and equal laws and ordinances, acts, constitutions and offices, from time to time, as shall be thought most meet and convenient for the general good of the colony, unto which we promise all due subjection and obedience.

Cape Cod, the 11th November, 1620."

Their next object was to select a landing-place suitable for a settlement, a task the more difficult and wearisome on account of the ice with which the sea had already covered the shore. From their place of anchorage, they sent out several little expeditions for the exploration of the coast; and at length, after five weeks, they again weighed anchor on the 15th of December, to run into the harbor of Cape Cod. On the 20th they left the ship, and chose a hill which commanded the surrounding country and overlooked the Bay, as their place of settlement. Here, on the 23d of December, they laid the foundations of a town to which they gave the name of New Plymouth. The constancy and firmness of the settlers would, however, hardly have saved them from the fate of their predecessors, had not a contagious sickness shortly before swept away nine-tenths of the Indians in this region. A few months after, a treaty of peace was concluded with the remainder, which, with unimportant interruptions, (as for instance the war carried on in 1637, particularly in Connecticut, against the Pequots,) secured quiet to the colony, for more than half a century, that is, down to the great Indian war with King Philip, in the year 1675. These friendly relations were maintained by strict attention to justice in dealing with the Indians. The land needed for the settlement was purchased of them; a court of justice was established for protecting them against frauds by private persons; and in all their relations with them the English were subjected to the full rigor of the law. It was, moreover, regarded as a holy duty to communicate to the Indians the imperishable blessings of Christianity; and in truth, it was in New England that the first successful missionary efforts of the evangelical church had their birth.

On the other side, the settlers had to contend with difficulties and calamities, whose severity, especially during the first winter, threatened the very existence of the colony. The hardships incident to their voyage and settlement, the want of houses to protect them against the inclemency of the season, as well as of many necessities of life, and in addition, the unusual severity of the winter, had given rise to diseases which carried off, within the first four or five months, one half of their number. For several years they were obliged to depend for their subsistence chiefly upon hunting and fishing. Often, through the failure of their crops, they had scarcely corn enough for seed, and the supplies from England relieved only their most pressing necessities. But there was another want which they felt still more painfully. The greater part of their brethren who had remained in Leyden now shrunk from following them, and by this means, Robinson was prevented from coming to New England. He died on the 19th of February 1625, lamented not only by his own congregation, but by the Hollanders also, who testified at his funeral their appreciation and esteem for his character. For several succeeding years they were obliged to depend for their instruction and guidance on their Elder, Mr. Brewster, or on other gifted laymen. Among those who subsequently joined them from England, was a minister by the name of Ralph Smith, who in 1629 was chosen to be their preacher. As their circumstances improved, they dissolved connection with the Company of Merchant Adventurers, after refunding the money advanced by it for their assistance. Under Charles I the colony obtained a patent, which had been drawn in favor of Governor William Bradford, but was made over by him to the General Court of New Plymouth.

MASSACHUSETTS BAY COMPANY — SETTLEMENT OF SALEM AND CHARLESTOWN.

Soon after the founding of New Plymouth, several attempts were made to colonize the more northerly regions of Massachusetts Bay; but these undertakings, which originated solely in worldly aims, remained without any permanent fesult. This, however, did not discourage similar enterprises. When it became known that the colony of New Plymouth was beginning to prosper, the wish, stimulated by the continued persecution of the Puritans, of finding an asylum for religious freedom, became active in England. At this same time a Company for the establishment of larger settlements was formed, which soon extended its operations, as such attempts at new settlements began to prove more successful. On the 4th of March, 1629, this association was, by a royal charter, incorporated as a political body, under the name of "the Governor and Company of Massachusetts Bay in New England." Its members were empowered to choose yearly their governor, lieut. governor, and eighteen assistants or magistrates,[1] from the free citizens of the aforenamed company. They were to hold quarterly a general assembly, or supreme court; they could admit freemen, choose officers, apportion land, and as it seemed to them desirable for the welfare of the settlement, could make laws, these being not in contravention of the laws of England; while to all who might settle in this region, the right was guaranteed of worshipping God according to their own consciences. The provisions of this charter formed the basis of the subsequent constitution of the colony. Immediately after the choice of a governor, agents were sent over partly to aid the present settlers, partly to obtain more exact information. Two Nonconformist ministers, Higginson[2] and Skelton by name, were then persuaded to accompany the expedition of six ships which was about being sent out. With them went also the above-mentioned Ralph Smith, and thirty-five families from the Leyden church, which had been dissolved after Robinson's death. They landed on the 24th of June, 1629, and founded the towns of Salem and Newton, afterwards called Cambridge.

[1] These constituted the governor's council.

[2] The documents respecting these transactions are contained in a collection of original papers relative to the history of the colony of Massachusetts Bay. Boston, 1769. Here also is Higginson's diary of his journey.

With these new comers also, religion had been the moving cause of emigration. They immediately applied, therefore, to their Plymouth brethren for information respecting the church order and discipline here established, which had been derived from Robinson; and after several conferences on the subject, resolved to form a church after the same model. Higginson thereupon drew up the following covenant, as an expression of the sentiments of these colonists:—

"We covenant with our Lord and one with another; and we do bind ourselves in the presence of God, to walk together in all his ways, according as he is pleased to reveal himself unto us in his blessed word of truth; and do explicitly, in the name and fear of God, profess and protest to walk as followeth, through the power and grace of our Lord Jesus Christ.

"We avouch the Lord to be our God, and ourselves to be his people, in the truth and simplicity of our spirits.

"We give ourselves to the Lord Jesus Christ and the word of his grace for the teaching, ruling, and sanctifying us in matters of worship and conversation, resolving to cleave unto him alone for life and glory, and to reject all contrary ways, canons and constitutions of men in his worship.

"We promise to walk with our brethren with all watchfulness and tenderness, avoiding jealousies and suspicions, backbitings, censurings, provokings, secret risings of spirit against them; but in all offences to follow the rule of our Lord Jesus, and to bear and forbear, give and forgive, as he hath taught us.

"In public or private, we will willingly do nothing to the offence of the church; but will be willing to take advice for ourselves and ours, as occasion shall be presented.

"We will not in the congregation be forward either to show our own gifts in speaking or scrupling, or there discover the weakness or failings of our brethren; but attend an orderly call thereunto, knowing how much the Lord may be dishonored, and his gospel and the profession of it slighted by our distempers and weaknesses in public.

"We bind ourselves to study the advancement of the gospel in all truth and peace; both in regard of those that are within or without; no way slighting our sister-churches, but using their counsel, as need shall be; not laying a stumbling-block before any, no, not the Indians, whose good we desire to promote; and so to converse, as we may avoid the very appearance of evil.

"We do hereby promise to carry ourselves in all lawful obedience to those that are over us, in church or commonwealth, knowing how well-pleasing it will be to the Lord that they should have encouragement in their places by our not grieving their spirits through our irregularities.

"We resolve to approve ourselves to the Lord in our particular callings, shunning idleness as the bane of any state; nor will we deal hardly or oppressively with any wherein we are the Lord's stewards.

"Promising, also, unto our best ability to teach our children and servants the knowledge of God, and of his will, that they may serve him also; and all this not by any strength of our own, but by the Lord Christ; whose blood we desire may sprinkle this our covenant made in his name."

In presence of the delegates from the church of New Plymouth, the persons assembled thereupon declared solemnly and each one for himself, their agreement with this Confession of Faith. They then proceeded to choose Higginson and Skelton as their pastors, and ordained them to the office through the laying on of hands by certain brethren appointed by the church for that purpose. The church being thus constituted, a number more were accepted as members; some, on a declaration of their agreement with the covenant; others, on a written statement of their faith and hope; and others, again, on an oral relation before the church in regard to their spiritual state; but no one was admitted without satisfactory evidence of a blameless life and conversation. A sufficient warrant in regard to faith and life was the only condition of fellowship; in what form, was left to the discretion of the elders. They furthermore agreed with the Plymouth church in regarding the children of believers as church-members with their parents, and baptism as a seal of this membership. Only it was required that, before admission to the Lord's Supper, each one should be examined by the church-officers; if found to be sufficiently instructed in the essential doctrines of religion, free from open scandal, and willing to confess publicly to the covenant, he was then admitted.

It is obvious that the regulations here adopted were liable to fluctuation; for in matters of conscience, everything cannot be foreseen and a complete system formed at once. It appears, too, by comparing the words of Higginson when leaving England with the course pursued by his church towards members of the Episcopal communion, that such opposition resulted from no settled plan, but was more or less forced upon them. Mather[1] relates that Higginson, on setting sail from the Isle of Wight, looked back on his native land and exclaimed: "We will not say as the Separatists were wont to say at their leaving of England, Farewell Babylon! farewell Rome! but we will say, Farewell,

[1] Magnalia, Book III. p. 74. In the diary and letters of Higginson (collection of original papers,) nothing is found in relation to this point.

dear England! farewell, the church of God in England, and all the christian friends there! We do not go to New England as separatists from the Church of England; though we cannot but separate from the corruptions in it; but we go to practise the positive part of church reformation, and propagate the gospel in America." But they wished, nevertheless, to be free from that which had so agitated the Church of England, and hindered the full development of the Reformation. Soon after the formation of the church in Salem, some among the settlers opposed the establishment of public worship, because the Liturgy of the Church of England had been discarded. They charged the ministers with favoring separatism, out of which would soon grow anabaptism; and they declared that they would, for their part, adhere to the order of the English Church. But the ministers replied that "they were neither Separatists nor Anabaptists; that they did not separate from the Church of England, nor from the ordinances of God there, but only from the corruptions and disorders of that church; that they came away from the common prayer and ceremonies, and had suffered much for their non-conformity in their native land; and therefore, being in a place where they might have their liberty, they neither could nor would use them; inasmuch as they judged the imposition of these things to be a sinful violation of the worship of God." The leaders of the opposite party, two brothers by the name of Brown, attempted to set up a church of their own; but, by authority of the magistrates, in which the clergy unreservedly concurred, they were immediately sent back to England. Perhaps some civil offence was connected with this disagreement;[1] perhaps, also, men who had fled from per-

1 Neal, in his History of New England, I. p. 145, charges them with

secution, might find cause of apprehension in the establishment of a church which attached so high a value to the very things on account of which they had been persecuted and exiled. The government regarded the measure as one of self-defence.

GOVERNMENT OF THE COLONY TRANSFERRED TO NEW ENGLAND — FOUNDING OF BOSTON.

The Massachusetts Bay Company, which had been chartered by royal authority, on being informed of the prosperous condition of the settlements made in 1629, wished to adopt some special measures for their advancement. It was resolved to transfer the government of the colony to New England itself; and accordingly John Winthrop, who with many other distinguished and wealthy men was desirous of settling in New England, was chosen Governor. Harmonizing with the colonists in religious views, he had also had opportunity for showing, under very difficult circumstances, his capacity for this office, to which, with brief interruptions, he was reëlected for twenty successive years. A few days after the departure of the expedition (consisting of ten ships) a little writing was published,[1] entitled "The humble request of his Majesty's loyal subjects, the Governor and Company lately gone for New England, to the rest of their brethren in and of the Church of England; for the obtaining of their prayers, and the removal of suspicions and misconstructions of their intentions." "We desire," — such is its language — "you would be pleased to take notice of the principals and body of our company, as those who esteem it our

"endeavoring to raise a mutiny;" but this assertion is not sustained by evidence, and Mather says nothing of the kind.

[1] Hutchinson's History of Massachusetts, Vol. I., Appendix.

honor to call the Church of England, from whence we arise, our dear mother, and cannot part from our native country where she specially resideth, without much sadness of heart, and many tears in our eyes; ever acknowledging that such hope and part as we have obtained in the common salvation, we have received it in her bosom, and sucked it from her breasts. We leave it not, therefore, as loathing that milk wherewith we were nourished there, but, blessing God for the parentage and education as members of the same body, shall always rejoice in her good, and unfeignedly grieve for any sorrow that shall ever betide her; and, while we have breath, sincerely desire and endeavor the continuance and abundance of her welfare, with the enlargement of her bounds in the kingdom of Christ Jesus. You are not ignorant that the spirit of God stirred up the apostle Paul to make a continual mention of the church at Philippi, which was a colony from Rome; let the same spirit, we beseech you, put you in mind that are the Lord's remembrancers, to pray for us without ceasing, who are the weak colony from yourselves. — What goodness you shall extend unto us, in this or any other christian kindness, we your brethren in Christ Jesus shall labor to repay, in what duty we are or shall be able to perform; promising so far as God shall enable us, to give him no rest on your behalfs; wishing our heads and hearts may be fountains of tears for your everlasting welfare, when we shall be in our poor cottages in the wilderness overshadowed with the spirit of supplication, through the manifold necessities and tribulations which may, not altogether unexpectedly, nor we hope unprofitably, befall us."

The exiles who in this manner bade farewell to their native land, landed in Salem, July, 1630. From this place they settled Charlestown and Dorchester, and towards the end of the same year founded the town of Boston, which, as the seat of government, and through its superior commercial position, soon rose into great importance. In the years following, under the oppressive administration of Archbishop Laud, emigration became a still more pressing necessity; so that settlements were speedily formed, not only on the coast of Massachusetts Bay, but farther west, as at the mouth and on the shores of the Connecticut. These later colonies did not, however, rise into the rank of Massachusetts, which at the very outset had left the older settlement of New Plymouth far behind. But in tracing the historical development which the church-system of the Independents exhibited in New England, Massachusetts will preëminently demand consideration, not alone on account of her extent of territory, but because here the principles of the Independents were most distinctly expounded, and most powerfully defended; and it was from this chief theatre of outward assault and inward conflict, that the consequences of the struggle passed over to the rest of New England. But before attempting to portray these conflicts, we must now consider what appears as characteristic of this new church-party in America; and we must also, in connection with a retrospect of the original character of the Independents, particularly exhibit the change wrought in this respect by the emigration.

THE TWO FUNDAMENTAL PRINCIPLES OF CONGREGATIONALISM.

In separating from the Episcopal Church, the Church party of the Independents, as we have seen, not merely took ground against certain specific abuses, but assumed a peculiar character, through the two following positions, viz:

1. The several churches are altogether independent of one another.

2. Evidence of the requisite qualifications is required by the church, before admission to the Lord's Supper.

These principles, first announced in Holland, and brought thence to New Plymouth, found almost universal acceptance among such of the New England settlers as had forsaken their native land on account of religion. From the very outset their institutions were regulated, and the conflicts which arose were conducted, by these fundamental principles. The most explicit and decided expression of them is found in the platform of church discipline, proposed in a synod held at Cambridge, in Massachusetts, 1648, which was generally adopted. This Confession of Faith belongs, indeed, to a later period, and we shall have occasion to recur to it farther on;[1] but, as it expresses throughout, as we shall see, the principles of the early colonists unchanged,[2] we may here borrow from

[1] See Chapter V.

[2] In the *Collection of original papers* is found a document called *An Abstract of the Laws of New England,* probably from the year 1637. This abstract was printed in London in 1635, and is mentioned by the editor, William Aspinwell, as a work of Cotton, who will claim our notice farther on. Those of the enactments which relate to the Church, contain the germ of the Synodial-conclusions of 1648. Thus, among the duties of the governor is reckoned the preservation of religion, and the general court is to support him in maintaining the purity and the unity of religion. Civil rights belong alone to members of the churches which have been regularly formed with the concurrence of the churches already established; as such members those are designated who are admitted to the Lord's Supper. We here subjoin the following characteristic laws: According to Ch. 3. § 4. no one is to build his house above half a mile, at most a mile, from the place where the church assembles. Ch. 8. § 5. declares that heresy is the stubborn maintenance of a destructive error which subverts the foundations of the christian religion; if connected with attempts to seduce others, it shall be punished with death, such a heretic being no less than

it the official declarations of the same. In the second chapter, after making the distinction between the church militant and the church triumphant, as well as between the visible and the invisible church, it thus proceeds, in reference to fellowship in the church:

"5. The state of the members of the militant visible church, walking in order, was either, before the law (Gen. 18: 19, Ex. 19: 6), economical, that is, in families; or, under the law, national: or, since the coming of Christ, only congregational,[1] — therefore neither national, provincial, nor classical."[2]

"6. A congregational church is, by the institution of Christ, a part of the militant visible church, consisting of a company of saints by calling, united into one body by a holy covenant, for the public worship of God, and the mutual edification of one another in the fellowship of the Lord Jesus."

By the term "saints by calling" is to be understood, according to chapter 3, § 2: "1. Such as have not only attained the knowledge of the principles of religion, and are free from open and gross scandals, but also do, together with the profession of their *faith and repentance*, walk in *blameless obedience to the word.* 2. The children of such, who are also holy." The more particular determinations,

an idolater. § 6. Such members of the church as obstinately, after due admonition and conviction, refuse to submit to the will of the well grounded churches, and to their christian reproof and discipline, shall be cut off by banishment, or be punished according to the judgment of the court.

1 Here occurs in parentheses the words: "the term Independent we approve not." This change of names, Brownists, Independents, Congregationalists, is certainly not without significance.

2 The last term has reference to the synodical, classical, and congregational assemblies of Presbyterianism. The classes embrace several congregations and are subject to the synods.

in respect to the requisites for church membership, which are contained in the twelfth chapter of this platform, and have reference to a certain contrary view, previously mentioned, will be given in full presently. Respecting the other point, the limits of church government, we here notice the principle, laid down in chapter 3, § 4, that the bounds of a church shall not overgo such limits as that all the members may not conveniently meet together in one place. On a greater increase of the population they should, as indeed happened continually, form two churches. So also, through the choice of ministers, elders, and deacons, was maintained the direct participation of the whole body in church government. In regard to this, a distinction is made between the power exercised by the officers of the church, as such, and that belonging to all the members. Thus, chapter 5, § 2, it is said: "The latter is in the brethren, formally and immediately from Christ; that is, so as it may be acted and exercised immediately by themselves; the former is not in them formally or immediately, and therefore cannot be acted or exercised immediately by them, but is said to be in them, in that they design the persons unto office, who only are to act or to exercise this power." Even though it is said, chapter 10, that these two powers are supplementary to each other, yet has the church the right to dismiss her officers; not only because she has herself chosen them, but because in her resides the power of church government. This constitution, which is, in the proper sense of the word, democratic (so, indeed, it is expressly designated), essentially contributed to maintain, in the relations of the churches thus existing side by side, the principles of independency. It is true, several synods were soon called, and even empowered to "debate and determine controversies of faith and cases of conscience," to issue admonitions in reference to single churches, and even to exclude from fellowship such churches as departed from the right way. Still it is declared, in chapter 16, § 4, that the synods "*cannot exercise church censures, in way of discipline, nor any other act of church authority or jurisdiction.*"

THE CONGREGATIONALIST THEOCRACY.

The two principles here mentioned, which are still held by the Congregationalists of the present day, were cherished as of vital import by our colonists, to whom the affairs of religion, the exercise of their own form of worship, and the enjoyment of the divinely instituted means of grace, appeared the goal of all their efforts. They regarded themselves, moreover, not as single fugitives, but as a body politic — an idea brought out in the Instrument, subscribed at Cape Cod in 1620,[1] with a clearness which excites astonishment. What they wished was a State, which they could enjoy in common as an ordinance of God. But the State was to unfold within the church. As they regarded the government as God's servant, so likewise all citizens, as such, were to serve God. Thus "it was resolved in the General Court, at Boston, May 18," 1631, that "for the future no one shall be admitted to the freedom of this body politic, unless he be a member of some church within the limits of the same." Thus was here developed a State church. One evidence of this is furnished by this fact, among others, that the clergy were to be supported, not merely by the contributions of actual church members, but "all who are instructed in the Word must contribute for those by whom they are taught in all good things." [Platform, chap. 11, § 4.] The views then

[1] See p. 57.

entertained of the relation between the civil and the ecclesiastical government, serve to explain the measures pursued in the controversies, as well as in the development of the Congregationalist church in general. We here quote from the articles of the platform, thus giving the views, in their very words, of those who professed them. The 17th chapter treats of "*the power of the civil authority in church matters*," and maintains:

"1. That it is lawful, profitable, and necessary for Christians to gather themselves together into church estate, and therein to exercise all the ordinances of Christ, according unto the Word, although the consent of the magistrate could not be had thereunto; because the apostles, and Christians in their time, did frequently thus practise when the magistrates being all of them Jewish and pagan, and most persecuting enemies, would give no countenance or consent to such matters.

"2. Church-government stands in no opposition to civil government of commonwealths, nor any way intrencheth upon the authority of civil magistrates in their jurisdictions; nor any whit weakeneth their hands in governing, but rather strengtheneth them, and furthereth the people in yielding more ready and conscionable obedience to them, whatsoever some ill-affected persons to the ways of Christ have suggested, to alienate the affections of kings and princes from the ordinances of Christ; as if the kingdom of Christ in his church could not rise or stand without the falling and weakening of their government, which is also of Christ (Isa. 40: 23); whereas the contrary is most true, that they may both stand together and flourish, the one being helpful unto the other, in their distinct and due discriminations.

"3. The power and authority of magistrates is not for

the restraining of churches (Rom. 13: 4., 1 Tim. 2: 2), or any other good works, but for helping in and furthering thereof; and therefore the consent and countenance of magistrates, when it may be had, is not to be slighted or lightly esteemed; but, on the contrary, it is a part of that honor due to christian magistrates, to desire and crave their consent and approbation therein; which being obtained, the churches may then proceed in their way, with much more encouragement and comfort.

"4. It is not in the power of magistrates to compel their subjects to become church-members, and to partake of the Lord's supper (Ezek. 44: 7, 9); for the priests are reproved, that brought unworthy ones into the sanctuary (1 Cor. 5: 11); then it was unlawful for the priests, so is it as unlawful to be done by civil magistrates; those whom the church is to cast out if they were in, the magistrate ought not to thrust them into the church, nor to hold them therein.

"5. As it is unlawful for church-officers to meddle with the sword of the magistrate, so it is unlawful for the magistrate to meddle with the work proper to church-officers. The acts of Moses and David, who were not only princes but prophets, were extraordinary, therefore not imitable. Against such usurpation the Lord witnessed, by smiting Uzziah with leprosy for presuming to offer incense.

"6. It is the duty of the magistrate to take care of matters of religion, and to improve his civil authority for the observing of the duties commanded in the first, as well as for observing of the duties commanded in the second table.[1] They are called GODS (Ps. 88: 8.) The end of the magistrate's office is not only the quiet and peaceable life of the subject in matters of righteousness and honesty,

1 In other words, duties towards God as well as towards man.

but also in matters of godliness, yea, of all godliness (1 Tim. 2 : 2). Moses, Joshua, David, Solomon, Asa, Jehosaphat, Hezekiah, Josiah, are much commended by the Holy Ghost, for the putting forth their authority in matters of religion; on the contrary, such kings as have been failing this way are frequently taxed and reproved of the Lord. And not only the kings of Judah, but also Job (chap. 29 : 25), Nehemiah (chap. 13.), the king of Nineveh (Jonah 3 : 7), Darius, Artaxerxes (Ezra 7), Nebuchadnezzar (Dan. 3 : 29), whom none looked at as types of Christ (though were it so, there were no place for any just objection) are commended in the books of God, for exercising their authority in this way.

"7. The objects of the power of the magistrate are not things merely inward, and so not subject to his cognizance and view, as unbelief, hardness of heart, erroneous opinions not vented, but only such things as are acted by the outer man; neither is their power to be exercised in commanding such acts of the outward man, and punishing the neglect thereof, as are but mere inventions and devices of men, but about such acts as are commanded and forbidden in the Word; yea, such as the Word doth clearly determine, though not always clearly to the judgment of the magistrate or others, yet clearly in itself. In these he, of right, ought to put forth his authority, though ofttimes actually he doth it not.[1]

"8. Idolatry, blasphemy, heresy, venting corrupt and pernicious opinions that destroy the foundation, open contempt of the word preached, profanation of the Lord's day, disturbing the peaceable administration and exercise

1 This provision, as well as many others in these laws, is exceedingly indefinite. The application to single cases could only be determined by the spirit of the code, which is indeed sufficiently manifest.

of the worship and holy things of God, are to be restrained and punished by civil authority.

"9. If any church, one or more, shall grow schismatical, rending itself from the communion of other churches, or shall walk incorrigibly and obstinately in any corrupt way of their own, contrary to the rule of the Word; in such case the magistrate is to put forth his coercive power, as the matter shall require. The tribes on this side Jordan intended to make war against the other tribes, for building the altar of witness, (Josh. 22), whom they suspected to have turned away therein from following of the Lord."

From these declarations it is manifest that the government was THEOCRATIC. The settlers, whose aim it was to derive all their institutions from the word of God, here also universally appealed to the Jewish code.[1] It is from this point of view that we must contemplate those peremptory measures for the expulsion of every opposite tendency, which threatened to disturb the unity of the Church and the State governments, or but to cripple the efficiency of the latter. But here we must especially call attention to that peculiarity of this theocratic constitution, by which no one was permitted to exercise a civil office, or even to enjoy full civil rights, unless he were a member of some regular church, established and ordered in accordance with the principles of the Independents. In the case of State Churches elsewhere, whether of past or present

1 Collection of original papers, p. 161, where occurs the following quotation from a manuscript biography of John Davenport (p. 108,) by Cotton: "The Theocracy, that is, God's government, is to be established as the best form of government. Here the people, who chooses its civil rulers, is God's people, and, equally with those they choose, in covenant with him; they are members of the churches; God's laws and God's servants are enquired of for counsel."

time, membership is conferred by birth, and no one, while conforming to existing usages, and to the preponderating influence of the older members, is excluded except for some explicitly avowed contrariety of opinion. But in New England, one could not thus silently pass into the membership of the church. He was only admitted on the development in the individual of a definite conscious need for fellowship with the church, and when, after being examined by the minister and elders, he had publicly made confession of his faith before the church, and had given evidence of his religious state as that of a regenerate man. Thus, was the STATE also, as well as the Church, to be a COMMUNITY OF BELIEVERS.

It is the object of the following chapters to depict, first the conflict which arose with, and also within, this theocratic constitution; secondly, the dissolution of the same; and finally, the condition which resulted from its abrogation. But before proceeding to this development, we will preface it by some information in regard to the political relations of the Colonies during the first half of the period now under consideration, and briefly refer to their missionary undertakings, and to the founding of the theological Institution at Cambridge. The two latter do not indeed stand in the same immediate connection with the historical development now to be presented; but so far deserve special attention, as contributing to the more exact characterization of the New England Church.

POLITICAL DIVISION AND HISTORY OF NEW ENGLAND.

In its political character also, the government was purely democratic. In accordance with the charter before mentioned, the whole body of free citizens elected the Governor, the members of the Court of Assistants, and General Court,[1] which combined in itself the legislative and highest judicial power. What might have appeared wholly inadmissible in a commercial company in England, assumed a different aspect, when, by transplantation to the other side of the ocean, and by the growth of all the elements of a state, the PROPER RIGHTS OF SOVEREIGNTY had attached themselves almost unnoticed to the delegated privileges. These rights had from the first been exercised with steady firmness by the government in Boston, in the full conviction of proceeding in accordance with the laws of God, and in harmony with the letter and spirit of their charter. When, in the year 1630, the government of Plymouth put the question in Boston,[2] whether it possessed the competency to execute sentence of death on a convicted murderer, the answer was, that undoubtedly it had that right, though the warrant lay solely in the analogy of procedure by the Massachusetts government. Agreement with the laws of England was, it is true, expressly recognized as the rule in legislation; but more in theory than practice. An appeal to England was only resorted to exceptionally and by necessity. It may appear singular that this should not have been opposed at the very first, by the mother country. But before the consequences could be foreseen by Charles I., his power to carry even the most unimportant measure was entirely gone. The Republicans in England favored the development of this

1 More distinctive are the designations afterwards in use: Council and General Assembly. According to the laws of 1637, (see p. 68,) all governmental power is vested in and proceeds from the Supreme Court. When subsequently, in accordance with the charter of William III., the governors were appointed by the crown, the governor, council, and general assembly were often compared to the king, lords, and commons.

2 Baylies, I. p. 203.

free government, and thus it had become firmly established when, at a later period, it was assailed by Charles II.

The great distinction enjoyed by Massachusetts is strikingly illustrated by the fact, that many of the colonies which by degrees came into existence held, for a longer or shorter period, a dependent relation to her, more or less clearly defined. Thus New Hampshire, where single settlements had been formed soon after the founding of New Plymouth, and where in 1631 the town of Portsmouth was settled, subjected itself in 1640 to the jurisdiction of the General Court of Massachusetts. The detached settlements in Maine were longer held back from the same measure by private individuals; but in 1651 this colony also became attached to Massachusetts. Remaining thinly peopled down to recent times, it was not till 1820 that Maine was admitted as a proper state into the confederacy of the United States. Although both colonies were for a time again withdrawn from Massachusetts by royal decree, yet she understood how to maintain her authority over them, so long as she retained possession of her charter.

From the settlements first established, persons went farther westward to the river Connecticut, and in 1636, planted Hartford. In this they proceeded on a sort of warrant from the General Court at Boston; but soon finding that they were beyond the jurisdiction embraced in the charter of Massachusetts, they established a political organization after the model of that colony, made laws, and chose magistrates. Not long after, a company arrived from England with a patent for this same region; but as it did not answer their expectations, they sold their charter to the previous settlers. Still more destitute of legal authority was the colony of New Haven, which lay farther westward, bordering on the possessions then held by the Dutch. Hither, in 1637, had come a party of emigrants with their minister, John Davenport, under the guidance of Theophilus Eaton, afterwards their Governor, and had purchased of the Indians on this part of the mainland, as well as on the opposite island of Long Island.[1] Here they adopted as their model the government of Massachusetts, adhering to it still more strictly than the founders of Connecticut, who had at once ordained that civil rights should be enjoyed without reference to church membership.

Surrounded by the above-named colonies, lay PROVIDENCE and RHODE ISLAND, whose settlement will be treated of in the next chapter. Founded, so early as 1634 and 1637, by fugitives and exiles from Massachusetts, they had thus long sustained themselves in direct opposition to the other colonies, who refused all connection with them. They were denied admission to a proposed confederacy, which went into effect in 1643, when the four colonies of New Plymouth, Massachusetts, Connecticut, and New Haven combined themselves in a league, offensive and defensive, as the UNITED STATES OF NEW ENGLAND.

In this compact also, having for its object mutual protection, as well against the attacks of the Indians as against their northern neighbors the French and their western neighbors the Dutch, Massachusetts held a marked preponderance. During the changes in the government of England at the period of the first English revolution, the colonies submitted to the ruling authority, whatever it might be; and strong as must have been their sympathy with the Independent party, they greeted the accession of Charles II., in 1661, with a loyal address of congratulation.

[1] A part of the island was colonized from New Amsterdam; later it belonged wholly to New York.

Shortly after, charters were granted by the king to Rhode Island, Connecticut and New Haven, the two latter of which were in 1664 united into one colony. The same year New Amsterdam was captured by the English and named New York. In 1668 Holland relinquished her colonies at the peace of Breda, recaptured them indeed in 1674, but in the following year lost possession of them forever. But while the western frontier of New England was thus secured, within its borders raged a bloody war with the Indians, favored by the French and by the leadership of the enterprising Philip, king of the Wampanoags. With the death of the latter, in 1676, the power of the Indians within the territory itself was broken, and henceforth they only attempted war on the borders in connection with the French.

The later political relations of New England, so far as they serve for the illustration of its church-history, will be glanced at farther on.[1] About the year 1680, a year of great changes in many respects, New England consisted of the three united colonies of New Plymouth, Massachusetts with Maine and New Hampshire, and Connecticut with New Haven. The settlements of Rhode Island and Providence had also been united into one, since the year 1643.

MISSIONARY AND EDUCATIONAL EFFORTS.

Within every Christian communion, so soon at least as its interior organization has acquired a certain degree of solidity, and a fresh vigorous life, a tendency is developed to spread the gospel beyond its own limits. But this tendency takes different outward forms, not only according to the fields offered or sought for its operations, but also

[1] See Chap. VIII.

according to the character and relations of the churches themselves. The truth of this may be shown through the entire history of the christian church. The christianization of classical antiquity owed its peculiar form no less to the character of the apostolic age, as a period of preëminent personalities, than did the conversion of the Germanic world to the inflexibly rigid organism of the Romish church. In regard to the missionary activity of New England, it is to be noted as a peculiar characteristic, that it manifested itself at a very early period; only a few decades after the first formation of Independent churches, only a few years after the establishment of the larger churches in New England. In regard to the progress of this activity, it is especially worthy of note that the missionaries had to do with a foreign race, who lived beside and among Europeans, yet in respect to civilization standing most decidedly below them. The names of Eliot and of the Mayhew family have become generally known, as the most eminent preachers of the gospel among the Indians. These men, besides the gifts of religious heroism and unconquerable endurance, possessed also the ability to make what they taught intelligible and acceptable, and to form churches out of those whom they had gained as friends of the word of God. In this work, which was very early crowned with great success, they were sustained by many other distinguished men. In spite of the opposition of the former priests, who feared to lose the gains of their sorceries; in spite of their chiefs who feared to lose that unlimited power which they possessed over their property, various churches, some of them very large in numbers, were formed from the converted, or, as they were called, "praying Indians." It was not long before preachers were raised up from among the Indians themselves, who sought to make known the gospel to their countrymen. But it must here be remarked, that these missions were not merely the undertakings of individuals; the mother-country did not fail to encourage and sustain them. In the Massachusetts Charter, it was expressly made the duty of the settlers "to win and incite the natives of that country, to the knowledge and obedience of the only true God and Saviour of mankind." An association was formed in England, confirmed in the year 1647, under the name of the "Society for the spread of the Gospel in foreign lands," which contributed money for purchasing articles of various kinds, necessary to the support of English and Indian missionaries, and especially for procuring a translation of the Bible into the Indian tongue. The Congregational churches of New England made a similar expression of their sympathy, by the establishment of an Indian College for the education of native preachers. The later results did not indeed correspond to this noble beginning; for not only was the education of native missionaries given up and the Indian College abolished, but the Indian churches themselves fell into decay. In place of the original confidence reposed in the English, there sprung up gradually an enmity towards them, to which the border wars with the French and Dutch had greatly contributed. After King Philip's war, the former relation was not reëstablished, as indeed, from that time, the colonists no longer observed so strictly in their dealings with the natives those earlier principles of integrity, of which we have before spoken. The government was unable, either by prohibitions or punishments, to hinder the sale of brandy, which was furnished to the natives not only by the French, but at a later period by the people of New England also; and to such a degree did the Indians abandon themselves to intoxication, that it may be regarded as one of the chief causes of their gradual decay and ruin. In connection with that aversion to civilization, natural to tribes which have grown up in the forest, the Indians in general have been stigmatized as an idle race, — as Mather says, "they kept the command: Thou shalt sanctify the seventh day; but not the other: Six days shalt thou labor." An unconquerable pride, moreover, forbade their engaging in regular occupation, or the pursuits of agriculture. They were unfitted for admittance into the New England confederacy on terms of equality with the other members. Even for a special alliance, which, with increasing culture, might have developed itself into something farther, they were not sufficiently protected against hostile interference; not sufficiently isolated from the peaceful progress of European civilization. Yet, in contemplating the fate of this unhappy people, in general, as well as the inconsiderable results of missionary effort among them, we must not leave out of view the subsequent decay of Christianity among those to whose care they were committed. It is a striking fact that the fifth decade of the eighteenth century, which was distinguished by a special revival of the religious life in New England, produced also in Brainerd[1] a missionary who labored among the Indians with the gifts, the active zeal, and to a certain extent with the success of those earlier preachers of the word.

An index no less characteristic of the Congregationalists than their missionary activity, but in another direction, is seen in the early establishment of a scientific institution. So early as September 1630, that is, immediately after the founding of Boston, four hundred pounds sterling were

1 The diary of his labors and experiences is contained in the biography published by Jonathan Edwards, which we shall mention further on.

appropriated at an assembly of the General Court for the establishment of a college. But as this sum was insufficient for the purpose, and it could not then be increased, the execution of the plan was delayed some years. But in 1637, John Harvard, a minister who had shortly before arrived from England, bequeathed to this object seven hundred and eighty pounds; a committee was then formed, and contributions being added both by the colonial government and by private individuals, the work was now set forward without delay. Newtown, a place settled in 1629, was selected as the location, and was called Cambridge, in honor of the English University-town; the Seminary itself, in memory of the above-mentioned legacy as the main constituent of the first fund, received the name of Harvard College. A building was erected expressly for the purpose, where the pupils lived together as in the English universities. Even in its first years, this institution became a *schola illustris*, where polite learning and philosophy formed the substance of the course of instruction. The first charter of 1642 mentions a president and six ministers from the neighboring towns of Cambridge, Watertown, Boston, Charlestown, Roxbury and Dorchester, who in connection with the Boston Government were to have the oversight of the college. Thus the college received at once a theological character, a peculiarity which became yet more manifest on the confirmation and extension of the original charter in 1650 and 1672, after the Indian College above-mentioned was incorporated with it. At a still later period it received a yet farther enlargement in its general design and character. The right was granted it of conferring academic degrees, that of master being reached in order after a residence of seven years. The terms of admission were, ability to translate Cicero off-hand, and a knowledge of the elements of Greek grammar. This institution had been for many years the only school for the education of the clergy in New England, when Yale College, in New Haven,[1] was founded with a similar design, at the beginning of the eighteenth century. In all the vicissitudes experienced by the Congregationalists, Harvard College has had a living participation. The unbelief which, in the eighteenth century, extended itself over New England, obtained a footing here also, and increased to such a degree that gradually all the teachers and directors, indicated in the charter, became Unitarians. In their hands this university remains to the present day; while other colleges and seminaries have been established by the Congregationalists of the present time.

We now proceed to the development of the ecclesiastical polity of New England. We shall describe, in chapter third, such forms of opposition as separated from the connection, and in chapter fourth such as were repulsed from it; chapter fifth will treat of the suppression of the resistance to the theocratic relation; chapter sixth of the dissolution of this relation.

[1] See Chap. VIII. As early as 1651 very earnest efforts were made for the establishment of such an institution in New Haven, especially by the minister of that place, John Davenport. But the resources of this colony were insufficient for the purpose, and even after its union with Connecticut it could do no more than to establish a grammar school.—*Trumbull's History of Connecticut,* Vol. I. Ch. 13.

CHAPTER III.

EXPULSION OF ROGER WILLIAMS AND THE ANTINOMIANS—RHODE ISLAND.

THE ESTABLISHED THEOCRACY FIRST CONTESTED BY ROGER WILLIAMS; HE IS BANISHED, AND FOUNDS PROVIDENCE ON NARRAGANSET BAY.

THE controversies of the dominant church with Roger Williams and the Antinomians gave occasion to the settlements on Narraganset Bay, which subsequently united themselves to the colony of Rhode Island. The latter was based on principles, in regard to the relation of church and state, wholly different from those just exhibited; but the hostility and exclusive policy of the other colonies towards Rhode Island had an earlier source, viz., the circumstances in which this settlement originated. This will appear from the following explanation.

Roger Williams[1] was born in Wales in the year 1599. He devoted himself at first to the study of jurisprudence, but soon relinquished it for that of theology. He became a clergyman in the Episcopal church, but his puritanic principles constrained him, like so many others, to forsake his native land. On the 5th of February 1631, he landed in New England, and for a while resided in Boston. A few weeks after his arrival, the church of Salem invited him to

[1] Memoir of Roger Williams, by James D. Knowles. Boston: 1834. This biography is enriched with many documents.

become the assistant of their minister Mr. Skelton, Mr. Higginson,[1] the other pastor of the church, having died soon after its formation. As soon as this became known, the Boston Court was called together by Governor Winthrop, April 12th, and the following statement was made by its order to the church: "That whereas Mr. Williams had refused to join with the congregation at Boston, because they would not make a public declaration of their repentance for having communion with the churches of England while they lived there; and, beside, had declared his opinion that the magistrate might not punish a breach of the Sabbath, nor any other offence, as it was a breach of the first table; therefore they marvelled they would choose him without advising with the council; and, withal, desiring they would forbear to proceed till they had conferred about it."

The first of these charges we do not find to have been again brought forward in the subsequent proceedings with Williams. As we have before had occasion to observe in the measures and declarations of the first Massachusetts settlers, the views of the colonists in relation to fellowship with the Church of England were vague and unsettled; nor does it appear how far this expression of repentance which he desired was to extend. While at Plymouth, during the following years, he maintained intercourse and fellowship with members of the Boston church; but the demand itself is in keeping with that decision of character which is generally attributed to him, and which seems to have been connected with a certain vehemence of temper, at least in his early years. The other point in the accusation, that relating to the commands of the first table, is of more importance; and this we shall have another opportu-

[1] See p. 60.

nity for discussing, as it comes up again in connection with a subsequent action against Williams. The church at Salem, though informed of the step intended by the General Court, on that same 12th of April chose Williams as their pastor. It is a noticeable fact that it was on the 18th of May that he took his oath as citizen, exactly the time when the law was passed requiring every citizen to be a member of some regular church.[1] This act is of importance, in view of the principles with which he was afterwards charged; but it shows also that the Boston government took a course in this proceeding which, if not inconsistent, was at least wanting in decision. But scarcely had Williams been a few months in Salem, when he was obliged to leave that town and go to Plymouth. Manifestly this step was neither voluntary on his part, nor from the wish of the Salem church, as appears from their subsequent recall and continued attachment to him. The Boston government used their influence to carry out, in practice, the principles laid down in the Cambridge Platform, (Chap. 17, § 9) respecting schismatical churches.[2] But certainly these principles were at first yet more indefinite, in respect to the interference of the civil power, than after the passage of the above cited law; hence, nothing can be made out in regard to their customary application, there being no direct information even in respect to the present case.

Williams was well received in Plymouth, and acted as assistant to their minister, Mr. Ralph Smith.[3] Governor Bradford[4] said of him, "He was freely entertained among us, acording to our poor ability, exercised his gifts among us, and after some time was admitted a member of the church, and his teaching well approved; for the benefit whereof I shall bless God, and am thankful to him ever for

[1] See p. 71. [2] P. 75, f. [3] P. 59. [4] P. 59.

his sharpest admonitions and reproofs, so far as they agreed with truth." While Williams was still residing at Plymouth, the town was visited by Governor Winthrop,[1] Mr. Wilson the Boston minister, and other distinguished men. At this time no trace appeared of hostility or coldness. On a certain Sunday, when they celebrated the Lord's Supper together, the church was addressed both by the ministers above mentioned, and by the Governors of Boston and Plymouth. Williams remained two years at Plymouth, but the first favorable disposition towards him did not continue; the effect, probably, of the open expression of his views in regard to the relations of the civil magistracy. Mr. Brewster, the ruling elder, foreboded the farther spreading of these opinions, and expressed his fears "that Williams would run the same course of rigid separation and anabaptistry which Mr. John Smith, the Se-baptist[2] at Amsterdam, had done." A large part of the church now abandoned Williams, who, in August 1633, willingly accepted a call from the Salem church to assist their now infirm pastor, Mr. Skelton; this he did without being at first formally inducted into the office. Meanwhile, the Salem church continued to stand, to a certain degree, in an attitude of estrangement towards the other churches. When, in this same year, a number of ministers of Massachusetts Bay agreed to meet together once a fortnight for conference on the interests of the church, Skelton and Williams held aloof from it, out of fear that it might grow into a presbytery or ecclesiastical tribunal. Yet the others declared that they were all, decidedly and unanimously, of the opinion that no church or person can have any power over another church; nor did they,

1 Winthrop's Journal. This diary extends to the year 1644, and contains very interesting particulars in regard to the history of this period.

2 See p. 36.

in these meetings, attempt the slightest exercise of such jurisdiction. Shortly after, Williams was cited before the General Court at Boston, on account of a treatise addressed by him to the Governor and Council of Plymouth. In this he had maintained that the royal charter was invalid, and consequently also the colonists' title to possession, which could be based alone on an agreement with the natives. In the first patent, reference was indeed made to "the great sickness by which the country was depopulated, and thus deserted, as it were, of its natural inhabitants;" but the prevailing view was also therein expressed, that the colony had passed into the possession of the King of England, as that christian sovereign whose subjects had first visited the country. But, as already stated, the settlers had proceeded wholly in accordance with the principle now laid down by Williams.[1] On this point, therefore, they came to an understanding. He explained his irreverent expressions in regard to the king in a less offensive sense, or retracted them; he stated, moreover, that he had regarded the treatise as merely a private thing, not intended for publicity, and even expressed his willingness to burn it. Thus was this difficulty settled.

For a time he remained wholly undisturbed in his labors, and gained for himself the warmest affection of his hearers. On the death of Mr. Skelton, in August, 1634, the church chose him for their pastor. The government at Boston requested the church not to ordain him; but it remained unmoved, and Williams was installed in the usual manner. Soon after he was cited before the General Court, and this was repeated several times. In the charge instituted against him on the 8th of July, 1635, is contained a summary of the opinions advanced by him,

[1] See p. 58.

in which we find the four following points: 1. That the magistrate ought not to punish the breach of the first table, otherwise than in such cases as did disturb the civil peace; 2. That he ought not to tender an oath to an unregenerate man; 3. That a man ought not to pray with such, though a member of his own family; 4. That it was not necessary to give thanks after the sacrament, nor in general after meat.

The first of these points is the most important, as it is also the most significant of the views and principles held on both sides. Those of the dominant party are contained in the Cambridge Platform[1] and it cannot be questioned, that to impugn this right of the magistracy was to assail the existing theocratic government. Roger Williams, on the other hand, as appears from his later writings as well as in the founding of his new settlement, regarded the entire separation of church and state as the necessary condition of complete religious liberty. Hence, they could come to no agreement in this respect; though the Congregationalists were compelled gradually to adopt these same principles, which now prevail in all church-parties throughout the United States.

The second point holds a certain relation to the third; but it seems also to have had reference to a special exigency, viz., an attempt made by the government, just at this time, to procure a change in the freeman's oath hitherto in use. Information having come to the General Court of the intrigues of certain partisans of the Episcopal church, or other malcontents, against the country, it was resolved as a measure of safety, to tender to each man a new oath of fidelity, in which was promised, in place of obedience to all legal ordinances, obedience to all whole-

[1] See p. 68, ff.

some ordinances of the existing government. No public office was to be entrusted to one who refused this oath. This plan was opposed by Williams, and his influence so prevailed with members of the General Court, that it could not be carried through. Its origin is probably to be found in a commission granted by Charles I. to Archbishop Laud and others, conferring on them plenipotentiary authority over the colonies; but the mode by which they sought to defend themselves was as much at war with their original principles, as it was in accordance with the measures which had once made the Independents fugitives.

The positions charged upon Williams in reference to the unregenerate are worthy of note. They plainly appear like expressions originating in unwarrantable deduction from certain principles. That fundamental rule, by which the unregenerate were refused admission to the membership of the Congregationalist churches, Williams extended to every form of divine worship and religious service; for as such he regarded the oath. This confounding of that which constitutes qualification for church-fellowship with that which renders a religious reference possible in any case whatever, gained no footing,[1] and was discarded even by the late adherents of Williams.

1 We take occasion here to quote an extraordinary specimen of argumentation, which was made use of against Williams. He complained in court of having been wronged by a slanderous report, as if he had said it was unlawful for a father to call upon his child to eat his meat. Mr. Hooker, a minister who was present, replied: "Why, you will say as much again if you stand to your own principles, or be driven to say nothing at all." Mr. Williams protesting the contrary, Mr. Hooker proceeded to reason thus: "If it be unlawful to call on an unregenerate person to pray, since it is an action of God's worship, then it is unlawful for your unregenerate child to pray for a blessing on his own meat. If it be unlawful for him to pray for a blessing upon his meat, it is unlawful for him to eat it, for it is sanctified by prayer, and without prayer, unsanctified (1 Tim. 4: 4, 5). If

The fourth point probably grew out of opposition to an effort for uniformity. In May, 1635, an act was passed by the General Court at Boston, "intreating the brethren and elders of every church within this jurisdiction, that they will consult and advise of one uniform order of discipline in the churches, agreeable to the Scriptures, and then to consider how far the magistrates are bound to interpose for the preservation of that uniformity and peace of the churches."

Notwithstanding the ultimate success of Williams's principles, it is certainly not to be denied that in his own time he was not in a condition to secure currency for opinions which were not entirely systematized and clear in his own mind, and which, to some extent, led him to pernicious conclusions. His personal qualities preserved the attachment of the church at Salem unimpaired. It so happened that during the above-mentioned transactions, this town applied for the assignment of a parcel of land belonging to it; but the Court answered, that their choice of Mr. Williams, and their perseverance in the same, showed such contempt of authority, that the petition could not be granted; nor in truth was their claim admitted till after the settlement of this affair. The Salem church now addressed letters to the other churches, calling their attention to this invasion of their rights and liberties, and urging them to admonish the magistrates, as church-members, for such a course of proceeding. Williams was still

it be unlawful for him to eat it, it is unlawful for you to call upon him to eat it; for it is unlawful for you to call upon him to sin." Mather, Book VII. Chap. II. § 6. Mather waxes indignant over the behavior of Williams, who chose to hold his peace, rather than make any answer. The ministers of Boston who were present at the trial, agreed unconditionally with the government.

more vehement. Being at that time confined by sickness, he wrote to his church, "that he could not communicate longer with the churches in the Bay, neither would he with themselves except they would refuse communion with the rest." Therefore, in October, he was again called before the Court, and there, in presence of the assembled ministers of the vicinity, was required to retract the opinions expressed in his two letters. This he refused, as also the offer of a respite with a view to a subsequent disputation. After an unavailing attempt, by a public conference, to bring him to submission, the Court, with the concurrence of all the ministers present, one alone excepted, passed sentence on him as follows: "Whereas, Mr. Roger Williams, one of the elders of the church of Salem, hath broached and divulged divers new and dangerous opinions, against the authority of magistrates; as also writ letters of defamation, both of the magistrates and churches here; and that before any conviction; and yet maintaineth the same without any retraction; it is therefore ordered, that the said Mr. Williams shall depart out of this jurisdiction within six weeks now next ensuing, which if he neglect to perform, it shall be lawful for the governor and two of the magistrates to send him to some place out of this jurisdiction, not to return any more without license from the Court."

The church at Salem retracted their former expressions, and submitted to the decision against their minister, though not without great previous excitement and agitation. Williams having requested permission to remain in Salem till spring, was allowed to do so, on condition of refraining from all expression of his views; but in January 1636, being charged with holding assemblies in his own house for the propagation of the offensive doctrines, it was resolved by the Court that he should be sent forthwith to England. During this interval, he had brought more than twenty persons to the determination of following him to Narraganset Bay, southward from the Plymouth colony, for the purpose of founding a settlement. As he did not answer to a warrant for his appearance in Boston, a pinnace was sent to Salem under a commission for his apprehension. But before its arrival he had left the town; a measure advised by Governor Winthrop himself, as the one most conducive to the public peace and to his own personal interests.

Proceeding through the yet uncultivated regions of Massachusetts in a southerly direction, he succeeded in establishing, on Narraganset Bay, the colony of Providence, which was soon joined by a considerable number of persons from the older colonies. With the same conscientiousness which he had required from others, he purchased lands from the Indians, and so entirely won their confidence, as to be able at a later period to render most important services to the other colonies in the minor wars with the Indians. We shall return to the subject of his personal opinions, and his relation to the other settlements, after having first described another controversy in Boston, which led to a second settlement on Narraganset Bay.

ANTINOMIAN AGITATIONS — ANNE HUTCHINSON.

Soon after the expulsion of Williams from Massachusetts, there arrived among the numerous emigrants to New England a young man of distinguished family, whose name often appears in the subsequent history of England. Henry Vane abhorred the oppressions of Episcopal domination, and resolved to found a settlement in Connecticut. His father, who was a partisan of the king, was induced by him to consent to the undertaking; for at that time Charles I. seems to have favored the removal of his opposers from England.[1] Vane landed at Boston, in 1636, and although still a young man, was immediately chosen Governor of Massachusetts. Though not himself an adherent of the Antinomian doctrines, which were at this time spreading in Boston, these made great progress under his government. It appears also, from a correspondence between him and Williams, with whom he was on terms of close friendship, that he took the same ground with him in regard to unconditional freedom of religious worship and of church discipline. His high rank secured him many adherents among the members of the General Court, who used their most strenuous efforts to secure his reëlection as governor the following year (May, 1627); but after considerable agitation, John Winthrop, the well-tried founder of this colony, succeeded to the office.[2] Under him the Antinomian controversy reached its crisis and termination.

These views had become associated with the preaching of the most eminent and respected minister of Boston. John Cotton had been some years settled as a clergyman at Boston, in England,[3] when he embraced, and applied in public worship, the nonconformist view respecting certain ceremonies in the Episcopal church. He, nevertheless, remained several years undisturbed in his office, beloved and esteemed by his congregation, and much valued by Wil-

1 Subsequently the king threw hindrances in the way of such emigration. In 1639, as is well known, he obliged Cromwell to relinquish his intended voyage to New England.

2 Vane soon after returned to England, and as a member of the Long Parliament, took very decided ground against the royal government. After the Restoration, he was executed, June 11th, 1662, although he had not been one of the judges of Charles I.

3 In Lincolnshire.

liams, the Bishop of his diocese, who was himself inclined to Puritanism.[1] But at length, a person against whom the magistrates of Boston had instituted some proceeding, swore before the High Commission in London, that the clergymen and magistrates of Boston did not kneel at the sacrament, and, in other respects, departed from uniformity in ceremonies. Before a warrant could arrive, Mr. Cotton fled disguised to London; but was there told by his friends, among whom were some very distinguished men, that "if he had been charged with crime, they could have obtained his pardon; but the sin of being a Puritan was unpardonable." Following the counsel of these friends, he embarked for America in the year 1636, having then exercised the office of a clergyman almost twenty years. Soon after his arrival in Boston, he began to act as assistant to Mr. Wilson, then minister of the church. The reputation of great learning, which Cotton brought with him from England, secured him high distinction: while he won the love and confidence of his flock, by activity in his office, and by his preaching, which was admired for its freedom from Latin phrases, and displays of scholastic learning then in vogue, thus being intelligible to every class of hearers.[2]

It was the custom in Boston for members of the church to hold weekly meetings for conversation on the subjects which had been brought before them in public worship. This practice was particularly observed in connection with Mr. Cotton's preaching, even among the female members under the guidance of one Mrs. Anne Hutchinson, who

[1] Williams was afterwards himself called to account, and was heavily fined and thrown into prison; being set at liberty by the Long Parliament, he became, in 1641, archbishop of York.

[2] His name was so well known in England, that after the Revolution broke out, he was requested by many distinguished men to return; but he never again left his adopted country. He died in Boston in 1652.

had arrived in the country in 1636. She was in the habit of praying before assemblies of sixty to eighty persons, and of repeating Mr. Cotton's discourses, to which she then added explanations and reflections of her own. Here Antinomian tendencies soon developed themselves[1] in the doctrines, "that the person of the Holy Ghost dwells in a justified person; that the command to work out our salvation with fear and trembling refers to such only as stand under the law of works; that sanctification is no sufficient evidence of a justified state." With these teachings was connected a fanatical tendency, exhibited in the claim to special revelations. While Vane was governor, these views, which were propagated under the honored name of Cotton, found favor in many quarters; the party which cherished them branded the rest as "legalists, who were acquainted neither with the spirit of the Gospel, nor with Christ himself." "People under a covenant of works" were distinguished from "people under a covenant of grace." The dispute having soon spread through the whole town and even among members of the government, Cotton found it necessary to express his opinion in regard to it. He rejected the new doctrines as erroneous; but as he had at first formed a very favorable judgment of Mrs. Hutchinson and her followers, and as she professed, when admonished by him, to acquiesce in his views, he expressed himself with great moderation. In the crisis to which the controversy had now come, his explanation satisfied neither party; though it would seem, from his being sent from Boston to New Haven, for the purpose of procuring a change in the measure there adopted at this time, that the personal estimation which he had enjoyed remained unabated.

[1] Hutch. II. p. 46.

The Antinomian doctrines had just then found an advocate in a minister by the name of Wheelwright, brother-in-law of Mrs. Hutchinson. He maintained in a sermon, that "the magistrates and ministers of the country walked in such a way of salvation, as was no better than a covenant of works." He compared them to the Jews, to Herod, to the Philistines, and exhorted all who stood in the covenant of grace to contend against them as against their greatest enemies. Thereupon he was summoned by the magistracy before the General Court at its next session, and his defence having been heard, his sermon was pronounced "seditious and tending to the disturbance of the public peace." All attempts to bring him to a sense of his error were unavailing; still he was allowed the time to the next session for considering whether he would give in his submission, or expect the sentence of the Court. The adherents of the Antinomian party were so excited by this attack on their minister, that they assembled the same evening and drew up a petition or rather a protest against the proceedings of the Court, wherein they expressed their opinion that "Wheelwright had neither been guilty of any seditious act whatever, nor did his doctrine contain anything seditious, being no other than the word of Scripture; it had, moreover, had no seditious consequences, for none of his followers had drawn the sword, or attempted to set free their innocent brother. They therefore besought the Court to consider how great was the danger attending such an intermeddling in the affairs of the prophets of God, and to remember that even the apostle Paul was called a pestilent fellow, a mover of sedition, and the ringleader of a sect." This petition was presented to the Court a day or two after the censure had been passed on Wheelwright's sermon; but though signed by above sixty names, and even by some members of the Court, it was rejected by the majority.

FIRST NEW ENGLAND SYNOD — EXPULSION OF THE ANTINOMIANS.

But the government was itself aware, that a division which had gone so far could not be settled or suppressed by ordinary means. It was resolved, therefore, to call a synod of ministers and lay-delegates of the churches, from which they might secure the necessary support for a vigorous course of proceeding. This first synod of the Independents met at Newtown,[1] on the 30th of August 1637. To this assembly, besides the regular members, the magistrates also were admitted for the purpose of maintaining quiet and order; and they were not only allowed to hear, but as occasion offered, to express their views. A particular space was reserved for the adherents of the new opinions, and free entrance was granted to all who wished to be present. On the first day, Thomas Hooker, minister of Hartford in Connecticut, and Peter Bulkley of Concord, Massachusetts, were chosen moderators, and a list of eighty-two erroneous opinions then prevailing in different parts of the country was read before the synod. On the following morning, a committee employed itself in drawing up the grounds of refutation, and in the afternoon presented their arguments to the synod. The next day, the other party gave in their reply, and to this followed a rejoinder to the reasons thus alleged by the Antinomians. Thereupon the final action was taken by a unanimous condemnation of all the new opinions, to which the whole body of ministers present gave their subscription. Only Mr. Cotton declared, that while he "disrelished the greater part of the new opinions, some of which were heretical,

1 Called Cambridge in the following year. See p. 84.

some blasphemous, some erroneous, and all of them incongruous," yet he could not condemn them *in toto* and without qualification. In reference to the doctrine of justification, he maintained, in contrariety to the general opinion, that "there may be a union of man with God, before faith." It was felt that the dissent of a man like Cotton had a momentous bearing on the decision of the controversy, which could thus be prosecuted by the disaffected under his name even more successfully than before. But by repeated conference on the contested points, Mr. Cotton was brought to an agreement with the rest in the following declaration: "That we are not united and married to the Lord Jesus Christ without faith, giving an actual consent of soul unto it; that God's effectual calling of the soul unto the Lord Jesus Christ, and the soul's apprehending by an act of faith the offered righteousness of the Lord Jesus Christ is in order of nature before God's act of justification upon the soul; that in the testimony of the Holy Spirit, which is the evidence of our good estate before God, the qualifications of inherent graces, and the fruits thereof, proving the sincerity of our faith, must ever be coëxistent, concurrent, coäpparent, or else the conceived testimony of the Spirit is either a delusion or doubtful." Having thus yielded his assent to the general conviction, Mr. Cotton promised also to unite his testimony with that of his brethren against the erroneous opinions. The synod had been three weeks in session. On the last day, Mr. Davenport, minister of New Haven, preached a discourse from Phil. 3: 16., "Nevertheless, whereunto we have already attained, let us walk by the same rule, let us mind the same thing." He then read aloud the decisions of the synod, which were so drawn up that after the statement of each particular error, the judgment followed: "We find this contrary to such and such a text of Scripture." Finally, he exhorted the ministers and lay-delegates to labor in their respective churches for a uniformity with the views of the synod, and then dismissed the assembly.

Now, whatever a synod lacked in legislative power, according to the fundamental principles of the Independents, it gained in this case through the unanimity of its members. But neither did Wheelwright change the character of his preaching, nor Mrs. Hutchinson discontinue her meetings, especially as both of them still found no inconsiderable support in Boston. On this account, the General Court assembled on the 2d of October in Newtown. Their first step was to exclude three members from Boston, by one of whom the petition above mentioned, had been drawn up and signed, and by both the others publicly defended. After some resistance, the people of Boston were induced to supply the places thus made vacant by a new election. Wheelwright was now required to give a categorical answer to the interrogatory previously put, whether he would acknowledge his error in respect to that seditious sermon, or expect the judgment of the Court. He replied, that "he was guilty neither of sedition nor insubordination; he had preached nothing but christian truth; as to the application, that was made by others, not by himself." He was then required, for the sake of the public peace, to leave the colony voluntarily. This being refused, sentence was passed, declaring his forfeiture of civil rights, his banishment from the commonwealth, and his immediate imprisonment in failure of furnishing security that he would depart before the end of March. From this decision he appealed to the King of England, but it was replied that his case was not of a character admitting of appeal. He then declined giving the required security, and was accordingly lodged in prison; but on the following day he yielded, recalled his appeal, and declared himself ready to submit to simple banishment. The Court dismissed him on the promise, that if he did not leave the commonwealth within fourteen days, he would himself return to prison, and there await the decision of his case. He chose to go into banishment.[1]

This matter being disposed of, the petitioners were called before the Court; after a part had made their submission, the rest were punished, some by dismissal from their offices, some by fines, some by banishment. Mrs. Hutchinson had not been concerned in the petition; but it could no longer be overlooked that she still continued her weekly meetings. She was accordingly called up and charged with being the cause, through the preaching of her errors and her slander of all the ministers of the country, of the late disturbances and disorders in church and state. In her defence, so far from retracting anything or promising to remain quiet in future, she indulged freely in bitter reflections against the Court. She thus compared her case with that of the prophet Daniel:[2] "When the princes and presidents could find nothing against him, because he was faithful, they sought matter against him concerning the law of his God, to cast him into the lions' den." Then she assumed the prophetic tone: "Take heed how you proceed against me; for I know that for this you go about to do to me, God will ruin you and your posterity, and this whole state." The Court ordered her to be silent, and as there appeared to be no hope of her recantation, required her to depart from that jurisdiction

[1] Seven years after, on his apologizing for remarks made against the Government, his sentence was revoked; and he returned and continued to live many years as minister of the Church in Hampton and afterward in Salisbury.

[2] Dan. 6: 4, 5.

within six months. At the same time, the church at Boston, of which she was a member, declared her guilty of heresy, as having maintained twenty-six of the doctrines condemned by the synod. She drew up, indeed, a recantation, but added to it the protestation "that she was never really of any opinion contrary to the declaration she had now made." Being convicted of the contrary by witnesses, her recantation was rejected, and she was excommunicated as a public liar, with the full consent of the church. Other members of the church shared the same fate, not so much on account of erroneous opinions, as of offences in conduct.

These exiles betook themselves, some to Connecticut, some to New Hampshire, but the greater part repaired to Roger Williams, in Providence. Here they resolved to settle on an island in Narraganset Bay hitherto called Aquatneck,[1] to which they gave the name of Rhode Island. After having purchased it from the Indians by the help of Roger Williams, they founded here a colony, which, though holding the most friendly relations to that of Providence, was, at first, wholly distinct from it. It was, however, the wish of both colonies to be united. In 1643, Williams went to England, and through his acquaintance with Sir Henry Vane obtained from parliament a charter for the colony of Rhode Island, under which name were included all the settlements in Narraganset Bay. This charter was confirmed by Charles II., in 1662, and although annulled in 1684, was restored after the accession of William III. Their constitution, which is thoroughly democratic, has maintained

[1] Mrs. Hutchinson, for some reason not known, removed from Rhode Island in 1642, after the death of her husband, to the Dutch settlements, and took up her abode in the neighborhood of New York. The following year, she was murdered, with her whole family, by the Indians, one daughter excepted, who was carried into captivity.

itself unchanged till near the present time, which is the case with no other state of the North American Union.

RELATION OF RHODE ISLAND TO THE OTHER COLONIES.

We have already noticed the antagonism in which Rhode Island found itself continually placed in respect to the other colonies. The declaration of a total separation of church and state, and of unconditional liberty in religious worship, seemed like an unheard of novelty. The speedy dissolution of the new settlement was confidently anticipated in Boston, and it was judged necessary to keep rigidly aloof from all connection with them, in order not to be involved in the same ruin. The General Court of Massachusetts expressed itself on this point in a resolution adopted May 12th, 1638. One of the exiles, John Green by name, who had settled in Providence, wrote from this place to the government at Boston, charging them "with arrogating to themselves the power of Christ over the churches and the consciences of men." Thereupon it was ordered, that "the said John Green shall not come into this jurisdiction upon pain of imprisonment and further censure; and because it appears to this Court that some others of the same place are confident in the same corrupt judgment and practice, it is ordered, that if any other of the inhabitants of the said plantation of Providence shall come within this jurisdiction, they shall be apprehended and brought before some of the magistrates; and if they will not disclaim the said corrupt opinions and censure, they shall be commanded presently to depart; and if such persons shall after be found within this jurisdiction, they shall be imprisoned and punished as the Court shall see cause."

The following chapter will show the application of this enactment on the appearance of another party opposed to the Congregationalist Theocracy, which, judging from Roger Williams's course, it was supposed might justly be associated with his name. It seems probable that during the first years of his residence in Providence, Williams had established no separate church,[1] the number of inhabitants being perhaps too small, or too diverse in their views, or too much occupied at first in providing for the absolute necessaries of life. Religious meetings were held, however, under the guidance of Mr. Williams. As the settlers increased in number, as well by emigration from England as from the other colonies, several opposers of infant baptism were found among them, and Williams now declared himself of their way of thinking. That he had previously advocated the doctrines of the Anabaptists is not probable, the above-mentioned charge of Brewster notwithstanding; for, in that case, it would certainly have been made to bear more decidedly against him. It was resolved to organize a new church; and as there was no minister among them, one of the lay brethren first administered the rite of baptism to Mr. Williams, who then did the same for the rest. This was in May, 1639. Scarcely was this done, when scruples arose in his mind respecting the validity of his baptism, which induced him two or three months after to withdraw from the new church; and though not differing on essential points of faith from the Christians around him, he never again entered into the church relation. The grounds of this course are to be found in his writings. Thus he

[1] We may at least draw the conclusion that those residents of Providence, who had previously been members of the Salem church, were not excluded till after Williams went over to the Baptists. The older narrators, for the most part, only take notice of the affairs of Rhode Island in connection with the other colonies; and even Knowles, the biographer of Williams, has not been able to settle this point with certainty.

maintained, that the proper ministration of the word of Christ was interrupted for many centuries by the reign of antichrist; the proclamation of the Gospel might still be continued and lead souls truly to heaven; but never again will there exist a true and genuine church, till after a new special revelation from God. This fanatical opinion seems, however, to have exercised no material influence either on his private or his public life. He maintained a regular correspondence with distinguished individuals in the other colonies, particularly with the governor of Connecticut, a son of Governor Winthrop of Boston, and received from him many tokens of regard. He exhibited great wisdom in composing the disorders and contentions which were rife in the new state; and at his death, early in the year 1683, he left the settlement which he had planted in a flourishing condition.

The prejudice excited in Boston against everything which proceeded from Rhode Island, as shown in the foregoing narration, exercised no little influence on the measures of the government in the controversies which form the subject of our next chapter. We shall now pass immediately to the conflicts with the Anabaptists and Quakers; though in the order of time, they follow the events and measures which mark the first firm organization and subsequent change of the theocratic constitution. But for the sake of presenting, in an uninterrupted view, the progressive inward development of that which belonged to the organism of the church itself, we must first dispose of an assault from without, which it successfully repelled. Whatever in its constitution serves for the illustration of the measures adopted for this purpose, has been already exhibited in the extracts from the platform of church discipline contained in chapter second.

CHAPTER IV.

EXCLUSION AND PERSECUTION OF ANABAPTISTS AND QUAKERS.

DREAD OF THE ANABAPTISTS CONNECTED WITH THE HISTORY OF THE RE-BAPTIZERS OF GERMANY; MEASURES FOR THEIR SUPPRESSION.

THE Anabaptist church, formed by Williams in Providence,[1] continued to exist after his withdrawal from it; and in consequence of the banishment of the Antinomians from Boston, still another arose in Newport, the principal place in the island of Rhode Island. This was under the care of John Clarke, formerly a physician, who had been a resident of Boston during the two years previous to the rupture which has been described. The exact date of its origin cannot be determined, but it was not far from the year 1644, and may have been even earlier. In the settlements on Narraganset Bay, the principle there dominant, of a total separation between church and state, had developed in the Anabaptists no hostile tendency towards civil government in general.

But when, during the same period, this party began to increase and extend itself in Massachusetts, the government,

[1] The adherents of adult baptism have successfully appropriated to themselves the name of Baptists, and repudiated that of Anabaptists: on the grounds, 1st, that it is not their design to re-baptize; and 2d, that the name Anabaptist was associated with certain practical results, or with doctrines and acts of the German re-baptizers. The truth of this will appear from the ensuing narration.

remembering what had happened in Germany, apprehended not merely an antagonism to the existing theocratic relation, but an overthrow of civil order and government. We see a manifestation of this fear in the following law passed by the General Court in 1644: —

"Forasmuch as experience hath plentifully and often proved, that since the first rising of the Anabaptists, about one hundred years since, they have been the incendiaries of the commonwealths, and the infectors of persons in main matters of religion, and the troublers of churches in all places where they have been, and that they who have held the baptizing of infants unlawful, have usually held other errors or heresies together therewith, though they have (as other heretics use to do) concealed the same till they spied out a fit advantage and opportunity to vent them, by way of question and scruple; and whereas, divers of this kind have, since our coming into New England, appeared amongst ourselves, some whereof (as others before them) denied the ordinance of magistracy, and the lawfulness of making war, and others the lawfulness of magistrates and their inspection into any breach of the first table; which opinions, if they should be connived at by us, are like to be increased amongst us, and so must necessarily bring guilt upon us, infection and trouble to the churches, and hazard to the whole commonwealth; it is ordered and agreed, that if any person or persons, within this jurisdiction, shall either openly condemn or oppose the baptizing of infants, or go about secretly to seduce others from the approbation or use thereof, or shall purposely depart the congregation at the ministration of the ordinance, or shall deny the ordinance of magistracy, or their lawful right and authority to make war, or to punish the outward breaches of the first table, and shall appear to the Court wilfully and obstinately to continue therein after due time and means of conviction, every such person or persons shall be sentenced to banishment."

In the year 1646, the government, in replying to the complaints of certain disaffected persons whose petition will be mentioned in the following chapter, thus vindicates this law:[1] "The great trouble we have been put unto and hazard also, by familistical and anabaptistical spirits, whose conscience and religion hath been only to set forth themselves and raise contentions in the country, did provoke us to provide for our safety by a law, that all such should take notice how unwelcome they should be unto us, either coming or staying. But for such as differ from us only in judgment, in point of baptism or some other points of less consequence, and live peaceably amongst us, without occasioning disturbance, etc., such have no cause to complain; for it hath never yet been put in execution against any of them, although such are known to live amongst us."

To this explanation of the law in words, we now add the actual application of it.

The Anabaptists first came into collision with the government in Plymouth colony. Obadiah Holmes,[2] once a student in Oxford University, had experienced, while still a youth, that inward conflict through which he attained to the consciousness of sin and of salvation. On his landing in New England he became a member of the Salem church. Here he remained six or seven years, and then removed, 1645, to Rehoboth, a newly-settled town of New Plymouth, on the border of Rhode Island. Here also he lived some

1 Collection of original papers relative to the history of the colony of Massachusetts Bay, Boston, 1769, p. 216.

2 Backus, I., 208 ff., gives some account of his life by himself, preserved in the family in his own handwriting.

four years in connection with the church under the care of Mr. Newman; but at length, Holmes, in connection with other members of the church, charged this minister with having, by the aid of a few others, proceeded in an unjustifiable manner in the name of the church. Being outvoted in this attempt, they resolved on forming a separate church, a measure certainly not at variance with the principles of the Congregationalists. But general scandal was excited when the seceding members submitted to immersion (probably at the hands of John Clarke), and proceeded to form an Anabaptist church. Holmes was excommunicated by the Congregationalist church, and on the 4th of June, 1650, was presented, with two others, before the General Court of New Plymouth. Four petitions had been addressed to that body, urging the speedy suppression of the existing schism; one from the town of Rehoboth, one from the neighboring church in Taunton, one from the collective ministers of New Plymouth, two excepted, and one finally from the General Court at Boston. Still Holmes and his followers were mildly dealt with; only they were obliged to leave the colony. They took refuge in Newport, and connected themselves with the church there, under the care of Mr. Clarke.

There lived at Lynn, a place eight or ten miles north of Boston, an Anabaptist, by the name of William Witter, who wished to connect himself with a church of his own persuasion, but, on account of his advanced age, could not undertake the journey to Newport. At his request, Clarke and Holmes, in company with a third by the name of Crandall, made him a visit on the 19th of July, 1651, and the day after, being Sunday, held divine service in his house; but, while Clarke was preaching, two constables made their appearance, who, after producing their warrant from the local magistrate, apprehended the three men, and took them as prisoners to the ale-house.[1] Here they were required to attend the afternoon service, and were obliged to do so, although Clarke declared that he would make known his dissent in the meeting, "by word and gesture." He did both. When they had been shown into the seat appointed for them, Clarke put on his hat again,[2] which was then struck off by a constable. Prayer, singing, and sermon being ended, he desired leave to address a few words to the congregation. On being answered that no objections could be heard against what had been delivered, he replied that this was not his purpose; but, as he had already signified his dissent from them "by gesture," he now wished to declare the grounds of the same by words. He then proceeded: "First, from the consideration we are strangers to each other, and so strangers to each other's inward standing, in respect to God, and so cannot conjoin and act in faith; and what is not of faith is sin. And, in the second place, I could not judge that you are gathered together and walk according to the visible order of our Lord." At this point, the magistrate informed him that he could say no more, and commanded silence. Two days after, he sent them to Boston, with a mittimus, wherein were the foregoing incidents. Here, on the 31st of July, they received sentence, Clarke to pay twenty pounds, Holmes thirty, and Crandall five; or, in default of payment, to be "well whipped." The acts recited in the mittimus are set forth as the grounds of this sentence, to which is added: "That the said John Clarke, on the following day, at the house of Witters, and in contempt of

[1] It is clear that the town was provided with no prison, and thus it was that the prisoners were able to hold another meeting.

[2] These statements are taken from an account by Clarke himself.

authority, being then in custody of the law, did there administer the sacrament of the Lord's Supper to one excommunicated person (Holmes), to another under admonition (Crandall), and to a third, that was an inhabitant of Lynn and not in fellowship with any church; and yet, upon answer in open Court, did affirm, that he never rebaptized any, although he confessed that he did baptize such as were baptized before, and thereby did necessarily deny the baptism that was before to be baptism, the churches no churches, and also all other ordinances and ministers, as if all were a nullity; and also did, in the court, deny the lawfulness of baptizing of infants; all this tends to the dishonor of God, the despising of the ordinances of God among us, the peace of the churches, and seducing the subjects of the commonwealth from the truth of the gospel of Jesus Christ, and perverting the straight ways of the Lord."

According to Clarke's report, Governor Endicott added, in an excited manner: "You have deserved death; we will not have such trash brought into our jurisdiction. You go up and down, and secretly insinuate into those that are weak; but you cannot maintain it before our ministers. You may try and dispute with them." Accordingly, on the following day, Clarke wrote to the Court, desiring the official appointment of the time and place of disputation; but to this they demurred. After a consultation on the matter, Clarke was again called up, and questioned whether he wished to dispute upon the specifications in his sentence, and defend what he had done; "for," it was added, "the Court sentenced you, not for your judgment and conscience, but for matter of fact and practice." Clarke replied, that matter of fact and practice was but the manifestation of his judgment and conscience; and he proposed to draw up a written statement of the main points of his belief, which might serve as a basis of the disputation. He then returned to prison, and thence sent to the Court four conclusions. The first of these was directed against encroachments on the offices of Christ, especially on his office as king; the second declared baptism by immersion, which was to be administered to true believers only, to be a command of Christ; the third maintained that each believer, after the measure of his gifts, might, yea, was bound to preach the word, both in and out of the church; the fourth protested against all outward penalties in matters of religion and conscience. He received, for answer, a dismission from prison, some of his friends having paid his fine without asking his consent. He now made known his intention of leaving Boston and returning to his family, but expressed his readiness and desire to defend his cause in the manner proposed, either now or at a later period. It was replied that the proffers made him merely had reference to private conferences, for his instruction and conviction. A willingness was expressed, however, to grant him a public disputation; but so hampered as to the way in which it should be conducted, and with such restrictions in regard to rigid adherence to the questions in debate, that Clarke felt himself obliged to decline it. Crandall was likewise dismissed, under promise of appearing before the next court, and both returned to Rhode Island. But Obadiah Holmes would neither pay his fine, nor allow others to do it for him, and consequently remained in prison till the next sitting of the Court. The threatened sentence of corporeal punishment was then publicly executed on him;[1] nay,

[1] The detailed account of his sufferings is given in a letter addressed to the brethren of his own faith in England.

even two of the spectators, who praised God for the constancy of his faith, were arrested, and only escaped similar dealing through the payment, by friends, of forty shillings fine. Thereupon, the adherents of these doctrines were banished in a body from Massachusetts, and went to Rhode Island.

In November, 1651, Clarke accompanied Williams to England, for the purpose of settling certain disputes respecting the boundaries of Rhode Island, and there published a book, entitled "Ill News from New England; or, a Narrative of New England's Persecutions." What impression these accounts made on the English Congregationalists, may be seen from the following letter, addressed by Sir Richard Saltonstall, formerly first magistrate of Massachusetts, to the Boston ministers, Cotton and Wilson:

"Revered and dear friends, whom I unfeignedly love and respect, —

"It doth not a little grieve my spirit to hear what sad things are reported daily of your tyranny and persecutions in New England, as that you fine, whip, and imprison men for their consciences. First, you compel such to come into your assemblies as you know will not join you in your worship; and when they show their dislike thereof, or witness against it, then you stir up your magistrates to punish them for such (as you conceive) their public affronts. Truly, friends, this your practice of compelling any in matters of worship, to do that whereof they are not fully persuaded, is to make them sin, for so the apostle (Rom. 14: 23) tells us, and many are made hypocrites thereby, conforming in their outward man for fear of punishment. We pray for you and wish you prosperity in every way; hoped the Lord would have given you so much light and love there, that you might have been eyes to God's people here, and not to practise those courses in a wilderness which you went so far to prevent. These rigid ways have laid you very low in the hearts of the saints. I do assure you I have heard them pray in the public assemblies, that the Lord would give you such meek and humble spirits, not to strive so much for uniformity as to keep the unity of the spirit in the bond of peace."

The reply of Cotton to this letter is striking and characteristic:

"Honored and dear sir, —

"My brother Wilson and self do both of us acknowledge your love, as otherwise formerly, so now in the late lines we received from you, that you grieve in spirit to hear daily complaints against us. Be pleased to understand we look at such complaints as altogether injurious in respect to ourselves, who had no hand or tongue at all to promote either the coming of the persons you aim at into our assemblies, or their punishment for their carriage there. Righteous judgment will not take up reports, much less reproaches against the innocent. The cry of the sinners of Sodom was great and loud, and reached up to heaven; yet the righteous God (giving us an example what to do in like case), he would first go down to see whether their crime were altogether according to the cry, before he proceed to judgment. And when he did find the truth of the cry, he did not wrap up all alike promiscuously in the judgment, but spared such as he found innocent. We are amongst those whom, if you knew us better, you would account peaceable in Israel. Yet neither are we so vast in our indulgence or toleration, as to think the men you speak of suffered an unjust censure. For one of them (Obadiah Holmes) being an excommunicate person himself, out of a church in Plymouth Patent, came into this jurisdiction, and took upon him to baptize, which I think himself will not say he was compelled here to perform. And he was not ignorant that the re-baptizing of an elder person, and that by a private person, and under excommunication, are all of them manifest contestations against the order and government of our churches, established (we know) by God's law, and (he knoweth) by the laws of the country. As for his whipping, it was more voluntarily chosen by him than inflicted on him. His censure by the Court, was to have paid, as I know, thirty pounds, or else be whipt; in which case, if his suffering of stripes was any worship of God at all, it could be accounted no better than will-worship. The other (Mr. Clarke) was wiser in that point, and his offence was less, so was his fine less, and himself (as I hear) was contented to have it paid for him, whereupon he was released. The imprisonment of either of them was no detriment. I believe they fared, neither of them, better at home, and I am sure Holmes had not been so well clad of many years before.

"But be pleased to consider this point a little further. You think to compel men in matter of worship is to make them sin. If the worship be lawful in itself, the magistrate compelling him to come to it compelleth him not to sin; but the sin is in his will that needs to be compelled to a christian duty. If it do make men hypocrites, yet better be hypocrites than profane persons. Hypocrites give God part of his due, the outward man; but the profane person giveth God neither outward nor inward man. You know us not if you think we came into this wilderness to practise those courses here which we fled from in England. We believe there is a vast difference between men's inventions and God's institutions; we fled from men's inventions, to which we should else have been compelled; we compel none to men's inventions. If our ways (rigid ways, as you call them) have laid us low in the hearts of God's people, yea, and of the saints, (as you style them), we do not believe it is any part of their saintship. Nevertheless, I tell you the truth, we have tolerated in our churches some Anabaptists, some Antinomians, and some Seekers, and do so still at this day. We are far from arrogating infallibility of judgment to ourselves, or affecting uniformity; uniformity God never required, infallibility he never granted us."

Into such expressions did an unyielding polemic zeal betray even such a man as Cotton; a man of whom Williams, though his earnest opponent, and exchanging with him controversial writings on their respective principles, has spoken with the highest estimation.[1] It is the clearest exponent of that generally prevailing opinion, which a few years later expressed itself, with reference to a new form of opposition, in measures of even yet greater severity. It is noticeable, that Cotton Mather's history of New England, ordinarily so diffuse in narrating the most unimportant particulars, passes over the foregoing story in total silence. The same, according to Backus, was the case with the earlier historians of Massachusetts, with Captain Johnson, who wrote in 1654, and with Morton, in 1669, although his object was the refutation of charges made against New England. Hubbard, in 1680, only makes a distant allusion to it; Governor Hutchinson, in his history of Massachusetts, mentions the year 1665 as the date of the first persecution of the Anabaptists. Yet, in a third volume, he gives, among other legal documents, some which have re-

[1] Backus, I. p. 472. [2] Ib. II. p. 253.

ference to the occurrences of 1651. Neal alone, in his history, has taken particular notice of Clarke's account. In the following chapter we shall, moreover, have occasion to show that hostility to Anabaptism was not without influence on the decisions of the Congregationalists in regard to Infant Baptism, when this became from an entirely different point of view the subject of discussions and proceedings.

PERSECUTION OF THE QUAKERS.

We pass now to the last persecution in New England, properly so called, the most violent, and the longest in duration. But in order to understand the constantly increasing severity of the measures against the Quakers, we must not only give a full exhibition of what occurred in New England, but must glance briefly at the origin and growth of this sect in the mother-country. Just at the period when insurrection and civil war had brought the political relations of England to the verge of anarchy and dissolution, George Fox, a Lancashire shoemaker, began to publish his claim to an inward revelation, and travelled through the country to spread his doctrines. Of these the central point was, the inward enlightening of man by the Spirit of God as the proper source of divine knowledge, rather than the Scriptures; as also, that our salvation is rather through the Christ *within*, than the Christ without. From this followed a depreciation of the historical Christ, as well as of everything stated and prescribed in divine service, of the sacraments, of appointed times and places for public religious worship. With the denial of the proper ground-truths of Christianity in regard to the redemption of man, connected itself a fanatical opposition to all civil order and to all prevailing customs. The word of Scripture they called a dead letter; yet in their own appeals to it, they could use the letter, that is, the words, violently wrested from their connection. The preaching of the first Quakers is not indeed to be made a reproach to the later "Friends," as remoulded both in respect to doctrine and practice by Barclay and Penn; but in the period with which we are concerned, their advent can only be regarded as a movement of wild fanaticism.[1] Some of their number appeared in parliament, and announced before the Protector the downfall of the State, to which they were called by the Spirit to contribute. In order to give public offence, they opened shops on Sunday, and one woman even appeared in church wholly destitute of clothing. In the year 1565, they acknowledged one James Naylor,[2] a former soldier of Cromwell's army, as the manifested Son of God. Being called before the court, he declared that every honor offered to him as a created being, he declined; but if the hearts of others were moved by the Father thus to honor him, it was not in his power to refuse it; it had been commanded him, through the power of the Lord, to allow this homage to be paid him. He was required to recant, was put in the stocks, placed backwards on a horse and led through London, his tongue was bored, his forehead

[1] The conflict of Roger Williams with these people is significant in respect to both parties. He too maintained, from the word of God, the worship of that time to be unchristian, and thus placed himself in opposition to every existing church-organization; and in connection with this, he advocated freedom of conscience to the extremest limit. Yet he subsequently took most decided ground against the Quakers, both in oral disputations and in his writings against George Fox, who, in 1668, had visited Rhode Island. It is here to be remarked that the founder of a settlement and body politic can be no friend of disorder and contempt of civil government; and also that Roger Williams, while separating from all churches, held fast to the fundamentals of Christianity, and did not neglect to support them by his testimony.

[2] Neal's History of the Puritans, IV. 154.

branded, he was whipt through Bristol; but nothing could move him. He was then condemned to imprisonment with hard labor, being allowed nothing for his sustenance except what he earned himself. After two years, however, he acknowledged that the honor which had been paid him was wrong and sinful, and professed his shame for having encouraged it. He was then dismissed from prison, but died soon after.

The restless spirit of this sect had already carried its adherents to the colonies in America, and it happened that their first appearance was in Rhode Island, whence they sought to push their way into the jurisdiction of Plymouth. At the same time they appeared also in Barbadoes in the West Indies; and in 1656, two women, Maria Fisher and Anna Austin by name, came in a ship from this island to Boston, and there, by books and tracts, disseminated the doctrines of the Quakers. This coming to light, the Governor ordered their arrest, and also that the books, about one hundred in number, should be burned. Then calling his Council, it was resolved that the prisoners should remain in confinement till a good opportunity offered for sending them away; and the ship-captain who had brought them was to give bonds for their departure in one hundred pounds. But before this could be effected, four men and four women of the same principles had made their way to Boston from Rhode Island, who as soon as discovered, were put in prison, and then sent out of the country. The government designed by these measures to keep the Quakers at a distance, and not supposing any of the inhabitants themselves to be infected with their opinions, believed that by sufficient rigor they could reach their end. Accordingly, on the 14th of October 1656, they passed a law which was in substance as follows: —

"Every master of a vessel bringing in Quakers, shall pay a fine of one hundred pounds. Every Quaker, immediately on his arrival shall be lodged in the House of Correction, to be severely whipped on his entrance, and to be kept close at hard labor; no one to be allowed to speak or hold any intercourse with him. Whoever knowingly brings in, spreads, or conceals Quaker writings shall be fined five pounds. Whoever undertakes to defend the doctrines of the Quakers, shall for the first offence be fined ten shillings, and for the second, four pounds; for the third, he shall be committed to prison, till a suitable opportunity is found of transporting him out of the country, which is then to be done forthwith."

When this law was proclaimed with beat of drum through the streets of Boston, Nicholas Upshall, a man some sixty years of age, came forth from his house, and protested openly to the officers "that the execution of this law would be the forerunner of judgments on the land; wherefore he besought them to beware what they did, lest they might be found among those who were fighting against God." This was regarded as an attack upon the government; Upshall was called before the court, and as he would neither acknowledge his offence nor beg forgiveness, he was fined twenty pounds, and ordered to leave the jurisdiction within one month.

The following year, the above-cited law was put in practice. A tailor's wife named Maria Clarke, who had abandoned her husband and six children in London, in order, as she said, to deliver a message from the Lord, was put in prison, whipped, and banished. The same punishment was soon after inflicted upon two men, Holden and Copeland, who belonged to the Rhode Island Quakers, and had been already once banished. They made their appearance at Salem, where they even took it upon themselves to speak in a public religious meeting. It now became evident, from the numbers who frequented their meetings, that their opinions had found favor among the residents. These private gatherings were immediately interrupted; each person present was fined five shillings for absenting himself from public worship; every one who had taken part in them was sent to the House of Correction at Boston.

But all the attempts of the government for the suppression of this sect, were frustrated by the persistency of the Quakers in returning from banishment. Hence, in October, 1657, a law was passed that: "whoever brings a Quaker into this jurisdiction shall pay one hundred pounds, and be kept in prison till the penalty is discharged; whoever harbors or conceals a known Quaker shall pay forty shillings for every hour's entertainment, and remain in prison until payment of the same. Every Quaker, who shall become such in the colony, is to be treated in like manner with those who come in. For the first and second offences, when the criminal has been punished according to the laws previously enacted, if a man, he shall lose first one, and then the other ear; if a woman, she shall be severely whipped; the third time, man or woman, shall have the tongue bored through with a hot iron. In all cases, they shall be kept in prison till such time as they can be sent away at their own cost."

But neither had this law the expected effect of terrifying the Quakers; for on the 16th of September 1658, three men, two of whom were Holden and Copeland, being identified as having been previously banished, had their right ears cut off. The same disturbances continued. In the year 1658 two women attempted to hold forth publicly during divine service. The same was done by a Quaker from Barbadoes, by the name of Harris. When lodged in prison and required to labor, he could not be induced by any means whatever to comply, and neither he nor his friends would pay their fines, or the costs of their removal from the country, when freedom was offered them under these conditions. Their contumacious behavior being reported by the jailer to the magistrate, he gave order that such prisoners as would not labor should be whipped twice a week, the number of strokes to be increased each time. But this treatment also was without influence on Harris, who would probably have allowed himself to be whipped to death, had not some of his acquaintances paid the fine, and thus procured his release. It was customary with the Quakers, while steadfastly refusing to pay their fines, to allow the penalty to be discharged for them. But on the inquiry being made by magistrates of smaller towns, what they should do, in cases where there were no friends at hand to give this aid, they were empowered to sell the offenders to the English settlements in Virginia and Barbadoes. This, however, only served as a bugbear, and was not carried into execution.

During this time, meetings were again held here and there in the country, and, in consequence, the laws above mentioned were put in execution particularly against the residents, and in some respects with increased rigor. Thus the fines were made so exorbitant, that numbers were thereby reduced to poverty. But nothing could check the continual return of these desperate people, nor put a stop to their illegal and offensive conduct. At the tribunals, they derided and scoffed at the magistrates; women appeared naked in the streets, and in one case, at Newbury, Massachusetts, even in the church. Nor were these disturbances confined to that colony. The matter had been already discussed in a meeting of commissioners from the four united colonies, held in 1656, and a demand made upon Rhode Island, in the name of peace and for the welfare of the whole country, to take part with them in some common measures against the Quakers. To this the General Assembly which met at Portsmouth on the 13th of March, 1657, returned answer as follows:[1] —

"Whereas, freedom of different consciences to be protected from inforcements was the principal ground of our charter, both with respect to our humble suit for it, as also to the true intent of the honorable and renowned parliament in England, in granting of the same to us, which freedom we still prize as the greatest happiness that man can possess in this world; therefore, we shall, for the preservation of our civil peace and order, the more especially take notice that those people, and any others that are here, or shall come among us, be impartially received, and to our utmost, constrained to perform all civil duties requisite. And in case they refuse it, we resolve to make use of the first opportunity to inform our agent residing in England."[2] On a second demand from the commissioners of the four colonies, they again replied, on the 13th of October 1657: —[3]

"As concerning these Quakers (so called) which are now among us, we have no law among us whereby to punish any for only declaring by words, etc., their minds and understandings concerning the things and ways of God, as to salvation and an eternal condition. And we find, more-

1 Backus, I., 312.

2 Clarke, who in 1652 had gone with Williams to England, remained there after the return of the latter, as agent of the Rhode Island colony, till 1654.

3 Knowles, Memoir of Williams, p. 294.

over, that in those places where these people, aforesaid, in the colony, are most of all suffered to declare themselves freely, and are only opposed by arguments in discourse, there they least of all desire to come; and we are informed that they begin to loathe this place, for that they are not opposed by the civil authority, but with all patience and meekness, are suffered to say over their pretended revelations and admonitions, nor are they like or able to gain many here to their way. And surely we find, that they delight to be persecuted by the civil powers, and when they are so, they are like to gain more by the conceit of their patient sufferings, than by consent to their pernicious sayings."

The Rhode Island government conceded that the doctrines of the Quakers tended to the prejudice of the civil authority, and promised to take the matter into consideration at the next General Assembly, and to adopt suitable measures for preventing any "bad effects from their doctrines and endeavors." But, notwithstanding the threat of exclusion from all commercial intercourse with the rest of New England, they adhered inflexibly to their former policy. Though Rhode Island, with her principles of toleration, had actually suffered less than the other colonies, the latter had now gone so far in the path on which they had entered, that it was difficult to turn back; to them it seemed impossible to stand still. As all four colonies were disquieted by the Quakers, though Connecticut and New Haven suffered less than the others, the commissioners closed their proceedings at a conference held in Boston, September, 1658, with the following resolution:[1] —

"Whereas, there is an accursed and pernicious set of heretics lately risen up in the world, who are commonly

[1] Backus, I. 317.

called Quakers, who take upon them to be immediately sent of God, and infallibly assisted, who do speak and write blasphemous things, despising government, and the order of God in church and commonwealth; speaking evil of dignities, reproaching and reviling magistrates and the ministers of the gospel, seeking to turn the people from the faith, and to gain proselytes to their pernicious ways: And whereas, the several jurisdictions have made divers laws to prohibit their coming among them; (but they refusing obedience and still making disturbance) it is therefore propounded, and seriously commended to the several General Courts to make a law, that all Quakers formerly convicted and punished as such, shall, if they return again, be imprisoned, and forthwith banished or expelled out of the said jurisdiction, under pain of death." This was signed by seven of the commissioners; but John Winthrop, a son of the above-named governor of Massachusetts, and the only commissioner from the colony of Connecticut added: "Looking at the last as a query and not as an act, I subscribe, John Winthrop." Connecticut and New Haven failed to carry out this resolution; but in 1658 it became law in Massachusetts. The government designed to commit the application and execution of this law to the acting magistracy, and an ordinance to that effect did in fact pass the Court of Deputies by thirteen voices against twelve; but when the minority declared they would protest against the bill, it was agreed that the accused, in cases occurring under this law, should be brought before a court specially sworn for the purpose. Plymouth also persevered in persecuting the Quakers. Captain James Cudworth, a magistrate of that colony, thus laments over it in a letter to a friend who was absent on a journey to England: "I entertained two Quakers in my house, in order to become better acquainted with their principles; for this I was called before the court. My declaration that I was no Quaker and my behavior not unlawful, since, according to the existing ordinances only such could be punished as received Quakers and kept them in their houses after warning by the magistrates, they indeed allowed. But when I spoke against the persecutions, they increased all the laws against Quakers, imposing for each attempt of the same to teach, and for each communication with them, the hardest imprisonment and most exorbitant fines, and yet without hindering or lessening the evil. In the Massachusetts, after they have whipped them and cut off their ears, they have now gone the farthest step they can, they have banished them, upon pain of death if they ever come there again; we expect we must do the like; we must dance after their pipe, for it is well if in some there be not a desire to be their apes and imitators, in all their proceedings of this nature. They have banished six on pain of death, and I wish that blood be not shed." The first of these apprehensions was not realized; the second proved itself but too well founded, as will appear from the narration of the last occurrences of this persecution in Boston.

Among the persons banished from Massachusetts by the late statute, were William Robinson, a merchant from London, Marmaduke Stevenson, from Yorkshire, and a woman named Mary Dyar,[1] from Rhode Island. All three returned, however, and when questioned as to the reason, replied that "they came in obedience to the Lord." Governor Endicott said to them: "We have made divers laws, and sought manifold ways to keep you at a distance from us; but I find that neither whippings, nor dungeons, nor

[1] She belonged to the Antinomians who were banished in 1637. Hutch. I. 184.

cutting off ears, nor banishment on pain of death, helps; I wish not your death." No farther defence could be drawn from them; only Stevenson declared, in writing, that, "in a vision, as he was following the plough, he heard a secret voice within him. Thereupon, he had forsaken his family and calling, and gone, in the year 1658, to Barbadoes, and thence to Rhode Island, where, as he was tilling the ground, the word of the Lord came unto him, saying: 'Go to Boston, with thy brother, William Robinson;' for obedience to which, contrary to the commands of men, he now suffers bonds nigh unto death." This paper was subscribed: "Prison, at Boston, October, 1659, Marmaduke Stevenson; but a new name has been given unto me, which the world knoweth not, and is written in the Book of Life."

All three were thereupon condemned to death. The two men were executed on the 27th of October, 1659. The woman, when at the foot of the gallows, was pardoned, at the intercession of her relatives, from Newport, in Rhode Island, whither she was then sent. But she came back the next spring, and suffered the penalty of death on the 1st of June, 1660.

The general surprise and indignation, occasioned by this first application of the new law, obliged the Massachusetts government to publish the following declaration:

"Though the justice of our proceedings against William Robinson, Marmaduke Stevenson, and Mary Dyar, supported by the authority of this Court, the laws of this country, and the laws of God, may rather persuade us to expect encouragement and commendation from all prudent and pious men, than convince us of any necessity to apologize for the same; yet, forasmuch as men of weaker parts, out of pity and commiseration (a commendable and christian virtue, yet easily abused, and susceptible of sinister and dangerous impressions), for want of a full information, may be less satisfied, and men of perverser principles to calumniate us, and render us as bloody persecutors; to satisfy the one, and to stop the mouths of the other, we have thought fit to declare, that, about three years since, divers persons, professing themselves Quakers (of whose pernicious opinions and practices we had received intelligence from good hands), both from Barbadoes and England, arrived at Boston, whose persons were only secured, to be sent away by the first opportunity, without censure or punishment, although their professed tenets, turbulent and contemptuous behavior to authority, would have justified a severer animadversion; yet the prudence of this Court was exercised only in making provision to secure the peace and order here established, against their attempts, whose design (we were well assured by our own experience, as well as by the example of their predecessors in Münster), was to undermine and ruin the same; and, accordingly, a law was made and published, prohibiting all masters of ships to bring any Quaker into this jurisdiction, and themselves from coming in, on penalty of the House of Correction till they could be sent away. Notwithstanding which, by a back door they found entrance; and the penalty inflicted on them proving insufficient to restrain their impudent and insolent obtrusions, was increased, — which also, being too weak a defence against their impetuous and fanatic fury, necessitated us to endeavor our security; and upon serious consideration, a law was made that such persons should be banished on pain of death, according to the example of England, in their provision against the Jesuits; which sentence being regularly pronounced at the last Court of Assistants against these parties, and they either returning, or continuing presumptuously in this jurisdiction after the time limited, were apprehended, and owning themselves to be the persons banished, were sentenced by the Court to death, — which hath been executed upon two of them. Mary Dyar, upon intercession of a son, through the grace and mildness of this Court, had liberty to depart within two days, and accepted of it. The consideration of our gradual proceedings, will vindicate us from the clamorous accusation of severity. Our own just and necessary defence calling upon us (other means failing) to offer the point, which these persons have violently and wilfully rushed upon, and thereby become *felones de se*, as well as the sparing of one upon an inconsiderable intercession, will manifestly evince we desire their lives absent, rather than their deaths present."

The weakness of this declaration, both in respect to the relations of crime and punishment, and to the appeal to a law in England, appears from the following judicial proceeding: At the beginning of the year 1661, William Leddra, a Quaker who had been already several times punished and banished from the commonwealth, returned to Boston. Being seized and brought before the Court, he was asked by Governor Bradstreet "whether he were willing to go to England." He answered that "he had nothing to do there." Upon the offer of being set at liberty, if he would promise not to return again, he replied: "I stand not in my own will, but the will of the Lord. If I am set at liberty, I will go, but such a promise I cannot make." Bradstreet then told him "that if he would neither go to England, nor remain out of the jurisdiction, he would fall under the full rigor of the law." Leddra appealed to the laws of England in respect to his judicial examination, but the appeal was not allowed. Much time was spent in endeavoring to persuade him either to recant his errors, or submit to the laws of the land, or to promise not again to return; but he remained obstinate. "What," said he, "join myself with such murderers as ye are! Then let each one who meets me say: Lo, this is the man who forsook the God of his salvation." Finally, sentence of death was pronounced upon him, and on the 14th of March, 1661, he was executed; declaring under the gallows that it was "for confessing the Lord, against liars and deceivers, that he was brought hither to death." While Leddra was still under examination, another Quaker, Wheelock Christison by name, came boldly before the Court with his hat on his head, and warned the magistrates to shed no more innocent blood. He refused to take off his hat, and on being questioned if his name was not Christison, and whether he had not been banished on pain of death, he replied to both in the affirmative, and was committed to prison. Being required to state in defence of himself any reasons why he should not suffer the penalty of the law, he asked them by what law they would condemn him to death. When the Court appealed to the recent law enacted against the Quakers, he desired to know how they were empowered to make such a law, and whether the law itself were not in contrariety to the laws of England. The Governor replied that there was a similar law in England, according to which Jesuits were hanged. "But," said Christison, "ye condemn me, not as a Jesuit, but as a Quaker; I appeal to the laws of my country." The Court offered him a lawful trial by court and jury, but he persisted in appealing to the laws of England, and repeating that he had never heard or read of a law in England for hanging Quakers. The Court, however, overruled his objection, and the jury declared him guilty. When the sentence of death was announced to him, he urged upon them the consequences of this measure against the Quakers. "For the last man that was put to death," said he, "here are five come in his room; if ye have power to take my life from me, God can raise up the same principle of life in ten of his servants, and send them among you in my room, that ye may have torment upon torment."

The 13th of June, 1661, was appointed as the day of his execution; but before it arrived, Christison, with twenty-seven other Quakers then lying in prison, was set at liberty and carried beyond the limits of the jurisdiction. The government seems to have become convinced, by this time, that their measures were as odious as they were ineffectual; they resolved to deal with the Quakers henceforth as vagabonds, to whip them through the towns of the colony, and then drive them out of its bounds. The above-mentioned executions occasioned great dissatisfaction in England; and Charles II., who had recently acceded to the throne, interposed his authority by a letter, dated the 9th of September, 1661, to the Governors and Magistrates of New England collectively: "Having received information of the imprisonment and execution of Quakers, his majesty hereby commands, as well in respect to any who may be already condemned as to those still in prison, that all proceedings with them be stopped, and that the above-named persons be sent, together with the accusations made against them, to England, in order there to receive their sentence." The general cessation of persecution, properly so called, forestalled the execution of this order; but the government, in its congratulatory address to Charles II., justified the measures which had been adopted. In our judgment of these occurrences, in addition to all which may be said with truth against the Quakers, we must bear in mind the utter perplexity of the government in regard to means for protecting themselves against these obstinate and impracticable fanatics.

We shall have occasion further on (Chap. VII.), to mention the subsequent persecutions and oppressive measures of the government against the Anabaptists. First, however, after having thus exhibited the secessions and expulsions from the theocratic government, we must consider the opposition developed in its own bosom, which led the way to an essential change of its constitution.

CHAPTER V.

SUPPRESSION OF THE INTERNAL OPPOSITION TO THE THEOCRATIC GOVERNMENT; SUSTAINED BY THE SYNOD OF 1648.

CHANGE IN THE ORIGINAL IDEAS, RESULTING FROM LATER IMMIGRATIONS; GOVERNMENTAL MEASURES FOR COUNTERACTING IT.

Two things in the founders of New England particularly strike the observer; their devotion to the common weal as citizens, and to the interests of the church as Christians. They regarded themselves, not as individual fugitives from oppression and persecution, but rather as confederates in a political association and members of a religious community. In both respects they were favored with the guidance of men equally upright and gifted, by whose influence this feeling, alike of their political and their ecclesiastical responsibilities, was maintained and developed in living power. This twofold relation had given birth to the Theocratic constitution. In exhibiting the characteristics of this constitution, we have already made use of the decisions of a synod held in 1648, as the clearest manifestation of the peculiarity of the civil government. But it is evident, not only from expressions in contemporary correspondence, but from the laws of Massachusetts, that this same view had prevailed universally from the very first. Indeed, we find it acted on, so early as the first controversy with Roger Williams.

Another point in this platform of church-discipline, the

question respecting church-membership, must now be particularly considered; as the decision in regard to it was expressly intended to counteract an attempt, peculiar in its character, to subvert the theocratic relation.

As every theocracy is exposed to the resistance of certain members of its connection, so was it the case here. But we must not lose sight of the fact, that the characteristic feature of the New England Theocracy, by which it was distinguished from every other, formed also the fundamental principle of the Congregationalists, and was regarded by them as a necessary step in the progress of the reformation. The requirement, that only such shall be admitted to the visible church as are members of that which is invisible, can be carried out in its full strictness no where on earth. But if, in addition, only these same church-members are allowed the enjoyment of civil rights, it can be maintained no longer than a controlling religious interest in the church-relation continues to penetrate all the individuals of the community. As we have already seen, the members of the Leyden church and the first settlers of Massachusetts Bay felt themselves called to such an attempt, and they were men fitted to accomplish it. But the subsequent immigrations from England did not originate solely in devotion to religious interests; nay, even in the second generation in America, the view had begun to lose ground, that connection with the church was man's first and only necessity. It was inevitable, therefore, that from that class of persons who could not claim to be church-members, must proceed a reaction, founded on the natural and necessary desire to be citizens of the State in which they lived.

But besides this anti-theocratic party, properly so called, another, an anti-Congregationalist party, might espouse and defend the opposition, on other grounds. It could not but happen, in a social state so decidedly Christian, that the wish should be felt by many, even among those who had little personal interest in religion, to hold a certain connection with the church, whose requisitions for actual membership they were, nevertheless, unable or unwilling to meet. So also, the desire must be felt, among those who were not church-members, that their children should be admitted to the privilege of baptism; while, on the other hand, the church might well refuse the rite, as being unable to regard those as future members, who were to be trained under the influence of persons themselves standing aloof from her. This question: 'Who are the proper subjects of baptism?' we shall see more particularly discussed at a later period. It was the answer to this question which caused the subversion of the original connection between church and state.

Before depicting the assault made on the theocracy from the political side, we will here mention a single instance of opposition, which, though without results, is of a noteworthy character. In 1637, a minister at Weymouth, Massachusetts, by the name of Lenthal, broached the doctrine that baptism constitutes the door of entrance to the visible church. Hubbard reports[1] that this view was immediately embraced by several others, and the plan was in agitation of forming a church, into which all baptized persons were to be admitted to communion, without any additional test. But when Lenthal was applied to for farther counsel in the matter, it was found that he had been con-

[1] According to Backus, I., 114. Here it is also remarked that Lenthal went in 1640 to Rhode Island, and from thence soon after to England. His views were in direct contrariety also with those of most of the North American church parties of the time.

ferred with by several magistrates and ministers, and had retracted his opinions. Having read his recantation[1] publicly before his congregation, he was exempted from further censure. This doctrine was in too decided contrariety to the prevailing view to have spread extensively, although strictly speaking, it was not directed against the theocracy as such.

How thoroughly the ruling powers were impressed with the idea, that church and state must constitute an undivided unity, appears from the two following laws passed in Boston, Sept. 1638: 1. "Whereas it is found by sad experience, that divers persons, who have been justly cast out of some of the churches, do profanely contemn the same sacred and dreadful ordinance, by presenting themselves over-boldly in other assemblies, and speaking lightly of their censures, to the great offence and grief of God's people, and encouragement of evil-minded persons to contemn the same ordinance; it is therefore ordered, that whosoever shall stand excommunicated for the space of six months, without laboring what in him or her lieth to be restored, such person shall be presented to the Court of Assistants, and there proceeded with by fine, imprisonment, banishment, or further, for their good behavior, as their contempt and obstinacy upon full hearing shall deserve." This law was indeed soon after abrogated. Not so the second, which long survived the real dissolution of the theocracy, and formed, in subsequent times, the chief occasion for the renewal of internal divisions. By this statute, all the inhabitants of a town, whether freemen or members of the church or not, were required to contribute equally to all necessary expenditures for church and state.

In close connection with the passage of this latter Act,

[1] So related in Neal's History of New England, I., p. 196.

stands a movement which threatened the overthrow of the theocratic relation, but became the occasion of its formal and explicit confirmation. In the colony of Plymouth also, as well as in Massachusetts, there had been always some, though not a large number, who took exceptions to the theocratic relation on the above-mentioned grounds; and the disaffected of the two colonies were in understanding with each other.[1] Individual complaints had already become loud, when, in 1646, the matter came before the notice of the General Court at Boston. A petition was sent in by certain inhabitants of Hingham, in Massachusetts, near the borders of New Plymouth,[2] which, after some preliminary compliments, in general terms, on the administration of the government, proceeded to designate the present condition of affairs as one of manifold grievances, alleging three specific causes for the same, and praying for the repeal and change of the following relations and ordinances. First, there exists great uncertainty in all respects, arising from neglect to recognize the laws of England as the basis of government, or to act on them as such; hence a want of that security and confidence in the enjoyment of life, freedom, and property, which is the right of every free-born Englishman, and a constant apprehension of illegal burdens and unjust punishments. Second, there are in these settlements many thousands of free-born, quiet, peaceable Englishmen, who though upright in their dealings, and disposed to promote the public weal, see themselves debarred from all civil employments; nay, are not permitted to occupy the lowest office, nor to have a voice in the election of magistrates, of captains, or other

[1] Hutchinson, I., 136.

[2] Collection of original papers relative to the History of Mass. Bay, Boston. 1769, p. 188 ff.

civil and military functionaries. The petitioners pray, therefore, that civil freedom and civil right be granted to 'all truly English,' without the imposition of any oath or covenant, which does not appear to accord with the Patent and the original oath of allegiance; such oath and covenant they were ready to assume, as should express their desire for the furtherance of the honor of God and the prosperity of the settlement, their loyalty to England, their love to their country. In the ordinances referred to, they foresee disruption from England; and they pray, in case their petition is rejected, that they may be regarded as foreigners, and be exempted from all charges. Third, there are divers good people, rich in knowledge and no way blamable in life and conversation, who as members of the church of England are in agreement with the last and best reformation in England and Scotland, but are yet excluded from the Supper on the pretence that they do not assent to the church-covenant, for which they see no foundation in the word of God, and moreover, this very covenant differs in different churches. Not only so, but they are constrained by penalties to attend public worship; and particular pains are used that they shall be present at times when baptism is administered, although their own children cannot be baptized. In some places they are obliged to contribute to the maintenance of the minister, in order to be regarded as brethren. With a brief reference to the necessary tendency of such a course to promote Anabaptism, they pray, therefore, to be received into the churches, and allowed a participation in all the privileges and ordinances which Christ has purchased for them and in whose name they have been baptized, that the Lord may be one and his name one in this place, and that so the seals of the covenant (the sacraments) may be enjoyed by them and their posterity. If this may not be, they request permission to form churches after their own manner. They conclude with the remark, that if repulsed here, they shall feel themselves constrained to apply to the honorable Houses of Parliament, who will, without doubt, take their unhappy state into consideration.

Among the seven petitioners, one possessed the rights of a free citizen without being a church-member, having become a freeman previous to the law before cited;[1] but the remainder seem to have been by no means the only ones in the colony, who were opposed to the established relations. This is clear from the popular excitement which, after this matter was decided, manifested itself in Boston against Governor John Winthrop, the most powerful and distinguished defender of the existing constitution. A letter addressed to him by a magistrate in Ipswich,[2] proves by its lamentations over the disorders thus occasioned, that the number of the malcontents was not small.

A preponderating majority of the government, as well as among the citizens generally, were decidedly averse to the principles set forth in this petition, and were indignant at its charges, for which it was believed no occasion had been given. We recognize the simplicity of the time in the circumstance, that the General Court felt itself called on to refute the petitioners and justify their own conduct by a lengthy public explanation. This document[3] gives a reflection at once of the prevailing views of the period, and of its peculiar style of argumentation. It begins with a reference to the complimentary expressions of the petitioners, which however, are declined, as being shown by what follows to be merely an unworthy *captatio benevolentiae*. Thus in regard to the first point, the laws of

[1] See p. 68. [2] Collection of orig. papers, p. 218. [3] Ib. p. 196, ff.

England are held up in opposition to the ordinances prevailing here, especially in relation to the declaration of personal freedom. A verbal agreement in this respect is out of the question; but the legislators of New England were firmly persuaded that they had met the spirit of the English constitution in their enactments, and their additional enactments in reference to ecclesiastical relations they regarded as resulting necessarily from their religious principles. They claim it as their due, that the manifold misfortunes of the last year may not be laid to their charge; and while acknowledging that grievances may still exist, remind their readers that as Rome was not built in a day, it would not be strange if within sixteen years from the foundation of the colony, much yet remained to be done. The objections of the petitioners, they say, are stated in terms so general that a proper refutation of them becomes impossible. The demand for universal right of suffrage, the government regards as an attempt to gain favor with the populace, and directs attention to the fact, that it lies with the petitioners themselves whether they shall be furnished with the requisite qualifications. The third point is most largely discussed. In accordance with the prevailing view of the time, it is assumed that by answering complaints in reference to the terms of church-membership, all objections in reference to the denial of political rights are also disposed of. The alleged title of many to the privileges of the church, is rebutted by the assertion that "some are hypocritical in their walk, others are notoriously corrupt in their opinions, other still, grossly ignorant of the fundamental doctrines of religion, and that, fourthly, if some did possess such knowledge and such gifts, they did not make the same known by a public profession before the church or elders, and consequently, their qualifications were unknown. "Our churches," it proceeds, "cannot blindly or upon the testimony of others, receive persons who refuse to give that account of their faith or repentance, which is so expressly required. 1 Pet. 3: 15. Matt. 3: 6. Acts 8: 37. Matt. 16: 16–18."

But it was not the manner of the leaders of New England to stop with such a vindication, and the petitioners were summoned before the Court. When they appealed to the right of petition, it was answered that they were not complained of for having presented a petition, but on account of their contemptuous and seditious expressions; and security was demanded for their good behavior. But while under indictment for a criminal offence, pardon was offered them if they would make full and frank confession of their fault. Declining to do this, they were fined, some in smaller, some in larger sums. Their appeal to the commission, appointed by the English government for all colonies, was not admitted. A number of them then resolved to carry their complaints to England; but their papers were seized by the government. Among them was a memorandum which contained, besides a complaint in reference to the late proceeding, a recapitulation of the points above mentioned; nay, they had gone so far as to propose changes involving the entire subversion of the present form of government. The supreme power of the General Court at Boston was represented as unauthorized, since even the charter of Massachusetts had not been confirmed by Parliament; and it was therefore requested that a Governor might be appointed from England. A copy of this memorandum, subscribed by some twenty-five non-freemen (such is the term they use), in behalf of themselves and many thousands, found its way to London. But the Massachusetts agent there resident was provided from Boston with arguments to meet it; and his skilful management, together with his influence with many members of parliament and other distinguished men, prevented all prejudicial consequences to the colony. The public mind was, moreover, too much occupied with the popular disturbances in England itself to bestow much attention on these petitioners.

But in Boston these proceedings were met by the loud expression of dissatisfaction, even among the members of the government; and this directed itself against a man so generally esteemed and honored as Winthrop, who was that year deputy-governor. In open assembly, he was charged with an attempt upon the liberties of the people, and was required, against all order, to exonerate himself by an explanation on the spot. Winthrop yielded to the demand, after having showed them that he might properly have refused. The result of his vindication was his public acquittal.[1] On resuming his seat as deputy-governor, Winthrop felt himself called on to make the following address:

"I shall not now speak anything about the past proceedings of this Court, or the persons therein concerned, only I bless God that I see an issue of this troublesome affair. I am well satisfied that I was publicly accused, and that I am now publicly acquitted. But though I am justified before man, yet it may be the Lord hath seen so much amiss in my administrations, as calls me to be humbled; and, indeed, for me to have been thus charged by men, is of itself a matter of humiliation, whereof I desire to make a right use before the Lord. If Miriam's father spit in her face, she is to be ashamed. But give me leave before you go, to say something that may rectify the opinions of many

1 "Notwithstanding, the touchy jealousy of the people about their liberties lay at the bottom of this prosecution," says Mather, Magn. Book II. Ch. IV. § 9.

people from whence the distempers have arisen, that have lately prevailed upon the body of this people. It is you who have called us unto this office; but, being thus called, we have our authority from God; it is the ordinance of God, and it hath the image of God stamped upon it; and the contempt of it has been vindicated by God with terrible examples of his vengeance. I entreat you to consider, that when you choose magistrates, you take them from among yourselves, men subject unto like passions with yourselves. If ye see our infirmities, reflect upon your own, and you will not be so severe censurers of ours. We count him a good servant who breaks not his covenant; the covenant between us and you is the oath you have taken of us, which is to this purpose, that we shall govern you and judge your causes according to God's laws and our own, according to our best skill. As for our skill, you must run the hazard of it; and if there be an error, not in the will but only in the skill, it becomes you to bear it. Nor would I have you to mistake in the point of your own liberty. There is a liberty of corrupt nature which is affected both by men and beasts, to do what they list; and this liberty is inconsistent with authority, impatient of all restraint; by this liberty *sumus omnes deteriores;* 't is the grand enemy of truth and peace, and all the ordinances of God are bent against it. But there is a civil, a moral, a federal liberty, which is the proper end and object of authority; it is a liberty for that only which is just and good; for this liberty you are to stand with the hazard of your very lives, and whatsoever crosses it is not authority, but a distemper thereof. This liberty is maintained in the way of subjection to authority; and the authority set over you will, in all administrations for your good, be quietly submitted unto by all but such as have a disposition to shake off the yoke, and lose their true liberty by their murmuring at the honor and power of authority." From this time to his death in 1647, Winthrop was yearly chosen governor.

SYNOD CALLED, MAY 1646.

These agitations now called forth decisions on the part of the church, sustaining the prevailing views. Reference has already been made to an act passed by the Court in March, 1635, "entreating the brethren and elders of every church within this jurisdiction, that they will consult and advise of one uniform order of discipline in the churches, agreeable to the Scriptures, and then to consider how far the magistrates are bound to interpose for the preservation of that uniformity and the peace of the churches." This measure has a manifest connection with the controversies occasioned by Roger Williams,[1] which, however, had been allayed without farther intervention on the part of the churches. It is not unlikely, indeed, that an avowed movement towards the establishment of a uniformity may have been met with disfavor; at all events, the act did not then go into effect. Much as it might be for the interests of the church, as connected with the existing theocracy, the interference of the civil magistrate in her internal affairs was never welcome, even with the prospect of her own increase in distinction and power. The same spirit now manifested itself in 1646. When the government, on occasion of the disturbances caused by the above-mentioned petition, issued an order for a synod, some of the deputies objected, on the ground that to concede such a power to the magistracy might be opening the way for them at any time to establish new ordinances respecting ecclesiastical matters, an office for which the civil government was not appointed by Christ, and thus

[1] See Knowles Memoir of Roger Williams p. 70; and the present work p. 92.

might be imposed on the church a uniformity in things which Christ has left undetermined. After a debate on this exception, the Court agreed to convene the Synod, 'by way of a motion merely,' and not in the form of an order. This motion, May 15, 1646, began with these words:

"The right form of church government and discipline being agreed part of the kingdom of Christ on earth, therefore the establishing and settling thereof by the joint and public agreement and consent of churches, and by the sanction of civil authority, must needs greatly conduce to the honor and glory of our Lord Jesus Christ, and to the settling and safety of church and commonwealth, where such a duty is diligently attended and performed." For want of such a form, — thus it proceeds — great differences in opinion and in practice appear in the churches, and still greater are to be expected; and that not merely in respect to unimportant matters, but in points of weightiest moment and grave significance; as, preëminently, in the question respecting admission to the ordinance of baptism. Some baptized those whose grandparents were actual members of the church, though the immediate parents were not so; or held the opinion that under certain terms and conditions the children of those might be baptized, who had indeed been members of a congregation in England, but here were not found qualified for participation in the Lord's Supper. On the other side, it was maintained by some that whatever might be the state of the parents, baptism ought not to be dispensed to any infants whatever. The Synod was therefore called upon to "discuss, dispute, and clear up by the word of God, such questions of church government and discipline, in the things aforementioned, or any other as they shall think needful and meet, and to continue so doing, till they, or the major part of them, shall have agreed upon one form of government and discipline, for the main and substantial parts thereof, as that which they judge agreeable to the Holy Scriptures." At the conclusion of such conference, the result was to be laid before the General Court, in order to receive from it, as agreeable to the word of God, such approval as is meet: "that the Lord being thus acknowledged by church and state, to be our judge, our lawgiver and king, he may be graciously pleased still to save us, as hitherto he has done."

The same call was sent to the churches in the other colonies, and was there followed by the same result. One of the three ministers who afterwards drew up for the Synod the model of church government as the basis of its action, was from the town of Duxbury in New Plymouth.[1] But though the government had sent out this summons merely in the form of an invitation, it was met by no inconsiderable opposition in Boston. Indeed, the church at first declined to choose delegates for the Synod. But John Norton,[2] a distinguished minister, who had come over from England in 1634 and received an official call from the church in Ipswich, preached with such effect before a very numerous assembly in Boston, on the nature of synods, that delegates were elected. Accordingly, at the beginning of the winter of 1646, the Synod assembled; but after a session of fourteen days it adjourned to the 18th of June, 1647; and the summer proving sickly on account of the great heat, they then adjourned again. But in September, 1648, they met once more, and prosecuted the

[1] John Partridge; Mather Mag. Book III. Part II. Ch. XI.

[2] Ibid. Book II. Part I. Ch. II. §16. He was called, after Cotton's death in 1652, to the church in Boston, where he lived ten years, an esteemed and beloved preacher of the Gospel.

business with which they were charged till its completion in October.

The first step was, to take into consideration the confession of faith adopted by the assembly of divines at Westminster.[1] Each article was read aloud by itself, and the unanimous concurrence of all present was expressed in the following resolution: "This Synod having perused and

1 This assembly was called by order of parliament in 1643. It consisted of ten peers, twenty members of the lower House, and one hundred and twenty clergymen; but the number of the latter was soon diminished by the secession of those inclined to episcopacy. At the very beginning, they took in hand a revision of the Thirty-nine Articles, but without completing it. Later, the Assembly was joined by the Scotch. The predominance thus gained by the Presbyterians was contested by the influence of the Independents, which was constantly strengthening under the countenance of Cromwell; who, however, were not able to carry through their principle of the independence of the single churches. On the contrary, both in the decisions respecting the ordination of ministers and public worship, the principles of the Presbyterians were adopted, according to which the assembly of the ministers and elders of one church were subjected to the presbyteries of several churches, and these again to a synod. Before the close of the assembly (in February 1648), the Independents, being outvoted, had withdrawn. So also did the Erastians, who allowed to the clergy only the office of preaching the word and administering the sacraments, but wished all church-government to be transferred to the state. The Confession of Faith laid before parliament in 1646, which was assented to by the Presbyterians and Independents, takes very decided ground against Arminianism, and exalts the doctrine of predestination in opposition to the views then current in the Episcopal Church. But with this concord, we see on both sides a tenacious adherence to their different doctrines in regard to church-government; as in all English church-parties, the constitution has ever been the main question. The Independents of England complained at that time of persecution; in the year of Cromwell's death, 1658, they held an assembly at London, and adopted the Savoy Confession, which agrees in all essential points with that of Westminster. The stand it takes against open communion seems to hold a certain connection with the opposition to Arminianism; making an unconscious application of the doctrine of predestination, by seeking to exclude all but the elect from membership in the visible church.

considered (with much gladness of heart and thankfulness to God) the confession of faith, published by the late reverend assembly in England, do judge it to be very holy, orthodox and judicious, in all matters of faith, and do therefore freely and fully consent thereunto for the substance thereof. Only in those things which have respect to church-government and discipline, we refer ourselves to the platform of church-discipline agreed upon by this present assembly; and we do therefore think it meet, that this confession of faith should be commended to the churches of Christ among us, and to the honored Court, as worthy of their due consideration and acceptance."

The Synod then applied itself to the completion of the work for which it had especially been called together. Besides the above mentioned Partridge, John Cotton and Richard Mather[1] were appointed to draw up, each by himself, an outline of Church-Discipline agreeable to the Holy Scriptures. The Synod compared these three models with one another, and thus arose the platform of Church-Discipline which, in October 1648, was presented to the General Court for consideration and acceptance. Its conclusions received indeed no such unanimous approval, in reference to each particular point, as the Articles of Faith; but, on the other hand, no decided opposition arose from any quarter, and when laid before the churches, it was accepted by all.[2]

PLATFORM OF CHURCH DISCIPLINE (THE CAMBRIDGE PLATFORM), ADOPTED IN 1648.

We have already had occasion to bring forward those points of this Platform, which contain an exhibition of the

[1] Grandfather of the church historian, Cotton Mather.

[2] Neal's History of New England, I., 292.

theocratic relation.[1] Our first object must now be to show how the question was answered, which, according to the declaration of the General Court, occasioned the preparation of the Platform, viz., the question respecting qualifications for church-membership. The answer is found in the fourth and twelfth chapters of the Platform; the one treating of the form of the visible church; the other, of the admission of members into the church. The fourth chapter thus speaks:

1. Saints by calling must have a visible political union among themselves, or else they are not yet a particular church, (1 Cor. 12: 27. 1 Tim. 3: 15. Eph. 2: 22. 1 Cor. 12: 15, 16, 17.) as those similitudes hold forth which the scripture makes use of to show the nature of particular churches; as a *body*, a *building*, *house*, *hands*, *eyes*, *feet*, and other members, must be united, or else (remaining separate) are not a body. Stones, timber, though squared, hewn and polished, are not a house, until they are compacted, and united: (Rev. ii.) so saints or believers in judgment of charity, are not a church, unless orderly knit together.

2. Particular churches cannot be distinguished one from another, but by their forms. *Ephesus* is not *Smyrna*, nor *Pergamos Thyatira*, but each one a distinct society of itself, having officers of their own, which had not the charge of others: virtues of their own, for which others are not praised: corruptions of their own, for which others are not blamed.

3. This form is the *visible covenant*, agreement or consent, whereby they give up themselves unto the Lord, to the observing of the ordinances of Christ together in the same society, which is usually called the *church-covenant:*

[1] See p. 68, ff.

(Ex. 19 : 5, 8. Deut. 29 : 12, 13. Zec. 11 : 14, and 9 : 11,) for we see not otherwise how members can have church-power over one another mutually. The comparing of each particular church to a *city*, and unto a *spouse*, (Eph. 2 : 19. 2 Cor. 11 : 2,) seemeth to conclude not only a form, but that that form is by way of covenant. The covenant, as it was that which made the family of *Abraham* and children of *Israel* to be a church and people unto God, (Gen. 17 : 7. Eph. 2 : 12, 18,) so it is that which now makes the several societies of Gentile believers to be churches in these days.

4. This voluntary agreement, consent or covenant, (for all these are here taken for the same) although the more express and plain it is, the more fully puts us in mind of our mutual duty; and stirreth us up to it, and leaveth less room for the questioning of the truth of the church-estate of a company of professors, and the truth of membership of particular persons; yet we conceive the substance of it is kept, where there is real agreement and consent of a company of faithful persons to meet constantly together in one congregation, for the public worship of God, and their mutual edification: which real agreement and consent they do express by their constant practice in coming together for the public worship of God, and by their religious subjection unto the ordinances of God there: (Exod. 19 : 5, and 20 : 8, and 24 : 3, 17. Josh. 24 : 18—24. Psal. 50: 5. Neh. 9 : 88, and 10 : 1. Gen. xvii. Deut. xxix.) the rather, if we do consider how scripture-covenants have been entered into, not only expressly by word of mouth, but by sacrifice, by hand-writing and seal; and also sometimes by silent consent, without any writing or expression of words at all.

5. This form being by mutual covenant, it followeth, it is not faith in the heart, nor the profession of that faith,

nor cohabitation, nor baptism. 1. Not *faith in the heart*, because that is invisible. 2. Not *a bare profession*, because that declareth them no more to be members of one church than another. 3. Not *cohabitation*, atheists or infidels may dwell together with believers. 4. Not *baptism*, because it presupposeth a church-estate as circumcision in the *Old Testament*, which gave no being to the church, the church being before it, and in the wilderness without it. Seals presuppose a covenant already in being. One person is a complete subject of baptism, but one person is incapable of being a church.

6. All believers ought, as God giveth them opportunity thereunto, to endeavor to join themselves unto a particular church, and that in respect of the honor of Jesus Christ, in his example and institution, by the professed acknowledgment of, and subjection unto the order and ordinances of the gospel: (Acts 2: 47, and 9: 26. Mat. 3: 13, 14, 15, and 28: 19, 20. Psa. 133: 23, and 87: 7. Mat. 18: 20. 1 John, 1, 3.) as also in respect of their good communion founded upon their visible union, and contained in the promises of Christ's special presence in the church; whence they have fellowship with him, and in him, one with another: also in the keeping of them in the way of God's commandments, and recovering of them in case of wandering, (which all Christ's sheep are subject to in this life) being unable to return of themselves; together with the benefit of their mutual edification, and of their posterity, that they may not be cut off from the privilege of the covenant. (Psa. 119: 176. 1 Pet. 2: 25. Eph. 4: 16. Job 22: 24, 25. Matt. 18: 15, 16, 17.) Otherwise, if a believer offends, he remains destitute of the remedy provided in that behalf. And should all believers neglect this duty of joining to all particular congregations, it might follow therefrom, that Christ should have no visible, political churches upon earth."

Still more decided is the view of the Synod, on the points in question, expressed in the twelfth chapter of the Platform. As it is through these decisions that the subsequent controversies are seen in their proper light, we will here give this chapter at length.

1. The doors of the church of Christ upon earth do not, by God's appointment, stand so wide open that all sorts of people, good and bad, may freely enter therein at their pleasure, (2 Chr. 29 : 19. Matt. 13 : 25, and 22 : 12.) but such as are admitted thereto, as members, ought to be examined and tried first, whether they be fit and meet to be received into church-society or not. The Eunuch of *Ethiopia* before his admission, was examined by *Philip*, (Acts 8 : 37.) whether he did believe on Jesus Christ with all his heart. The angel of the church at *Ephesus*, (Rev. 2 : 2. Acts 9 : 26.) is commended for trying such as said they were apostles and were not. There is like reason for trying of them that profess themselves to be believers. The officers are charged with the keeping of the doors of the church, and therefore are in a special manner to make trial of the fitness of such, who enter. Twelve angels are set at the gates of the temple, (Rev. 21 : 12. 2 Chr. 23 : 19.) lest such as were *ceremonially unclean* should enter thereinto.

2. The things which are requisite to be found in all church-members, are *repentance* from sin, and *faith* in Jesus Christ: (Acts 2 : 38—42, and 8 : 37.) and therefore, these are the things whereof men are to be examined, at their admission into the church, and which then they must profess and hold forth in such sort, as may satisfy *rational charity* that the things are indeed. *John Baptist* admitted men to baptism confessing and bewailing their sins: (Matt. 3 : 6. Acts 19 : 18.) and of others it is said that *they came and confessed, and showed their deeds.*

3. The weakest measure of faith is to be accepted in those that desire to be admitted into the church (Rom. 14: 1.); if *sincere*, they have the substance of that faith, repentance and holiness, which is required in church-members; and such have most need of the ordinances for their confirmation, and growth in grace. The Lord Jesus would not quench the smoking flax, nor break the bruised reed, (Matt. 12: 20. Isa. 40: 11.) but gather the tender lambs in his arms and carry them gently in his bosom. Such charity and tenderness is to be used, as the weakest Christian, if sincere, may not be excluded nor discouraged. Severity of examination is to be avoided.

4. In case any through excessive fear, or other infirmity, be unable to make their personal relation of their spiritual estate in public, it is sufficient, that the elders having received private satisfaction, make relation thereof in public before the church, they testifying their assents thereunto: this being the way that tendeth most to edification. But where persons are of greater abilities, there it is most expedient that they make their relations and confessions personally with their own mouth, as *David* professeth of himself. (Psal. 66: 6.)

5. A personal and public confession, and declaring of God's manner of working upon the soul, is both lawful, expedient and useful, in sundry respects and upon sundry grounds. Those three thousand, (Acts 2: 37, 41.) before they were admitted by the apostles, did manifest that they were pricked at the heart by *Peter's* sermon, together with earnest desire to be delivered from their sins which even wounded their consciences, and their ready receiving of the word of promise and exhortation. We are to be ready to *render a reason of the hope that is in us, to every one that asketh us;* (1 Pet. 3: 15. Heb. 11: 1. Eph. 1: 18.) there-

fore we must be able and ready upon any occasion to declare and show our *repentance* for sin, *faith* unfeigned, and *effectual calling*, because those are the *reason* of a well grounded *hope*. *I have not hidden thy righteousness from the great congregation.* (Psalm 40: 10.)

6. This profession of faith and repentance, as it must be made by such at their admission, that were never in church society before; so nothing hindereth but the same may also be performed by such as have formerly been members of some other church, (Matt. 3 : 5, 6. Gal. 2 : 4. 1 Tim. 5 : 24.) and the church to which they now join themselves as members, may lawfully require the same. Those three thousand, (Acts ii.) which made their confession, were members of the church of the Jews before; so were those that were baptized by *John*. Churches may err in their admission; and persons regularly admitted may fall into offence. Otherwise, if churches might obtrude their members, or if church-members might obtrude themselves upon other churches without due trial, the matter so requiring, both the liberty of the churches would thereby be infringed in that they might not examine those, concerning whose fitness for communion they were unsatisfied: and besides the infringing of their liberty, the churches themselves would unavoidably be corrupted, and the ordinances defiled, whilst they might not refuse, but must receive the unworthy: which is contrary unto the scripture, teaching that all churches are sisters, and therefore equal. (Cant. 8: 8.)

7. The like trial is to be required from such members of the church as were born in the same, or received their membership, or were baptized in their infancy or minority by virtue of the covenant of their parents, when being grown up into years of discretion, they shall desire to be

made partakers of the Lord's Supper: unto which, because holy things must not be given to the unworthy, therefore it is requisite (Matt. 7: 6. 1 Cor. 11: 27.), that these as well as others should come to their trial and examination, and manifest their faith and repentance by an open profession thereof, before they are received to the Lord's Supper, and otherwise not to be admitted thereunto. Yet these church-members that were so born, or received in their childhood, before they are capable of being made partakers of full communion, have many privileges which others, not church-members, have not; they are in covenant with God, having the seal thereof upon them, viz., baptism; and so, if not regenerated, yet are in a more hopeful way of attaining regenerating grace, and all the spiritual blessings both of the covenant and the seal: they are also under church-watch, and consequently subject to the reprehensions, admonitions, and censures thereof, for their healing and amendment, as need shall require."

If now we sum up the results of this Synod, we shall find in the Platform the confirmation, as well of the theocratic views which had all along been recognized in practice, as of the undisputed Congregationalist principles respecting the self-competency and independence of the churches, in regard to the exercise of the fullest and highest ecclesiastical authority. But the Platform also decides, as we see from the two chapters just quoted, the question respecting the qualifications for church-membership. We see here as little deviation from the conditions laid down by Robinson, as from those which still prevail among Congregationalists at the present day. The great value and blessing of baptism is indeed acknowledged; but the baptized are nevertheless put essentially on a level with others, who stand outside the church-communion and are obliged to submit to the same tests.

Before passing to the consideration of the repeated counter-movements against this decision, and to the determinations of the following synod, we will attempt to draw from the Platform a view of certain other ecclesiastical relations, which did not so essentially affect the progressive development of the church. The gradual and partial change experienced here, was, indeed, not so much expressed in special decisions, as introduced, step after step, by usage.

In regard to officers in the church, four of these are mentioned in the Platform. The sixth chapter treats of pastors and teachers, who (§ 5) are distinct from each other in this respect, that upon the former lies the duty of exhortation, administering therein of the word of wisdom; upon the latter, the care of doctrine, administering therein of the word of knowledge: both participate in the administration of the sacraments, and the execution of church censures, that being only an application of the word preached. Still, it is expressly declared (§ 6) that the office of teacher is not limited to the schools; but both belong alike to the church. Two such servants of the word would, however, be found only in the larger churches; and since these, as before mentioned, were accustomed to divide, a ready explanation may be found, in the independency of each church, for the gradual disappearance of one of these offices. The third office in the church was that of ruling elder. The two servants of the church already mentioned were, it is true, also called elders, and took part in the government of the church; but this was the especial duty of the ruling elder, to whom it did not pertain to teach or to preach. What belonged to all three in common, found in the ruling elder its chief executor, or at least its principal organ of communication. His duty is stated to be (chap. 7, § 2) that of admitting and excluding members; of calling together and dismissing the church; of preparing business for the public meetings and maintaining quiet and order in the same; of representing the church; taking the oversight of its members in respect to life and doctrine; visiting and comforting the sick; admonishing, as occasion shall offer, out of the word of God. The ruling elders stood as agents between the church and the individual members. This office at first existed in most of the churches; but at the end of a half century it had fallen into almost total desuetude. The cause of this was, in part, the gradual transfer of its duties to the other church servants; in part, the unpleasant nature of some branches of the office; for instance, that of oversight of the members, which became more and more repulsive during the signal decay of the church life at a later period. The fourth office, that of deacons, had for its object the purely external relations of the church, especially the management of its property.

While the above named offices are declared to be those alone which are agreeable to Scripture, all others, as popes, cardinals, patriarchs, archbishops, lordbishops, archdeacons, officials, commissaries, and the like, are described as mere inventions and ordinances, which tend to the great dishonor of Jesus Christ, the Lord and King of his church. The appointment of deaconesses is, however, recommended where it is practicable. The election of church officers, according to the eighth chapter, naturally pertains to the church; neither the government, diocesan bishops, or patrons can claim it on the ground of Scripture. Ordination is to be performed by the elders; if these are wanting, by brethren, orderly chosen by the church for the purpose.

In the latter case, however, the end is reached, if the imposition of hands and prayer are performed by the elders of other churches. But it gradually became established usage, to commit ordination to the ministers of neighboring churches. The articles respecting the communion of different churches with each other are in conformity with the principles thus laid down and explained. They are bound to mutual care, consultation, admonition, and sympathy, as becomes christian brethren. If a member of any church has occasion to leave it in a regular manner, he shall be dismissed with a letter of recommendation, that he may be received into the church to which he goes; although the latter, as we have seen, is not unconditionally bound to accept him.

We will here add the articles respecting excommunication. It may be pronounced against one who sins against his brother, if refusing to hear him, the witnesses, and the church (Matt. 18 : 15—17); as also for public scandals. But it must proceed from the spirit of judgment and meekness. All intercourse with the excommunicated shall be withheld, except so far as is indispensably necessary. Still he is not thereby deprived of his civil rights, and, being regarded as a heathen and publican, he may be present at the preaching of the word. In the hope of his recovery, he shall not be accounted as an enemy, but admonished as a brother; and on the manifestation of repentance, he shall be reinstated in his former relations. It is added, that the scandalous walk of persons in the church is not sufficient ground for separation from it, nor for withdrawal from participation in the sacraments therein administered.

Thus have we endeavored to give a reflection of the spirit which rules in this platform. Its most important decision, however, that which respects the qualifications for church-membership, found and continued to find many opposers. The succeeding chapters will show the triumph of another view, in reference to the relation of baptized persons, and the consequences of this change.

CHAPTER VI.

DISSOLUTION OF THE THEOCRATIC RELATION, FROM THE ECCLESIASTICAL AND THE POLITICAL SIDE.

ECCLESIASTICAL AGITATIONS WITHIN THE COLONIES.

The Cambridge Synod of 1648 had, as we have seen, triumphed over the opposition which threatened to subvert the theocratic relation. That opposition was essentially political in its nature, being directed against a political advantage enjoyed by church-members, against the theocracy in general.

But there now appeared opposers of the existing relations from a properly ecclesiastical stand-point, directly affecting the specific form of the theocratic constitution, as developed from the ground-ideas of Congregationalism. This conflict, waged with other weapons, and as it were in another territory, had also a different issue from the one just narrated.

It appears, from contemporary accounts, that the principles of the theocracy were carried out in practice, however much it might seem, in the single cases, to be at war with the spirit in which the Independents had their origin. About the year 1651, the church at Malden was fined in a heavy sum, for having chosen a minister without the agreement and consent of the neighboring churches, and without permission from the government. It was therefore ordained by law, that no minister could be called to the office in any church without the approbation both of some members of the magistracy, and of the neighboring churches. On the strength of this decision, the General Court[1] refused to allow the North Church in Boston to choose for their pastor, a well-gifted though unlearned man by the name of Powell, and they were obliged to content themselves with making him ruling elder. Not only so, but the government took upon itself to nominate another from New Plymouth, thus exercising a direct influence on the election. In reference to this occurrence, Hubbard,[2] one of the earliest historians of New England says: "Let the experience of all reformed churches be asked, and it will appear, that disorder and confusion in the church can be avoided by no decisions, councils and assemblies of synods, or of other deputies of the churches, if that which is determined be not somewhat set forward by the civil authority. All men are naturally so prejudiced by their own notions, that the order and rule of the gospel is not obeyed, unless there is a necessary power of restraint."

At this same time, when the connection between church and state was thus steadfastly maintained, commenced the discussion of the question respecting qualification for membership in the church itself. It cannot but strike one with surprise, that the progress of so few years had sufficed to produce, in a large majority of the people, a change in respect to the organic principles which lay at the basis of Congregationalism. This departure from the original strictness, which we shall see as the result of the ecclesiastical agitations of this period, finds its explanation in the form and character of the opposition here developed. In accord-

1 Backus, I., 267. Hutchinson, I., 174.

2 A history of Massachusetts from his hand appeared so early as 1680.

ance with her fundamental principles, the church could admit to baptism only the children of her actual members, and no one was entitled by this sacrament to full fellowship. But, as before remarked, in process of time not only had many emigrants come from England without that religious impulse; but there was a decay of that predominating church-feeling, even in the second generation in America. It was, nevertheless, not so extinguished that there was not a desire among such for a certain personal connection with the church, partly for their own sakes, and partly to secure for their children a participation in the privileges of the christian body. The church, however, could not regard these children as members through their parents, or expect that they would subsequently fulfil the obligations requisite for the other sacrament. But though she might feel herself strong enough, especially in her connection with the state, to resist the claims and wishes of those who were directly interested in these questions, yet another consideration here presented itself in respect to the immediate consequences of a consistent denial of baptism. It was especially to be feared lest Anabaptism, that bugbear of New England, would quickly extend itself, being strengthened by members, who saw themselves as it were thus compelled by the church to postpone their baptism. The danger appeared the more imminent from the fact, that it now began to show itself in a form which gave no occasion to the reproach of fanaticism, or of a tendency to disorder. Henry Dunster, the first president of Harvard College, who had been a teacher in that institution from the year 1640, was, by the testimony of his contemporaries, a very learned man,[1]

[1] He was especially celebrated for his knowledge of Hebrew. A metrical version of the Psalms, prepared by him, came into use in public wor-

and had at first, as it seems, performed the duties of his office to general satisfaction. But at a later period, he rejected infant baptism, manifestly for the sake of carrying out consistently the Congregationalist principle; for the sacraments being in his view of equal rank, he held the same pre-requisites necessary for both. Although he seems to have expressed this change of opinion with great moderation, the most injurious and corrupting influence was apprehended from it in his position; and in the year 1654, he was required to resign his office. He yielded a ready assent, and withdrew to Scituate, a town in Massachusetts on the borders of Plymouth colony. Here he lived to the year 1675 undisturbed, and without giving occasion to any farther excitement.

Just about the time when the opposition thus developed in Massachusetts had been quelled, there sprang up a controversy in Hartford, the capital of Connecticut, whose progress led to conclusions which revolutionized the hitherto existing relation. In the year 1647, their minister, Mr. Hooker, one of the founders of this colony, and "the father and pillar of the Connecticut churches," had died. Some years after, a dissension arose between his successor Samuel Stone, and Goodwin a ruling elder in the church, which seems in its beginning to have had reference merely to unessential points, in regard to the reception of new members. The subsequent grounds of conflict were as yet undeveloped; hence also, its proper immediate occasion did not come to light.[1] Goodwin complained that the

ship, even after another had been attempted 1639. Mather, Book III., II., Ch. 12; and Book IV., §§ 3 and 5. Backus, I., p. 182.

[1] Mather, (Magn. B. III., Chap. XVI., § 8,) says: "They were both of them godly men; and the true original of the misunderstanding between men of so good an understanding has been rendered almost as obscure as

rights of the brethren were neglected in the admission of members, and the true principles of Congregationalism treated with contempt.[1] The case or cases, in which the primitive strictness seemed to Stone to have been neglected, are not known. But the controversy itself spread through the neighboring churches, and in all of them with scarcely an exception, both the Hartford parties found zealous adherents and advocates. The whole colony and even the General Court took part in it. To avert a formal division in the church, synods of the neighboring churches and elders were repeatedly called in the years 1654 and 1655; but the excitement at Hartford had risen to such a height, that both sides suspected all the elders and churches in Connecticut and New Haven of being in some way prejudiced in favor of their opponents. It was therefore thought expedient to call a council from the other colonies. Accordingly, in the year 1656, a number of ministers and elders from Massachusetts repaired to Hartford, to give their opinion and advice. This seems to have been favorable to the stricter party, but did not effect any permanent result. Hubbard says, moreover, of Massachusetts in the year 1656: "Baptism had to this time been imparted to those children only, whose immediate parents were admitted to full fellowship in the place where they lived."

the rise of Connecticut river." Trumbull, (Hist. of Connecticut, Vol. I., p. 322,) says that it does not indeed fully appear, what particular act or sentiment in Mr. Stone or the church gave elder Goodwin disgust and began the dissension; but that it is evident that it had reference to church membership and the rights of the brotherhood. P. 311, Trumbull suggests that perhaps Goodwin "imagined himself not to have been properly consulted and regarded."

[1] Stone's definition of Congregational church-government was, "A speaking aristocracy in the face of a silent democracy." Mather III., XVI. 9.—Tr.

Their advice was conformed rather to this existing usage than to the views recently broached. But the mutual animosity continued to increase; and indeed very distinguished men, among them even Webster, the governor of Connecticut, ranged themselves on the side of the stricter party.

Meanwhile, in Connecticut as well as in the other colonies, there was growing up a strong party, who desired that all persons of regular and blameless life might be admitted to full communion in the churches, on profession of their belief in the christian religion, without further examination in respect to a change of heart; and moreover that all baptized persons should be treated as members of the church. Some went still farther, and insisted that all persons who had been members of churches in England, or had been members of regular ecclesiastical parishes there, and contributed to the support of public worship, should be allowed the privileges of church-members in full communion. They demanded also, that all baptized persons, upon "owning the covenant," as it was called, should have their children baptized, although they did not come to the Lord's table. A list of grievances, having reference to this subject, was introduced into the Assembly. The choice of a minister furnished the occasion for these views to take a decisive form. It was urged that the church alone was not competent to make this choice; but as all the inhabitants had, both in respect to themselves and their children, an equal interest with the church-members in the qualifications of the minister, and were obliged to contribute their proportion to his support, they had also the right to a voice in his election. On the other hand, it was maintained that the call of pastors by any other than church-members was contrary to Scripture;

they were ordained over the churches only, and were termed angels of the churches. These points were discussed with the greatest warmth, in ordinary intercourse as well as in public debate. The wish of unproved persons to participate in the rights and honors of church-members, and to have their children baptized, seemed to those who beheld in these innovations the corruption and profanation of the churches, to call for counteractive measures of the most decided character.

The General Court of Connecticut held itself equally bound to take into serious consideration the division at Hartford, and these new controversies in the colony. At their session in May 1656, a committee of four distinguished citizens of Hartford was nominated, to consult with the elders of the colony respecting the alleged grievances, and with their help draw up a statement of the principal points. This was to be presented to the General Courts of the United Colonies for their advice, which was solicited to be given with the least possible delay. The greater haste was thought necessary in settling these disputes, on account of the Quakers, who as already mentioned, had just at this time begun to disturb the colonies, and against whom Connecticut and New Haven had likewise enacted severe laws. The General Court of Massachusetts, in reply to the heads of grievance which had been laid before them, advised a general council and sent letters to the other courts to this effect. New Haven sent answers to the several questions proposed, and considered this sufficient. In Connecticut, February 26th, 1657, the proposal of Massachusetts was agreed to. Four ministers, Warham, Stone, Blyeman, and Russel, were appointed to meet the delegates of the other colonies the following year at Boston, for deliberation on the proposed questions or others that might come before them, and to report the conclusions of the synod to the General Court of Connecticut. But especially were the delegates instructed to confer respecting the Hartford affair with the Massachusetts ministers, from whom a visit was to be requested for the purpose of assisting in a council at Hartford. The agitated church was, moreover, desired to take part in the synod at Boston, with the assurance that in case its decision was not satisfactory, the attempt should be repeated to heal the breach in Hartford itself. Yet even in the meeting of the General Court, several distinguished men avowed their dissatisfaction with the proposed measures, as neither grounded on the divine word, nor adapted to restore peace and quiet. Doubtless, in so doing, they intended not only to set themselves against what they esteemed an interference of the legislative authority in ecclesiastical affairs, but against a dangerous tendency to innovation. The General Court at New Haven was also most decidedly opposed to such a council. Here was felt the powerful influence of Mr. Davenport, whose firm adherence to the original principles of Congregationalism will come under our consideration farther on. The request on the part of Massachusetts, that elders might be sent to the synod at Boston, was therefore declined, in a long letter explanatory of their views on the petitions presented to the General Court of Connecticut. "They had heard the petitioners confidently hoped to obtain great changes, according to which the privileges of membership should be extended to all members of church-parishes, without any requirement of conversion." The fear was expressed "that a general council held at that time, would greatly endanger the peace and purity of the churches." The General Court of New Haven stated, moreover, "that they had sent an answer to all the questions proposed to the Court of Connecticut, but held, nevertheless, that the legislature and elders of that colony were sufficient to determine all those points without any assistance from abroad; they themselves could not spare any of their elders, on account of the recent removal of some of their ministers by death." With their letter, they sent the answers which they had prepared, and entreated for them a serious consideration. They urged, also, that the principles grounded on the Scriptures, which had been thus far received, should be preserved inviolate; since a departure from them would, it was feared, be followed by most unhappy consequences to the church.

SYNOD OF 1657; THE HALF-WAY COVENANT.

Connecticut and Massachusetts, however, persisted in calling a general council. Seventeen questions[1] were laid before this body, to which others were added during the discussion. They all had reference, either directly or indirectly to the qualifications for church membership, and to the privileges resulting from it. This synod convened at Boston on the 4th of June, 1657, and after a session of little more than a fortnight, gave an elaborate answer to twenty-one questions. The Connecticut delegates brought back an authentic copy of the result and presented it to the General Court, at its session on the 12th of August. The Court ordered copies to be sent forthwith to all the churches in the colony; if any one of them had objections to make to these answers, they were to be transmitted to the General Court at its session in October.

The answers were soon after printed in London, under

[1] Given in Trumbull's Hist. of Conn., I., 316, and 317.—Tr.

the significant title: "A disputation concerning church members and their children." The result of the discussions is expressed in the following words: "It is the duty of infants, who confederated in their parents, when grown up unto years of discretion, though not fit for the Lord's Supper, to own the covenant they made with their parents, by entering thereunto in their own persons; and it is the duty of the churches to call upon them for the performance thereof, and if being called upon, they shall refuse the performance of this great duty, or otherwise continue scandalous, they are liable to be censured for the same by the church. And in case they understand the grounds of religion, and are not scandalous, and solemnly own the covenant in their own persons, wherein they give up themselves and their children unto the Lord, and desire baptism for them, we see not[1] sufficient cause to deny baptism unto their children." We see then, that all baptized persons were to be regarded as members of the church, and as subject to its discipline. Of the privileges attached to this relation, participation in the Supper is alone withheld from them in express words. But the claim to a share in the choice of ministers, put forth by the disaffected, received an answer in general terms, more favorable to this party than a decision which was made at a later period. It was to this effect: "That though it was the right of the brotherhood to choose their pastor, and though it was among the arts of Antichrist to deprive them of that power, yet they ought to have a special regard to the baptized, by the covenant of God under their watch."

Thus had the Synod struck out a middle course for the removal of the difficulties which had arisen. The wishes

[1] In Backus, I., 332, we here find, in parenthesis, the words: "with due reference to any godly learned that may dissent."

of those who feared or disliked the strictness of Congregationalism, had prevailed. Without examination on the part of the church, and without any statement in regard to their spiritual condition, they were church-members; civil rights could no longer be withheld from them, and their children were allowed the privilege of baptism. On the other hand, a distinction was made between such persons and members in full fellowship,[1] for which, as also for admission to the Supper, the earlier requisitions remained in force. But although a large number of persons, indeed the great majority of the people of New England at that time, might be extremely pleased with this conclusion, it encountered a powerful opposition. Not only many ministers, but, more particularly, the churches saw in such a modification of their hitherto elementary articles, an innovation which, as being irreconcilable with the principles of Congregationalism, must lead to its destruction. But before we trace the farther consequences of this conflict in general, we will present the result of the above-mentioned decision on the special case which had occasioned the calling of the Synod.

So far were the conclusions of the council from producing peace and quiet in the Hartford church, that the strife assumed a still more decided form. The stricter party now separated wholly from the Hartford church, and from its minister Mr. Stone, and connected themselves with the church in the neighboring town of Wethersfield. On the other side, Stone and the Hartford church thought themselves justified in the exercise of church discipline, and proceeded to the infliction of ecclesiastical penalties. The whole colony being in a state of excitement which threatened to rise still higher, the General Court, March

[1] In distinction from members of the half-way covenant.

11th, 1658, interposed by an Act, forbidding all farther action by the church at Hartford against those who had withdrawn; as also the completion by the latter of connection with any other church, till the existing difficulty should be settled in some way appointed by the Court. As the first step, the elders of the colony were desired to come together; if this was done, which seems not however to have been the case, it was without effect. As little success attended another effort of the Court for reconciling the disaffected, by conferences with influential and distinguished men. With equal tenacity, Stone and the church adhered to their opinion, and in May 1658 presented to the General Court a complaint against the seceders. The Court did not favor this step, but proposed a mutual conference, in which each side should be represented by three ministers who had taken no part in the controversy; if either party refused to choose elders for this purpose, the Court would choose for them. This was in fact done for Mr. Stone and the church, while the aggrieved brethren chose for themselves; but this refusal of the church to concur prevented the meeting of the council. Thereupon the General Court resolved, March 1659, to return to their earlier plan, and invited ministers and elders from six churches in Massachusetts, to visit Hartford the following June. They complied with the request, and exerted themselves in the most earnest manner, to allay the animosity. Although they did not effect a reconciliation, yet they succeeded in producing a better state of feeling than had existed for years. This good result being perceived by the General Court, they invited the same ministers to come again to Hartford in August, and at the same time, ordered that the points of complaint against the seceding brethren should be drawn up for their consideration and answer; and that both parties should submit to their judgment, which was to be the final decision on the case. This council did indeed so far succeed in adjusting differences, that a separation of the church was prevented for the present. Some of the most influential members had, it is true, died or removed from the place; but others viewed the new decisions as a departure from the original principles of Congregationalism, and at a later period, we see a separation in the church on nearly the same grounds. The rise, progress, and settlement of these controversies exhibit the peculiar characteristics of the New England Church. Especially noticeable is the universal interest which they excited. Not only did the churches of Massachusetts, Connecticut, and New Haven use their most zealous efforts to effect a reconciliation, but the Commissioners of the United Colonies testified their heart-felt sorrow over these differences, and sought by friendly persuasion to promote peace and heal division. The final result was solemnized, in November 1659, by a day of public thanksgiving.

THE SYNOD OF 1662 RE-AFFIRMS THE DECISION OF THAT OF 1657.

But while these things had been progressing, the agitations produced by the decision of the Synod of 1657 still continued. In New Haven, little was felt of their influence, since here the original principles were adhered to in their full integrity, and that decision was ignored by the stricter party. But in Connecticut, and especially in Massachusetts, the opposition was openly expressed; for the commissioners of both colonies had taken part in the Synod, and those who opposed the new determinations were numerous, especially among the laity. The General Court at Boston, alarmed at the symptoms of a general rupture, now summoned 1662, a synod of all the ministers of that colony,[1] which resulted in most important consequences for the other colonies also. Two questions were here proposed, of which the latter, the least important for the time, had reference to the connection of churches among themselves. It was answered in conformity with the platform of church discipline of 1648; the principle of the independence of single churches in respect to the exercise of church government was strictly adhered to, though the connection and union of churches was declared to be of beneficial influence. The first question: "Who are the subjects of baptism?" was answered at length, as follows: "The answer may be given in the following propositions, briefly confirmed from the Scriptures.

1. They that, according to Scripture, are members of the visible church, are subjects of baptism.

2. The members of the visible church, according to Scripture, are confederate visible believers, in particular churches, and their infant seed; i. e. children in minority, whose next parents, one or both, are in covenant.

3. The infant seed of confederate visible believers, are members of the same church with their parents, and when grown up are personally under the watch, discipline, and government of that church.

4. These adult persons are not therefore to be admitted to full communion, merely because they are and continue members, without such further qualifications as the word of God requireth thereunto.

5. Church members who were admitted in minority, understanding the doctrine of faith, and publicly professing their assent thereto, not scandalous in life, and solemnly owning the covenant before the church, wherein they

1 Mather, Book . p. 62 ff.

give up themselves and their children to the Lord, and subject themselves to the government of Christ in the church, their children are to be baptized.

6. Such church members who, either by death or some other extraordinary providence, have been inevitably hindered from public acting as aforesaid, yet have given the church cause in the judgment of charity, to look at them as so qualified, and such as had they been called thereunto, would have so acted, their children are to be baptized.

7. The members of orthodox churches, being sound in the faith and not scandalous in life, and presenting due testimony thereof, these occasionally coming from one church to another, may have their children baptized in the church whither they come, by virtue of communion of churches; but if they remove their habitation, they ought orderly to covenant and subject themselves to the government of Christ in the church where they settle their abode, and so their children to be baptized; it being the church's duty to receive such into communion, so far as they are regularly fit for the same." This answer is based on fellowship in the church according to the primitive principles. The children of such members are entitled to baptism, and remain under the discipline of the church, only they cannot (§ 5) participate in the Lord's Supper; none the less, however, are their posterity (§ 5, 6) to enjoy the same privilege as themselves. There follows, as indicated at the beginning of this answer, the confirmation of the several articles from the Holy Scriptures. After showing, with special reference to the covenant of circumcision and the promises of the Old Testament, that all children in a visible church on earth are by the Lord's appointment to be members of the same; it is added by way of limitation to the second article, that the piety of ancestors does not suffice, unless the next parents continue in covenant. The grounds are as follows:

"1. Because if the next parent be cut or broken off (Rom. 11: 17, 19, 20), the following seed are broken off also (Ex. 20:5);[1] as the Gentile believing parents and children were taken in; so the Jews, parents and children, were broken off.

2. One of the parents must be a believer, or else the children are unclean (1 Cor. 7: 14).

3. If children may be accounted members and baptized, though the next parents be not in covenant, then the church should be bound to baptize those, whom she can have no power over and no hope concerning, to see them brought up in the true christian religion, and under the ordinances; for the next parents being wicked and not in covenant, may carry away and bring up their children to serve other gods.

4. If we stop not at the next parent, but grant that ancestors may, notwithstanding the apostasy of the next parents, convey membership unto children, then we should want a ground where to stop, and then all the children on the earth should have right to membership and baptism."

In the following proposition are enumerated the blessings accruing to children through baptism, among which, that of education within the church is particularly mentioned. But most clearly does the change appear in the exposition of the fourth proposition, which treats of the exclusion of such members from the Lord's Supper. "The truth of this decision" it is said, "is plain from 1 Cor. 11: 28, 29, where it is required that such as come to the Lord's Supper, be able to examine themselves, and to discern the Lord's body; else they will eat and drink unworthily, and eat and drink damnation, or judgment to themselves, when they partake of this ordinance; but mere membership is separable from such

1 "A jealous God, visiting the iniquities of the fathers upon the children."

ability to examine one's self and discern the Lord's body; as in the children of the covenant that grow up to years is too often seen. 2. In the Old Testament, though men did continue members of the church, yet for ceremonial uncleanness they were to be kept from full communion in the holy things, (Levit. 7: 20, 21; Numb. 9: 6, 7, and 19: 13, 20). Yea, and the priests and porters in the Old Testament had special charge committed to them, that men should not partake in all the holy things, unless duly qualified for the same, notwithstanding their membership, (2 Chron. 23: 19; Ezek. 22: 26; and 44: 7, 8, 9, 23), and therefore much more in these times, where moral fitness and spiritual qualifications are wanting membership alone is not sufficient for full communion. More was required to adult persons eating the Passover, than mere membership; therefore so there is now to the Lord's Supper. For they were to eat to the Lord (Ex. 12: 14), which is expounded in 2 Chr. 30, where keeping the Passover to the Lord (v. 5), imports and requires exercising repentance (v. 7), their actual giving themselves up to the Lord (v. 8), heart preparation for it (v. 19), and holy rejoicing before the Lord (vv. 21, 22). See the like in Ezra 6: 21, 22. 3. Though all members of the church are subjects of baptism, they and their children, yet all members may not partake of the Lord's Supper, as is further manifest from the different nature of baptism and the Lord's Supper. Baptism first and properly seals covenant-holiness, as circumcision did (Gen. 17) church membership (Rom. 15: 8), planting into Christ (Rom. 6); and so members, as such, are the subjects of baptism (Matt. 28: 19). But the Lord's Supper is the sacrament of growth in Christ, and of special communion with him (1 Cor. 10: 16), which supposeth a special renewing and exercise of faith and repentance, in those that partake of that ordinance. Now if persons even when adult may be and continue members, and yet be debarred from the Lord's Supper, until meet qualifications for the same do appear in them; then may they also (until like qualifications) be debarred from that power of voting in the church, which pertains to males in full communion. It seems not rational that those who are not themselves fit for all ordinances, should have such an influence referring to all ordinances, as voting in election of officers, admission and censures of members doth import. For how can they, that are not able to examine and judge themselves, be thought able and fit to discern and judge in the weighty affairs of the house of God (1 Cor. 11: 28, 31, with 1 Cor. 5: 12)."

In settling the political and ecclesiastical relations of New England, the relations and ordinances of the Old Testament had often been appealed to as authority. In the present case also, in the explanations to § 5, which treats of the right to baptism, the Synod appeals to the manner in which persons acquired membership under the old covenant. Here it is especially noteworthy, how entirely was overlooked the radical difference between the Jewish and the Congregational church-constitution; for the main condition of the latter, evidence of the actual experience of conversion, was, and in the nature of the case must be, wholly foreign to Judaism. In place of taking for the starting point their own doctrine respecting the Lord's Supper, though lying at the very basis of what was peculiar in Congregationalism, they compared baptism with Jewish circumcision. The church-membership of parents constituted the claim in both cases; hence, as little in the one case as in the other, should children when grown up cease to be church-members. The qualification thus acquired for personal admission to church privileges secured the same, moreover, (§ 6) to their posterity.

This answer to the questions thus proposed to the Synod was honored with the approbation of more than seven-eighths of the assembled ministers. But, beside the prevailing opposition to it in the churches themselves, there were found, among the few ministers who dissented, men of great influence, who raised their voices powerfully against these innovations. Charles Chauncey, president of Harvard College, in a treatise which he published on the subject, took ground against the Synod. Of the same mind were Eleazer Mather, minister at Northampton, and Increase Mather,[1] (afterwards the first Doctor of Theology in New England, and ambassador of the colony in London), sons of Richard Mather,[2] minister at Dorchester, who was himself, however, among the defenders of the council. By them and some others, the remonstrance of John Davenport and Street of New Haven, against the articles adopted, was zealously supported in the Synod. This being without effect, Davenport also came out with a treatise, under the title "Another essay for investigation of the truth," to which Increase Mather furnished a preface. From the extracts given by Cotton Mather, it appears that the point of view from which the decisions of the Synod must be judged, according to the principles of Congregationalism, was exhibited with great clearness by its opponents. While conceding a distinction between "mere and qualified membership," the conditions for the latter are required no less of those who are to be baptized than of those who desire admission to the Lord's Supper. A reply followed in defence of the conclusions of the Synod, which however, cannot be acquitted of the same inconsistency and departure from original principles, before mentioned. But it is a notice-

1 Father of the author of the *Magnalia Christi Americana.*

2 Emigrated from England in 1635.

able index of the essential change which had taken place in New England, that the large majority of the ministers sustained the new opinions, which indeed soon obtained a fresh accession of adherents. Even Increase Mather changed his views, and subsequently published two essays in defence of the conclusions of the Synod, declaring them to be the primitive doctrine of the church of New England, although being a church then but newly founded, its earlier practice had been otherwise.

POLITICAL INFLUENCES UNFAVORABLE TO THE THEOCRACY.

Through peculiar circumstances, the General Court of Connecticut was prevented from adopting at once the conclusions set forth by the Synod, though from the stand it had previously taken, it appears to have been decidedly inclined to a change of the early Congregationalist principles. Soon after the accession of Charles Second, this colony had sent Winthrop, its Governor, to London for the purpose of obtaining a definite royal charter, their Constitution having hitherto had, in fact, a very insecure basis.[1] Through the skill and activity of this ambassador the king was induced to declare the colony, April 20, 1662, an incorporated body politic, under the title: The Governor and Company of the English Colony of Connecticut in New England in America. This charter expressly confirmed to the Government the rights of sovereignty hitherto exercised; the magistracy was to be annually elected by the free citizens, whose privileges were to be enjoyed by every free born Englishman. But, at the same time, it was directed that New Haven should be united to Connecticut. This colony had incurred the royal displeasure, by

[1] See p. 78.

harboring certain of the judges of Charles First condemned to death by parliament; and the more so, since even the magistracy, if they had not openly opposed the search for the regicides, had drawn upon themselves, not without reason, the suspicion of having favored their escape. The accused colony was, moreover, so poor as not to be able at this time to defray the expenses of its officers, and hence, also, was unable to send an agent of its own to represent its interests in England. But it was none the less disposed, on that account, to maintain its former independence at whatever cost. A mere protest was not deemed sufficient. As Connecticut, encouraged by individuals in the colony of New Haven friendly to such a union, had taken decided steps towards carrying out the provisions of the charter, it was resolved to repel every act of aggression by force. At the same time, application was made by New Haven to the commissioners of the four united colonies, and she found here the most unequivocal recognition of her rights. But besides the wish to retain the independence so long enjoyed, there was an ecclesiastical interest for which the ruling party in New Haven were deeply concerned. Here was still existing the theocratic relation, which allowed only to members of the church, and indeed only to those in full communion, the exercise of civil rights. The exasperation increased with the embarrassments in which New Haven found herself involved, alike by want of money, and by the influence of a not inconsiderable party who favored the union; and it was resolved to break off all direct negotiations with Connecticut. But in the year 1664, there arrived in New England royal commissioners, whose object was, in part, to examine into the state of the colonies; in part, to secure the subjection of New Amsterdam to the crown of England; and it was feared that they were armed with instructions of the most dangerous character, in reference to the hitherto free constitutions. Massachusetts herself now counselled compliance, and urged the ruinous consequences and at the same time the uselessness of farther resistance, at a time when the colonies so much needed unity. As the commissioners of the united colonies likewise recommended a friendly and peaceful union, and the royal commissioners insisted positively on the provisions of the charter, New Haven at length submitted. On the 13th of December 1664, the union was assented to by the General Court, not, however without a solemn protest against the invasion of their rights, and the proceedings of Connecticut. These are indeed, not to be justified; yet the end being gained, nothing was left undone to effect a thorough reconciliation. The most influential citizens of New Haven were elected to the highest offices, and every Act which had reference to the quarrel was consigned to everlasting forgetfulness.

These transactions furnish the explanation of the fact, that Connecticut did nothing in reference to the result of the Synod, but left to the churches and elders the adoption of whatever steps might be necessary. The very general opposition of New Haven to the Synod being known, it was held to be in the highest degree impolitic to strengthen the disagreement by a declaration on ecclesiastical matters. It was not till the union might be confidently regarded as near its consummation, that the General Court, under date of October 13th 1664, published the following Act:

"This Court understanding, by a writing presented to them from several persons of this colony, that they are aggrieved that they are not entertained in church fellowship, this Court having duly considered the same, desiring that the rules of Christ may be attended, do commend it to the ministers and churches in this colony, to consider whether it be not their duty to entertain all such persons, who are of an honest and godly conversation, having a competency of knowledge in the principles of religion, and shall desire to join with them in church-fellowship, by an explicit covenant." After reciting the conclusions of the Synod, with which we are already acquainted, the Act concludes: "The Court desireth the several officers of the respective churches would be pleased to consider, whether it be not the duty of the Court to order the churches to practise according to the premises if they do not practise without such order. If they dissent from the contents of this writing, they are desired to help the Court with such light as is with them, the next session of this assembly." Here also the new principles, though not formally adopted, yet received a public expression; at the same time the established theocratic relation in New Haven gave way under the pressure of political circumstances.

In this same period, the Theocracy was abolished by law in Massachusetts. Already deprived by those ecclesiastical decisions of its proper significance, there came decrees from another quarter, which severed the existing connection between Church and State. Massachusetts, after receiving information of the accession of Charles Second, had delayed proclaiming him king. But, in November, 1660, having ascertained from reliable sources that the political relations of England were settled, and that no farther change in its government was to be expected, the General Court resolved on a highly loyal address to the king. To this a very gracious answer was returned on the 15th of February 1661. Very soon after, however, it was announced in Boston that the existing relations of the colony were in danger, partly through the suspicions excited in the royal party by its previous policy; partly through claims instituted by private persons on the ground of earlier patents. The proclamation was now no longer delayed. This being accomplished in August 1661, it was resolved to send two delegates to London to take in charge the interests of the colony. Simon Bradstreet[1] and the Rev. John Norton, who were chosen for this purpose, found a more favorable reception in England than they had anticipated. The answer of the king, communicated to them on the 28th of June 1662, contained a confirmation of the privileges of their charter, and an amnesty for all the past. But though these general provisions occasioned great joy in the colony, there were others at which offence was taken. Even the very natural requirement, that all governmental power should be exercised and justice administered in the name of the king, being something to which they were not accustomed, seemed strange and alarming. True, the Boston government complied thus far; but they could not bring themselves to yield to the demand, that "freedom and liberty should be given to all such as desired to use the book of Common Prayer, and perform their devotions in the manner established in England, and that they might not undergo any prejudice thereby; that all persons of good and honest lives and conversations should be admitted to the sacrament of the Lord's Supper, according to the Book of Common Prayer, and their children to baptism; that in the choice of governor and assistants, the only consideration should be of the wisdom, virtue and integrity of the persons to be chosen, and not of any faction with reference to opinions

1 See p. 131.

and outward profession; that all freeholders of competent estates, not vicious etc., though of different persuasions concerning church government, should have their votes in the election of all officers, civil and military."

Indeed a general dissatisfaction with the result of the embassy soon began to manifest itself. The benefits secured were forgotten, and the manifold difficulties with which the delegates had to contend were overlooked; and in such a manner did the discontent express itself, that Norton, soon after his return from England, died of grief. The opposition towards the mother country was still more increased, when the deprivation of the nonconforming clergy of the Episcopal Church, on the 26th of August 1662, drove many of these to New England, and awakened here the apprehension of restraints on freedom of conscience. The alarm rose to the highest pitch on the intelligence, received in the spring of 1664, that ships of war were on their way with commissioners from the king. It was resolved to put in order all the means of defence, a measure which was of course merely intended to prevent the disorders apprehended from the troops; and a day of general fasting and prayer was appointed. On the 23d of July the squadron appeared before Boston, bringing four royal commissioners, viz. Colonel Richard Nicholas, George Cartwright, Esq., Sir Robert Carr, and Samuel Maverick, Esq., son of one of the petitioners of the year 1646.[1] After laying their credentials before the government, they made known a part of their instructions in respect to the attack on New Amsterdam, and desired a reinforcement of troops. The General Court being convened on the 3d of August, the commissioners, about to take their departure, gave notice that on their return from Manhadoes they should have many ad-

1 See p. 139.

ditional communications to make, and urged a farther consideration of the royal epistle of June 28th 1662. The General Court granted two hundred men at the expense of the colony; but the march was forestalled by the capitulation of New Amsterdam on the 27th of August 1664. In accordance with the king's letter, the law respecting admission to citizenship was abrogated and another passed, whereby "English subjects, being freeholders, reliable to a certain value, certified by the ministers of the place to be orthodox and not vicious in their lives, were allowed to be made freemen, although not members of the church." Thus was the dissolution of the Theocracy declared by law, and this relation was abolished for all New England. When the royal commission made a similar demand of New Plymouth, the General Court of that colony replied, "we do consent, it having been our constant practice to admit men of competent estates and civil conversation, though of different judgments, to be freemen, and to have liberty to choose and be chosen officers both civil and military."

Before we proceed to describe the consequences to the church, of this alteration of the principles of Congregationalism, and of the Theocracy, something farther will be mentioned of the transactions of the royal commissioners with the General Court of Boston. The Court was obliged to defend the privileges of its charter against claims of the most diverse character. Its firmness was especially manifested, when the commissioners attempted to constitute themselves a court of appeal in certain criminal cases, and even cited the government to answer before them. So likewise it was maintained with unyielding determination, that the demand to admit to the Lord's Supper such as had not been tested, must be committed to the decision of the church. New Plymouth took the same ground on this point, though in other respects this colony showed itself more compliant. The eastern provinces of New Hampshire and Maine were visited by all the commissioners, except Nichols, whose greater moderation in all respects secured the popular regard, and who subsequently maintained, as Governor of New York, a friendly intercourse with Massachusetts. On their return to Boston, the General Court declared, that the exercise of the rights of sovereignty in those eastern provinces tended to the disturbance of the public peace, and they desired a conference on this account with the commissioners. To this Carr replied, that the king's pardon for what had passed during the last rebellion was only conditional, and rested on the future good conduct of the colony; even adding the threat, that the leaders and originators of all those acts of resistance, were exposed to the same penalties which had fallen upon so many in England who had shared in the rebellion. The General Court thereupon broke off all negotiations. In accordance with the reports of the commissioners, both Plymouth[1] and Connecticut[2] received royal letters of commendation, in which their loyal behavior was extolled as being set off with special lustre by the contrary deportment of Massachusetts. The king, in a letter, charged the latter colony with suspicious and contumacious proceedings; his final decision, however, he proposed to suspend, and desired that Massachusetts should send five delegates to London to defend her cause, two of whom were designated by name. But the General Court thought the affair had been already so clearly explained, that it could not be done better. The interference on the part of the king, which was to have been expected, did not follow at this

[1] Baylies' Memoir of New Plymouth. [2] Trumbull's Hist. of Conn. App.

time; and the colony sought in various ways, by the transmission of a large amount of provision to the royal fleet, as well as of money to London after the great fire, and by a cargo of masts, sixteen hundred pounds sterling in value, to regain his favor. But an unmistakable alienation had commenced, which led the king subsequently to adopt decisive measures. It had lasted, though with many interruptions, through an entire century, when a more important interest thrust into the background all the jealousies between the mother country and the colonies; but at length, it manifested itself fully developed, and resulted in a total separation. To the church, this state of things was of no small importance, since it involved the sympathies and interests of the inhabitants to such a degree, as to contribute essentially to promote the change in belief and life which followed the change in church-discipline.

The ecclesiastical events of the succeeding period are neither of so general importance, nor so characteristic in themselves. Its earlier portion still exhibits manifold reactionary influences from the preceding period; the latter portion shows an almost universal declension. The former will form the subject of the seventh, the latter, of the eighth chapter.

CHAPTER VII.

REACTIONARY INFLUENCES PROCEEDING FROM THE CONGREGATIONALIST THEOCRACY, AFTER ITS ABROGATION.

OPPOSITION TO THE ESTABLISHMENT OF THE THIRD CHURCH IN BOSTON ON THE NEW PRINCIPLE OF CHURCH-MEMBERSHIP.

So deeply rooted in New England, from the beginning, was the original principle of Congregationalism in reference to church-membership, that it could still boast its decided adherents, even after the determinations of the synods. These, although desired and sought for by the majority of the inhabitants, as well as favored and defended by the greater part of the clergy, found in many churches a vigorous resistance. Nor did it stop with the adoption and expression of the dissenting opinions by individuals. Controversies arose, which in both the chief towns of the colonies, Boston and Hartford, led to division, and the formation of separate churches.

There were in Boston a considerable number of church-members, who, in opposition to the synodial decisions, held that only members in full fellowship should be admitted to the church. But their minister, John Wilson, who came to New England so early as the year 1630, and had exercised his office in Boston from the time of its settlement, took ground, as member of the Synod of 1662, in favor of the innovations there determined on; and the weight of his influence had repressed the expression of opposition. At his death, in 1667, the church seemed indisposed to replace him by a young man; but desired one who had received his training in England, and who had developed, through a long ministry, special gifts for the office. There were few who could meet these requirements. The choice fell on John Davenport of New Haven. Evidently this measure originated with the party who adhered to the practice of former times; but in selecting a man so honored and distinguished throughout New England, they had also in view an easier victory over the opposition which was to be expected. This did not fail to show itself. Thirty members of the church declared themselves against the choice in terms as follows:[1] "We should walk contrary to Rev. 3: 3, not holding fast what we have received; nor should we, as we have received Christ Jesus the Lord, so walk in him. It (the doctrine of the synod) having been a received and a professed truth by the whole body of the church, who have voted it in the affirmative, and that after much patience with and candor towards those that were otherwise minded; divers days having been spent about this great *generation-truth*, which since hath been confirmed by the synod. Full liberty hath also been granted, unto those who scrupled, to propose their questions; and they were answered with such public satisfaction, that those few who remained unsatisfied, promised to sit down and leave the body to act, excepting one or two. Accordingly, there was an entrance upon the work; but the Lord lay it not to the charge of those that hindered progress therein, which, with great blessing and success, has been and is practised in neighbor churches."

The others persevered, however, and carried the resolu-

[1] Mather, Book V. p. 82.

tion to call Mr. Davenport, by a considerable majority. He was now in his seventieth year. Thirty years had he labored in his church, and had gained for himself universal esteem and affection. It is not strange, therefore, that opposition was made to his dismissal. There was indeed good ground for lamenting the separation; for there was not a minister now left in New Haven except Mr. Street, the co-pastor of Mr. Davenport; and after his death in 1674, it was eleven years before the town succeeded in choosing another. Davenport having come to Boston, twenty-eight members of his church requested to be dismissed from the connection, in order to constitute a new church. This was unanimously refused by the officers. The dissenting brethren hereupon called a council of the neighboring churches, and in accordance with their advice proceeded, after two meetings held for the purpose in Charlestown on the 12th and 16th of May 1669, to organize themselves into a separate church, under the name of the "Third Church in Boston." In their covenant they thus speak: "And for the furtherance of this blessed fellowship, we do likewise promise to endeavor to establish among ourselves and convey down to our posterity, all the holy truths and ordinances of the gospel committed to the churches in faith and observance, opposing to the utmost of our church power whatsoever is diverse therefrom, or contrary thereunto."

About the same time, seventeen ministers,[1] probably the members of the above-mentioned council, publicly declared their dissatisfaction with the conduct of the majority of the old church. This step had reference to the manner of Davenport's dismission from New Haven, which being expressed in somewhat vague terms, had not been fully

1 Among the number was Increase Mather.

communicated to the church by the ruling elder. The church published a defence against this charge, which, however, soon ceased to excite attention; the disagreement in reference to the synodial conclusions being the true point of controversy. This was not settled by the death of Davenport which soon followed. Measures being taken by the Third Church to erect a meeting-house, loud opposition was made to it on the side of the magistracy. Governor Bellingham, who was a member of the First Church, called together the council of the colony, "fearing," as he declared in the order, "a sudden tumult, some persons attempting to set up an edifice for public worship, which was apprehended by authority to be detrimental to the public peace." But the council resolved not to interfere; but "if any had offended against the laws, they advised to proceed against them in a due course of law. Those who were about to erect a new meeting-house, must observe the laws and orders of the General Court." On application of the new church to the selectmen of the town, it was voted July 26th 1669, that there was certainly need of a new meeting-house. But the opposers of the synodial conclusions had this year a majority in the General Court. At the May session, 1670, a committee was appointed "to enquire into the prevailing evils which had been the cause of the displeasure of God against the land." In the report brought in by this committee, they refer to "declension from the primitive foundation work, innovation in doctrine and worship, opinion and practice, an invasion of the rights, liberties, and privileges of the churches, an usurpation of lordly and prelatical power over God's heritage, a subversion of gospel order; and all this with a dangerous tendency to the utter devastation of these churches, turning the pleasant gardens of Christ

17

into a wilderness, and the inevitable and total extirpation of the principles and pillars of the Congregational way."

That, in alleging this as the peculiar evil of the time, they intended to designate the new church and those ministers who had given their assent to its organization, is clear from the conclusion of the report, which mentions by name "the late transaction of churches and elders in constituting the Third Church in Boston, as irregular, illegal, and disorderly." The adoption of the report by the Court increased the general public agitation. But at the next election, thirty out of the fifty members of the House of Deputies, were not reëlected; a change unprecedented hitherto, but in consequence of which, a wholly different view must necessarily predominate in the assembly of these popular representatives, especially as some of the reëlected were probably adherents of the synodial determinations. Fifteen ministers now presented an address complaining of the imputations cast upon them in that report, and which, they maintained, were the work of a party who wished to hinder the formation of the Third Church. After calling attention to the injurious influence of such a course upon the public mind and upon the labors of the ministry, they desired the Court to grant them redress, by requiring either a public vindication or a general synod. In its reply, the Court asserted its exemption from question by any person, for acts passed by its authority, as well as its indubitable right to freedom of debate; but acknowledged that in an hour of temptation an act might pass in one Court which, "according to principles of religion, prudence and state-interest, might be reviewed and upon mature deliberation be rectified by another. In respect to the case under consideration, the Court hold it its duty to declare, that several expressions in the votes referred to in the petition appeared exceptionable." It was therefore ordered that all papers relating to these matters should be regarded as cancelled, and not be used against the reverend elders as having been the cause of God's displeasure against the country. The Court furthermore declared their adherence to the original objects of their emigration, and to the sober principles of Congregationalism and the practice of their churches, "in their purest and most athletic constitution." But in spite of these last words, it is manifest from their decision that the new principles had achieved no doubtful victory. The Third Church soon after erected its place of worship, and was favored with an unusual degree of prosperity. Its request for recognition and fellowship by the First Church was, indeed, many times refused. But in the year 1682, the latter, alarmed by the increasing danger of encroachments on the civil liberties of New England, and by the efforts of the governor to procure the erection of an English church, itself proposed to the sister-church to forgive and forget the past; and a solemn reconciliation took place.[1] The First Church remained, nevertheless, steadfast in its principles; and it was not till 1730, that it resolved to "conform to the general practice, that is to say, of admitting members on the half-way covenant," which had been the usage of the second church in Boston since the year 1675.

UNSUCCESSFUL ATTEMPT IN CONNECTICUT TO INTRODUCE THE PRESBYTERIAN CHURCH-CONSTITUTION.

In Connecticut also, the new principle had to contend with much opposition, although here the proper issue had

[1] These occurrences are given at large by Hutchinson, I., 247 ff.; separately narrated, with very important additions, by Benjamin Wisner in his *History of the Old South Church in Boston*, 1830.

given place to another, and been lost sight of. Even before these controversies had broken out in Hartford and other places, an attempt on the part of the government had been witnessed, which endangered the other original principle of Congregationalism. The complete independence of each single church, in respect to property and the exercise of church-government, remained unquestioned in Massachusetts. We see from the preceding narration, that the opinions and acts of synods were invariably intermediatory in their character, and obtained recognition only as such. In Connecticut also, the conduct and settlement of all controversies were governed by the idea, that subordinacy to a higher ecclesiastical tribunal was a thing not to be admitted. Hence such a doctrine could not be openly and explicitly asserted. Still, the following may be regarded as the first step to the measures subsequently adopted for this object.

Scarcely was the first excitement consequent upon the union with New Haven allayed, than the General Court took into serious consideration the final termination of the still existing church dissensions. It was resolved, therefore, on the 11th of October 1666, to call a synod, wherein the questions to be laid before the ministers should be publicly discussed, and that under such rules and regulations as the synod should judge suitable to the orderly conclusion of the debates. It was accordingly voted, that the whole body of ministers in the colony should appear as members, and four from Massachusetts be invited to assist; a majority of the ministers of the colony being assembled, they should proceed as a synod; the questions to be submitted by the government were to form the subject of discussion. The third Wednesday in May 1667 was appointed as the day for assembling. But the ministers took offence at this order, regarding it as an assumption on the part of government, of conferring synodial power. The Court, to escape the difficulty, changed the name, May 9th, 1667, and called it an Assembly of the ministers of Connecticut; and the meeting took place at the appointed time. It was here resolved, after consideration of the questions submitted, not to discuss them publicly. They then adjourned to the autumn, with the purpose of then reässembling and preparing a report, if such should be the wish of the government. The adherents of the synodial decisions here placed themselves directly in opposition to this demand for new decisions, fearing a foreign influence, whether from the civil power or from Massachusetts. The churches made it known through their delegates, that they would maintain the right which gave to actual church-members alone the election of ministers, uncontrolled by any action of towns or parishes. The original principles of Congregationalism, moreover, still prevailed so generally in usage, that up to this time no case had occurred of admission to baptism where neither father nor mother were actual church-members. It was for the very object of bringing the new doctrines into practice, that the government had invited the Massachusetts ministers to take part in the synod. But although favored with a very skilful advocate of the less rigid view, in Mr. Mitchel minister at Cambridge, the government still thought they had cause to apprehend a want of correspondence to their wishes on the part of the synod; and accordingly formed the purpose of forestalling its probable action at the appointed meeting. In September, the commissioners of the united colonies met at Hartford and adopted the following resolution: "That when questions of public concernment, about matters of faith and order, do arise in any colony, the decision thereof should be referred to a synod, or council of messengers of churches, indifferently called out of the united colonies by an orderly agreement of all the General Courts; and that the place of meeting shall be at or near Boston."

Now, the opposition to the synodial conclusions seems to have so fallen into the background, that this party joined with the government. Certain ministers of Connecticut, and indeed those who had been most strict in regard to the admission of members, presented a paper to the General Court, requesting that a general synod might be called, and setting forth that they had wished for a public disputation at the last assembly in May, but had been overruled by the majority. The latter, who evidently had feared an influence from without, in opposition to this wish expressed to the General Court their opinion, that such publicity would not be serviceable to the peace and edification of the churches, or to the general interests of religion; a decision among themselves, as had been the usage hitherto, was much to be preferred. They coúld not but wonder, moreover, that certain ministers had demanded a general council, when the Assembly by its own resolution was to meet again in October; and, moreover, many new opponents of such a proposition would be added to the former large number. At the same time, they assured the Court of their readiness to obey all lawful commands, and desired information whether the Assembly should meet again or not. The Government, in return, expressed the wish that the various churches of the colony might send their ministers to a council, to be held in common with the ministers of Massachusetts and Plymouth. This, probably, was a pretext adopted to hinder the reässembling of the Connecticut synod. The object was effected, although the general council was not called. The Connecticut ministers feared the influence from Massachusetts; while, on the other hand, the government might not account that influence sufficiently powerful and effective to justify them in urging this concert of measures, at the risk, which was always impending, of a wider division and a yet more decided resistance.

But although the attempt to bring about a greater unity by this means was relinquished, the Connecticut government seems to have been very earnestly engaged for securing such a result. The design was formed of a general plan for unity of discipline also, by which they should be guided notwithstanding dissimilar views on points of minor importance. To this end, four ministers were authorized to meet together in Saybrook, and give their advice in relation to the way in which this desirable end could be attained. But even this preliminary and introductory measure failed for the present. It was not till many years after, that the government of Connecticut succeeded, through the Saybrook Platform,[1] in producing a change in the relations of the churches to one another, which approximated to the principles of Presbyterian subordination. It was the apprehension of this which had now called forth the decided opposition of both ministers and churches. The relaxed principle in reference to the admission of church members, however, found much favor; in many congregations, the other party seceded and formed a separate church. Thus also the controversies which had been formerly settled in Hartford again revived, and soon assumed so decided a form, that the assembly of ministers, convened on this account, advised a separation; which the government also then pronounced admissible. The second church now formed

1 See Ch. VIII.

in Hartford declared, 1670, in a solemn covenant, their unwavering adherence to primitive Congregationalism. About the same time, similar movements occurred in other places in Connecticut. But, gradually, the new principle obtained universal currency, as indeed it favored the interests of the majority of the inhabitants, those at least of the later immigrants, who had entered New England with far other than religious aims.

PERSECUTION OF ANABAPTISTS IN MASSACHUSETTS IN 1665 AND THE FOLLOWING YEARS.

But this result is also to be ascribed in great part to the fear of Anabaptism, whose spread could not but be promoted by the denial of infant baptism. Although the Baptists living in Rhode Island had manifested in practice none of that hostility to all civil order which had been charged upon them, yet the early prejudice against them still continued in the other colonies. The Anabaptists now made their appearance again, and founded churches both in New Plymouth and Massachusetts; but the two colonies differed in the policy observed towards them. At Rehoboth[1] in Plymouth, in the year 1663, a number of Baptists separated themselves from the church there established, and for several years maintained themselves, undisturbed, as a separate society. But in 1667, they were summoned before the General Court, and were fined for "establishing public meetings without the knowledge and approbation of the Court, to the disturbance of the peace of the place." They were required to discontinue these meetings within one month's time, as their continuance in Rehoboth, being very prejudicial to the peace of the church and the town,

1 Backus, I., pp. 350 ff. The place was also called Seawek. See Neal, II., 232.

could not be allowed. "Yet," thus concludes this Act of the General Court of Plymouth, "in case they shall remove their meeting into some other place, where they may not prejudice any other church, and shall give us reasonable satisfaction respecting their principles, we know not but that they may be permitted by this government to do so." As the result of this permission, these Baptists founded a church in Swansea on the borders of the colony of Rhode Island, and lived without farther molestation by the government, under the ministry of Mr. Miles, who had fled from Swansea in Wales after the Uniformity-Act of 1662.

Not by so easy a process did the Baptists in Massachusetts attain to a secure position and permanent form. On the contrary, they were here obliged to maintain through a course of years a conflict with the government, which, in spite even of the laws and of specific ordinances, sustained itself by the force of public opinion. There had always been individuals who held to the doctrine that only adults should be baptized. But when the royal commissioners[1] proclaimed entire freedom to all parties and sects, the Baptists in and around Boston[2] availed themselves of their presence and constituted a church. It is mentioned in their church records, as follows:—"On the 27th of the third month[3] 1665, the church of Christ in Charlestown, Massachusetts, commonly (although falsely) called Anabaptists, assembled and entered into brotherly communion and fellowship with one another, binding themselves to walk together in all the

1 See p. 187.

2 The account which follows is contained in full, with the documentary evidence, in Backus, Vol. I., Chap. VI. It is also alluded to by Hutchinson, and is briefly presented in Caleb Snow's History of Boston, 2d edition, 1828.

3 The 28th of May.

appointments of their Lord and Master, so as it shall have pleased him to make known to them his mind and will through his word and his Spirit." Four members, Gould, Osburne, Drinker, and George by name, were thereupon baptized, five others uniting with them who had belonged to the same party in England. Shortly after the departure of the commission, on the 20th of August 1665, an order was issued by the Government to the Charlestown constable, that he should endeavor to discover where these people assembled, and require them to be present at the established worship. On their refusal to comply with this demand, they were brought in September before the Court of Assistants or Governor's Council, where they exhibited a confession of their faith, and explained the points of their dissent. But, not submitting to the requirement to desist from their schismatical practices, they were cited before the General Court in October, which, after a rehearsal of their views declared that "the said Gould and company are no orderly church assembly; that they stand justly convicted of high presumption against the Lord and his holy appointment, as also the peace of this government, against which this Court doth account themselves bound to God, his trust and his churches here planted, to bear their testimony, and do therefore sentence the said Thomas Gould, William Turner, Thomas Osburne, Edward Drinker, and John George, such of them as are freemen, to be disfranchized, and all of them, upon conviction before any one magistrate or Court of their further proceeding herein, to be committed to prison, until the General Court shall take further order with them." One of the spectators having remarked openly: "The Court has not to do in matters of religion," he was arrested, and it was only upon his confession that he saw his fault and was sorry for it," that he was dismissed, with an admonition by the Governor. In April 1666, the accused persons were again called up on the charge of absenting themselves from public worship. When they alleged in defence their attendance at their own assemblies, it was construed as open contempt of the Court, and they were fined four pounds each. As they would neither pay, nor bind themselves to appear at the next Court, they were committed to prison. After some time, they were again dismissed; but several times during the next two years, they were recommitted for the non-payment of fines and for the repetition of their offence. In March 1668, Gould, the pastor of the church, appealed from a sentence of the county Court in Charlestown to the General Court in Boston. It is a singular fact, that the jury sworn in this case at first decided for the reversion of the former judgment, but when it was recommitted for their farther consideration, they confirmed it, though under certain conditions; however, the Court could now decide against Gould. At the same time a public disputation, with several ministers selected for the purpose, was granted the Baptists. The General Court, it was said, held itself bound by the law of God and of this commonwealth, to protect the churches of Christ here planted, from the intrusion thereby made upon their peace in the ways of godliness; yet was willing, by all christian candor, to endeavor the reducing of the said persons from the error of their way, and their return to the Lord and the communion of his people from whence they are fallen. This disputation resulted as usual, and as was to have been expected, without having effected any change of views. But in May of the same year, three of the Baptists, Gould, Turner and Farnum, were sentenced to quit the jurisdiction on the 20th of July; if found therein after that time, no bail was to be accepted, but they were to be forthwith committed to prison. Gould, who was in confinement at the time, was discharged in order that he might fulfil the first part of this order.

But these measures had not the effect of lessening the number of their adherents, nor even of disposing the Baptists to remove voluntarily. Turner was actually put in prison, and Gould was searched for, but in vain. The Baptist church then proceeded to assemble upon Noddle's Island, in the vicinity of Boston. Whether they remained really unnoticed, or were purposely overlooked, is uncertain. Gould also lived on this island, as pastor of the church. Various distinguished persons interceded for them; among them, Lieut-Governor Leverett did not scruple to express his dissent from the rigid views of Governor Bellingham. Thirteen Congregationalist ministers of London also expostulated against the persecution in a letter,[1] from which we learn, moreover, the relation in which the churches on both sides of the ocean stood to each other.

"We shall not undertake in the least," — so runs the letter, — "to make any apology for the persons, opinions, and practices of those who are censured among you. You know our judgment and practice to be contrary unto theirs, even as yours; wherein, God assisting, we shall continue to the end. Neither shall we return any answer to the reason of the reverend elders, for the justification of your proceedings, as not being willing to engage in the management of any the least difference with persons whom we so much love and honor in the Lord. But the sum of all which at present we shall offer to you, is, that though the Court might apprehend, that they had grounds in general,

[1] Mather, Book VII. Ch. 4, § 4.

warranting their procedure, in such cases, in the way wherein they have proceeded; yet that they have any rule or command rendering their so proceeding indispensably necessary, under all circumstances of times or places, we are altogether unsatisfied; and we need not represent to you how the case stands with ourselves, and all your brethren and companions in the services of these latter days in these nations. We are sure you would be unwilling to put an advantage into the hands of some, who seek pretences and occasions against our liberty, and to reinforce the former rigor. Now we cannot deny but this hath already in some measure been done, in that it hath been vogued that persons of our way, principles, and spirit, cannot bear with dissenters from them. And as this greatly reflects on us, so some of us have observed how already it has turned unto your own disadvantage. We leave it to your wisdom to determine, whether under all these circumstances, and sundry others of the like nature that might be added, it be not advisable at present to put an end unto the sufferings and confinements of the persons censured, and to restore them to their former liberty. You have the advantage of truth and order; you have the gifts and learning of an able ministry to defend them; you have the care and vigilancy of a very worthy magistracy to countenance and protect them, and to preserve the peace; and, above all, you have a blessed Lord and Master, who hath the keys of David, who openeth and no man shutteth, living forever to take care of his own concernments among his saints; and assuredly you need not be disquieted, though some few persons, through their own infirmity and weakness, or through their ignorance, darkness and prejudices, should to their disadvantage, turn out of the way in some lesser matters, into by-paths of their own. We only make it our hearty request to you, that you would trust God with his truths and ways so far, as to suspend all rigorous proceedings in corporal restraints or punishments on persons that dissent from you, and practise the principle of their dissent without danger or disturbance to the civil peace of the place. Dated March 25th 1669."

This letter had not, however, the results which were to be hoped for. On the contrary, several Baptists were imprisoned in the following year. But in December 1672, Governor Bellingham, their decided opposer, died; his successor, Leverett, was successful in introducing a milder policy, so that in 1674 a Baptist recorded that they were enjoying their freedom in peace. Gould died in October 1675. Encouraged by the lenient exercise of power under Governor Leverett, they resolved in January 1678, to erect a place of worship in Boston. The building was carried forward so prudently, that no one knew its object till it was completed. On the 15th of February 1679, they first met for the celebration of divine worship. But they were not long undisturbed. The leaders of the church were called before the Court in May, and admonished; and an order was given that no assemblies should be held in a house which had been erected without consent of the town wherein it stands, on penalty that the same shall be forfeited to the use of the public treasury, or shall be torn down. The Baptists refrained from their assemblies, till the king interposed by a letter, written July 24th, 1679, forbidding that any of his subjects, papists excepted, should be subjected to punishments of any kind for serving God in their own manner. When, upon this, the Baptists again ventured to come together, they were again called before the Court and required to desist. In March, 1680, the Court ordered their meeting-house to be nailed up, and affixed to the doors a placard with the following words: "All persons are to take notice, that by order of the Court, the doors of this house are shut up, and that they are inhibited to hold any meeting therein, or to open the doors thereof, till the General Court take further order, as they will answer the contrary at their peril." On the following Sunday, the members of the church assembled in the meeting-house yard; but the next time they found the doors open, and proceeded to make use of the house. At the session of the next General Court, they were again admonished, and required to abstain from their assemblies. But this was, in fact, the end of all persecution; for as the Baptists suffered this order to pass wholly unnoticed, so was it with them henceforth, on the part of the government.

It was during the very time when these efforts were made to suppress the Baptists, that the former opposition to the Quakers reäppeared, a law being passed in the year 1676[1] against their meetings. Since the prohibition of King Charles, they could not indeed be persecuted as heretics and schismatics; but they were punished, imprisoned, and banished as vagabonds. But the opportunity and the pretext for this mode of treatment, to which, it must be conceded, their own conduct at their first appearance gave occasion, were taken away when this religious party assumed the peaceful form of the Society of Friends. By degrees, interests of a wholly different character arose to claim the attention of the New England governments, which threw into the back-ground persecutions of every kind.

1 Hutchinson, I., p. 289.

POLITICAL CAUSES OF THE DECAY OF THE EARLIER CHURCH-LIFE; MEASURES FOR COUNTERACTING IT; SYNOD OF 1679, CALLED THE REFORMING SYNOD.

Thus have we seen, that it was a religious necessity which gave occasion to the founding of the Congregationalist churches; and farther, that it was an absorbing sympathy for Gospel and Church, which led those pilgrims to found a Theocracy in New England. It is not to be denied, that in the attempt to erect a State which should contain only church-members, — properly, indeed, only members of the invisible church, — lay an inward cause for that dissolution of the relation which soon followed. But if we review the Theocracy in its course of development and abrogation, we cannot regard it as a natural progression in the path which this church-party was, by virtue of its principles, bound to traverse. It was not the consciousness that distinct spheres of human development, or to speak in their own peculiar style, that diverse ordinances of God, were here arbitrarily intermixed and entangled together in their organization, in a way only apparently conformed to Scripture, which led to re-consideration and discussion. It was through an impulse from without; through interests, in part wholly distinct from the church, in part only externally connected with it, that this structure, standing unique and alone in church-history, received its overthrow. Half measures took the place of consistent principles; and when extending political relations gradually absorbed the whole attention of the inhabitants of New England, there could not but follow a total transformation of that original condition, which, sustained as it was by remarkable individualities, and stamped in noble institutions, presents a subject of contemplation to the attentive observer, in manifold respects equally instructive and delightful.

The great Indian war under King Philip (1675 and 1676), is to be regarded as the specific juncture from which this decay became apparent. The favorable termination of that war was purchased by fearful losses. In Massachusetts and New Plymouth, as also in Rhode Island, one eleventh of the men capable of bearing arms were dead; and, according to a moderate estimate, one eleventh of all the habitations were burnt down. Added to this, the colonies, including also Connecticut, which, directly, had suffered less from the war, and had contributed but a disproportionate amount of troops, had incurred an almost overwhelming load of debt. This war, moreover, had quashed the early attempts to introduce Christianity among the Indians, and had caused an alienation whose results are seen in the subsequent fate of that unhappy race. During the time when the colonies were seeking to recover from these disasters, they were all in constant apprehension of measures, on the part of England, which threatened the continuance of their political constitution. Especially was this the case with Massachusetts. The withdrawal of the settlements in New Hampshire from her jurisdiction in 1679, contrary to their own wishes, could not but be regarded as the herald of steps which were to follow. If we take into view the conflicting sentiments of the later immigrants, the alteration in the essential principles of the church, the desolation of the country, and a constant solicitude in reference to its most important interests, we find a sufficient explanation of the changed condition within the church. We introduce into the present chapter some notice of this decline, on account of a reäction which attended its commencement.

Although the first generation had died out even in its younger members, yet the earlier manner of judging of the relations and events of life had not gone with them. It is related that the period following the Indian war was visited with scarcity, losses at sea, and diseases of an extraordinary character. With the observation of these facts was connected a consciousness of a decline in morals; the two being viewed in reference to each other, those misfortunes were regarded as tokens of the anger of God. Hutchinson,[1] indeed, remarks on the matter, that there was no evidence of any extraordinary degeneracy; but he judged also of this mode of thinking from a remote period and from a different point of view. Meantime, all the governments adopted measures for the removal of these evils. Thus the government of Connecticut,[2] immediately after the close of the war in October 1676, recommended it to the ministers of the colony, to take special pains to instruct the people in the duties of religion, and to stir up and awaken them to repentance, and a general reformation of manners. They also appointed a day of solemn fasting and prayer, to supplicate the divine aid, that they might be enabled to repent and sincerely amend their ways. The same measures were recommended anew in May of the following year, and the people were admonished, under a deep sense of the abounding of sin and the dark aspects of Providence, to humble themselves before God and to call upon his name. The laws enacted in New Plymouth,[3] after the war, testify that here was felt a similar consciousness of decline, the remedy for which was sought in the same manner.

But more distinctly did the whole mental and practical

[1] Hutch., I. 292. [2] Trumbull, I., p. 493.

[3] Francis Baylies's historical memoir of the colony of New Plymouth, Boston: 1830, Part 4, p. 23 ff. This work contains a complete history for the period when this colony was independent.

peculiarity of the earlier times manifest itself in the measures adopted in Massachusetts. After a reformation had been here attempted by individuals and single churches, but without any general success, the General Court, in the year 1679, called a synod[1] for the discussion of the two following questions: "What are the evils that have provoked the Lord to bring his judgments on New England? And what is to be done, that so these evils may be reformed?" The synod met on the 10th of September, 1679, in Boston.[2] After a conference in reference to the two questions, a committee was chosen to draw up an answer, which was again reconsidered and then unanimously voted. Thirteen points are alleged in answer to the first question, wherein the external providences are discussed with reference to the general apostasy of heart from God. From pride and arrogance of heart has arisen dislike to the proper subordination appointed by God, as well as a general disposition to contention; the same crime displays itself also in outward apparel. The altered relations of the church are then particularly discussed. The neglect of church-fellowship is lamented, as also that the baptized children do not strive to qualify themselves for full membership. On the other hand, men incline to human inventions, — the meetings of the Quakers and Anabaptists being thus designated. The name of God is profaned by the common use of oaths; while the Sabbath is desecrated by worldly employments and recreations, as well as by irreverent behavior and inattention in the house of God during public worship.[3] Espe-

1 Called the Reforming Synod. The acts of that body are found in the Magnalia, Book V, Part IV.

2 On this occasion, some churches sent only their ministers to this assembly, and not, as these wished, lay-delegates with them; but the synod resolved that the latter were also to be sent by the churches.

3 On this point it is remarked: "We read of but one man in Scripture

cially in the family is seen an undue and unlawful indulgence towards children, and this is a fountain-head of the existing evils. The want of family discipline has made many Christians like to the Indians; on which account, perhaps, these have been chosen by the Lord as an instrument of punishment and correction. Inordinate passions manifest themselves by intemperance in bodily enjoyments, the frequenting of taverns, immodest apparel, increase of law-suits, promise-breaking, strivings after worldly gain through unreasonable profits in trade, and covetousness. Furthermore it charged an opposition to the work of reformation, a preference of personal interests over public good, and a contempt of the divine means of grace, which latter show themselves fruitless in a special manner on account of neglect of repentance, notwithstanding a manifest call of the Lord. "Finally," in answer to the first question it is said, "there are several considerations which seem to evidence that the evils mentioned are the matters of the Lord's controversy. 1. In that (though not as to all,) as to most of them, they are sins which many are guilty of. 2. Sins which have been acknowledged before the Lord on days of humiliation appointed by authority, and not yet reformed. 3. Many of them not punished, (and some of them not punishable,) by men, and therefore the Lord himself doth punish for them."

In answer to the second question, the following means are suggested, for checking the encroachments of corruption. First, those who are, in any way, in authority, are exhorted to furnish a good example in themselves and their families. As the older generation has died out, "a declaration of adherence to the faith and order of the gos-

that slept at a sermon, and that sin had like to have cost him his life. Acts 20: 9."

pel, according to what is in Scripture expressed in the platform of discipline, may likewise be a good means both to recover those that have erred from the truth, and to prevent apostasy for the future." Watchful circumspection must be used, that no one without personal and public profession of faith and repentance be admitted to the communion in the Lord's Supper. Church-discipline is to be exercised, especially towards the rising generation, a matter to which the founders of these churches attached so peculiar an importance. As a farther means of promoting reformation, care should be taken for a full supply of officers in the churches; in the larger ones should be appointed teachers[1] besides the pastor, but in all cases, there should be ruling elders, and provision should be made for the support of the ministry, as well as for schools and the promotion of every kind of knowledge. "When New England was poor," it is said, "and we were but few in number comparatively, there was a spirit to encourage learning, and the college was full of students, whom God hath made blessings, not only in this, but in other lands;[2] and it is deeply to be lamented that now, when we are become many, and more able than at our beginnings, that society and other inferior schools are in such a low and languishing state. Wherefore, as we desire that reformation and religion should flourish, it concerns us to endeavor that both the college and all other schools of learning in every place be duly inspected and encouraged." Solemn and explicit renewal of the covenant is also proposed as an appropriate means, to be performed with special reference to the sins of the times, the reformation of which should

[1] See p. 158.

[2] This refers not merely to the other colonies; some of those who had been educated at Cambridge went to England.

be promised before the Lord, in the name and by the help of Christ; and with the expression of unity in all things generally acknowledged. We add the conclusion of this answer: "Inasmuch as a thorough and hearty reformation is necessary, in order to obtain peace with God (Jer. 3: 10.), and all outward means will be ineffectual to that end, except the Lord pour down his Spirit from on high; it doth therefore concern us to cry mightily unto God, both in ordinary and extraordinary manner, that he would be pleased to rain down righteousness upon us, (Hos. 10: 12.) Amen." In the preface which accompanied the transmission of these answers to the General Court, it is said: "The things insisted on, have, at least many of them, been often mentioned and inculcated by those, whom the Lord hath set as watchmen to the house of Israel; though alas! not with that success which their souls have desired. It is not a small matter, nor ought it to seem little in our eyes, that the churches have in this way confessed and declared the truth, which, coming from a synod, as their joint concurring testimony, will carry more authority with it than if one man only, or many in their single capacities, should speak the same things. And, undoubtedly the issue of this undertaking will be most signal, either as to mercy or misery. If New England remember whence she has fallen and do the first works, there is reason to hope that it shall be better with us than at our beginnings. But if this, after all other means in and by which the Lord hath been striving to reclaim us, shall be despised or become ineffectual, we may dread what is like to follow. 'T is a solemn thought that the Jewish Church had, as the churches in New England have this day, an opportunity to reform if they would, in Josiah's time; but because they had no heart unto it, the Lord quickly removed them out of his sight. What God out of his sovereignty may do for us, no man can say; but according to his wonted dispensations, we are a perishing people if now we reform not." The conclusions of the synod having been presented to the General Court, this body, by a resolution of October 15th, 1679, commended it to the earnest consideration of all the churches and people of the jurisdiction; desiring of all persons, in their respective stations, a careful and diligent reformation of all the great evils herein named, according to the true intent of the words, that so the anger and displeasure of God, so many ways manifested, may be averted, and his favor and blessing obtained.

That this measure was not without effect, and that too in the majority of the churches, was seen not only by an increased fervency of religious life among the older full members, but by accessions to their number. In some churches, it is true, the renewal of the covenant which had been recommended was rejected as an innovation; but it was almost universally complied with, and in a very solemn manner. After the way had been prepared in a church by various religious meetings and days of fasting and prayer, one day was set apart for the special solemnity, which, being on different days in the several churches, was attended by great numbers from the vicinity. In the forenoon, the minister of the place, after praying and preaching with reference to the occasion, proceeded to read the covenant, to which the members of the church then expressed their assent, the men by lifting their hands, the women by merely rising. In some places, only the communicants took part in the transaction; in others, "the children of the church" also participated.

In the afternoon, it was usual for another minister to preach and inculcate the obligations of the covenant. The form of the covenant corresponded, in general, with that in earlier use; in reference to the special occasion, it was added: "That we will (Christ helping) endeavor every one of us to reform our heart and life, by seeking to mortify all our sins and laboring to walk more closely with God, than ever yet we have done; and will continue to worship God in public, private and secret, and this without formality or hypocrisy; and more faithfully and fully than heretofore, to discharge all covenant duties one to another, in church communion. Secondly, to walk before God in our houses with a perfect heart, and that we will uphold the worship of God therein continually, according as he in his word doth require, both in respect to prayer and reading the Scriptures, that so the word of God may dwell richly in us: and we will do what in us lies to bring up our children for Christ, that they may be such as they, that have the Lord's name put upon them by a solemn dedication to God in Christ, ought to be. And will therefore, as need be, catechise, exhort, and charge them to the fear of the Lord; and endeavor to set a holy example before them, and to be much in prayer for their conversion and salvation. Thirdly, to endeavor to be pure from the sins of the times, especially those sins which have been by the late synod solemnly declared and evidenced to be the evils that have brought the judgments of God upon New England; and in our places to endeavor the suppression thereof, and be careful so to walk, as that we may not give occasion to others to sin, or speak evil of our holy profession.—Now that we may observe and keep this sacred covenant and all the branches of it inviolable forever, we desire to deny ourselves, and to depend wholly on the power of the eternal Spirit of grace, and on the free mercy of God, and merit of Christ Jesus; and where we shall fail, there to wait upon the Lord Jesus for pardon, acceptance and healing, for his name's sake."

But this reaction, though proceeding from the one only ground, and availing itself, for the most part, of genuine ecclesiastical and spiritual means, did not reach the root of the evil. The decline of the church, properly so called, in life and doctrine, will form the subject of the following chapter.

CHAPTER VIII.

DECLINE OF CONGREGATIONALISM.

EFFECTS OF THE REFORMING SYNOD BUT TEMPORARY.

In the transactions of the synod related at the close of the foregoing chapter, there was still manifest something of the spirit in which the settlers of Massachusetts had sought New England, fifty years before. But, though it cannot be admitted that the religious interest and the church spirit had wholly disappeared or fallen into the background, yet it must be allowed that the condition of the settlements had become, in this respect, wholly different. The evils complained of, which it was the object and endeavor of that synod to correct, continued to increase, till at length, in the revivals, they suffered a characteristic reaction.

The political history of New England, during the earlier period, almost loses itself, as to its most important features, in the ecclesiastical. Of the period immediately following it might be said, that the ecclesiastical interests were merged in the political relations. The latter demand, nevertheless, special consideration, as a means of elucidating the condition of the church.

The apprehensions of an invasion of the constitution, long entertained by Massachusetts, were at length realized. In the year 1684, the charters of all the colonies were repealed by Charles II. Immediately on his death, which occurred on the 15th of February, 1685, James II. was proclaimed in Boston. But the expectation of any change in the measures of his predecessor, proved vain. Nor, general as was the popular discontent, could the explicit declaration of the royal will be resisted. Connecticut, being allowed to attach itself either to New York or Massachusetts, chose the latter colony, to which were united also, Rhode Island and Plymouth. Towards the end of the year 1686, Sir Edmund Andros landed in Boston, as governor, by royal appointment, of all New England. Under these circumstances, he must, of necessity, stand in direct opposition to a population which had grown up under an independent magistracy, chosen by themselves. This relation was still more embittered by the establishment through the influence of Andros, of a church in Boston with the ritual of the Episcopal Church. Agents were dispatched to England, among them Increase Mather as chief advocate, for procuring from the king a restoration of the earlier constitution; but this was without effect. But when tidings arrived in Boston of the victory of William of Orange over James II. a revolution broke out, in consequence of which Andros and his adherents were imprisoned, and a provisional government was formed, chiefly from the members of the earlier magistracy. The repeal of the charter having been executed in legal form, it was necessary to apply to William III. for its renewal. This was granted in 1691, accompanied with the expression of approval for the steps which had been taken; but with this essential alteration, that henceforth the governor was to be nominated by the crown. Plymouth remained united to Massachusetts; Connecticut, on the contrary, whose constitution had been abrogated without the observance of legal forms, again adopted it when

Andros was deposed, and continued, as was also the case with Rhode Island, under the administration of governors chosen by herself. The new constitution was at first received in Boston with exultation, but complaints soon followed in regard to the alteration. And although some of the succeeding governors had the ability to make themselves influential and beloved, there commenced an estrangement which spread through all the relations to the mother country, and yielded only to the pressure of temporary danger. On the one side, the government strove to increase the distinction and prerogatives of the governor; on the other, the General Court[1] of Massachusetts sought to maintain a certain independence. Thus, the efforts of the English crown, persevered in year after year, could not break up the practice of voting the support of their Governor yearly. In this period lay the germs of those disputes which afterwards led to a disruption from England. Covered up by the last war against Canada, they again started into sight when, on the removal of the rival who had been so many years the object of dread, the urgent occasion of unity between the colonies and the mother country was taken away. Such a state of things was exceedingly unfavorable to a revival of the religious and church interests, and could not but tend to counteract the spirit which had manifested itself at the last synod, in 1679.

That this attempt to revive the condition of the earlier time was productive of no general improvement, is manifest from a publication by the government of March 13th 1690,[2] a time when a painful uncertainty prevailed in respect to the political relations of the colony. "Corruption

1 Corresponding to the former General Court.

2 Mather, Book V. p. 97.

of manners, attended with inexcusable degeneracies and apostasies in too many of this people," are alleged as the cause of God's anger, which shows itself "by manifold judgments in such a time of probation." These remarks close with a call for reformation; in compliance with which assemblies of ministers were held, and in various places the covenant was renewed. But as appears from the frequent lamentations of the New England writers of the time, these efforts were fruitless.

WITCH-TRIALS.

Shortly before the arrival of Sir William Phipps the first royal Governor in Massachusetts, this province became the scene of an infatuation, no less remarkable than it was lamentable, by which the public mind was wound up to the highest pitch of excitement. New England had now to suffer the consequences of a delusion which at that very period was dying out in Europe. In the years previous, witches had occasionally been tried and executed; but in 1692, processes of this kind commenced, especially in Salem, on such a scale that by degrees towards one hundred persons were brought to trial. The accusers represented themselves as tormented by these persons in a very singular manner, and as having seen and watched their secret conclaves with evil spirits. Under the promise of pardon, some were persuaded to acknowledge a covenant with the devil. Counsel being asked of the ministers in reference to the course proper to be pursued, they allowed, in their answer, the possibility of such a covenant; but insisted at the same time on the greatest caution in the examination. But this advice was unavailing; by answers forced into the mouths of the accused through ensnaring questions, and by the admission of incompetent witnesses, sometimes even of children, matters came to such a pass, that during the months of June, July and August 1692, twenty persons were executed, among them a former minister, who was now accused as a wizard. But not one of the number confessed himself guilty. It was not till the accusers had gone to the length of impeaching numerous persons of wholly blameless life, church members and people of distinction, that people came to their senses. Public opinion then turned against the accusers, who, though they escaped due punishment, could not evade the reproach of having sacrificed the lives and property of their fellow citizens, and disturbed the public peace, not only with culpable recklessness, but also with most wicked and self-conscious fraud. The credulity of the judges was first acknowledged when, many years after, those who had been stripped of their property by these trials, sought restitution at the public cost. If it is pleaded that these occurrences reflect no peculiar blame on those among whom they happened, yet it may well be maintained, that the sound sense and the living religious sentiment of the earlier time would have arrayed themselves decidedly against such an infatuation.

FARTHER RESULTS OF THE CHANGE IN CHURCH-PRINCIPLES.

We pass now to the still farther consequences of the change in church principles, which has been explained in the preceding chapter. It might have been expect ed, as the result of that separation of church-members into those in full communion, and those on the halfway covenant, that, on the one hand, the former would continue to be regarded as those who properly constituted the church; on the other, that a still more rigid practice would be observed in respect to their admission. But this was not the case, in either respect. The principle of requiring evidence of conversion went gradually more and more into disuse; and so early as the year 1696, a church was formed[1] in Hartford without reference in any way to such a requisition. In like manner, at the formation of a church in Boston about the year 1699, it was declared to be unnecessary. Even when the principle was still adhered to, the practice declined. The custom of making a public confession of faith, and a relation of christian experience was gradually lost. It was left wholly to the clergy to judge of the qualifications for admission and to report thereon to the church; and at the same time, the church office of ruling elder fell into oblivion. So far at length, did this go, that even candidates for full communion[2] scarcely did more than express their assent to the confession of faith. It is noticeable that the consciousness in the church of this decline was accompanied by the expressed conviction of its connection with these aberrations. This was the case even prior to the time when by a conclusion hereafter to be mentioned, the opposition to the earlier views was carried to its extremest point. Jonathan Mitchel, minister at Cambridge and teacher in Harvard College, had been one of the chief advocates of the middle course at the Synod of 1662; but in the admission of full mem-

[1] This was done by "*owning the covenant*," as it was called. This church at its formation in February 1696, under the lead of Mr. Woodbridge, consisted of 69 persons. To these 83 more joined themselves on the 8th of March, and in the course of another month, they numbered 192 members. Trumb. Hist. of Conn., Ch. XIX.

[2] The oldest church in the country, the Old Church of Plymouth, changed its method of admitting members in November, 1705, introducing written relations in place of oral. Backus, II., p. 29.

bers, he was still most earnest for the maintenance of the original strictness in all its force.

Cotton Mather[1] gives from a manuscript of Mitchel's of the year 1664, a refutation by his hand of the opinion that a public declaration of faith in Christ or of sincere repentance for sin suffices for admission to the Lord's Supper. Mitchel supposes that he who can "groundedly" make such a confession can specify something more; and he who cannot do it groundedly, ought not to be admitted; nay, he sees in this laxness the fountain of formality and irreligion. Among other things he says: "The power of godliness will soon be lost, if only doctrinal knowledge and outward blamelessness be accounted sufficient for all church privileges, and practical confessions (or examinations of men's spiritual estate) be laid aside. For that which people see to be publicly required and held in reputation, that will they look after and usually no more, but content themselves with that." The Reverend Urian Oakes, who had presided over Harvard College from the year 1675, thus expressed himself in the discourse after his election:[2] "Consider what will be the end of the departures or apostasies from the church government settled among us. I profess I look upon the settlement of the Congregational way as the boon, the gratuity, the largeness of divine bounty which the Lord graciously bestowed upon his people that followed him into this wilderness; and a great part of the blessing upon the head of Joseph, and of them that were separated from their brethren. Those good people that came over here showed more love and zeal, and affectionate desire of communion with God in pure worship and ordinances, and did more in order to it than others, and the Lord did more for them than for any people in the world, in showing them the

[1] Book IV., p. 179. [2] Mather, B. IV., p. 165.

pattern of his house and the true scriptural way of church government and administrations. God was certainly in a more than ordinary way present with his servants in laying of our foundation and in settling the way of church-order according to the will and appointment of Christ. Consider what would be the sad issue of revolting from the way fixed upon, to one extreme or to another, whether it be to Presbyterianism or Brownism. As for the Presbyterians, it must be acknowledged that there are among them as pious, learned, sober, orthodox men as the world affords; and that there is as much of the power of godliness among that party and of the spirit of the good old Puritans as among any people in the world. As for their way of church-government, it must be confessed that, in the day of it, it was a very considerable step to reformation. The reformation in King Edward's days was then a blessed work. And the reformation of Geneva and Scotland was then a larger step, and in many respects purer than the other. And for my part I fully believe that the Congregational way far exceeds both, and is the highest step that has been taken towards reformation, and for the substance of it, it is the very same way that was established and practised in the primitive times, according to the institution of Jesus Christ. I must needs say that I should look upon it as a sad degeneracy, if we should leave the good old way so far as to turn councils and synods into classes and provincial assemblies, and there should be such a laxness in admission of members to communion, as is pleaded for and practised by many Presbyterians."

The first of the apprehensions here expressed, of a church-government similar to the Presbyterian, will be discussed hereafter.

In reference to the other principle of Congregationalism,

we will here introduce two witnesses in whose testimony the charges, expressed in general terms in earlier times, appear in an increasingly specific form. Increase Mather, so often mentioned already, who was also president of Harvard College, published in 1700 a book entitled: "Vindication of the order of the gospel in New England." In this he says: "The Congregational church discipline is not suited for a worldly interest, or a formal generation of professors. It will stand or fall, as godliness, in the power of it, does prevail or otherwise. That there is a great decay of the power of religion throughout all New England is lamentably true; if that revive, there will be no fear of departing from the holy discipline of the churches of Christ. If the begun apostasy should proceed as fast the next thirty years, as it has done these last surely it will come to that in New England (except the gospel itself depart with the order of it), that the most conscientious people therein will think themselves concerned to gather churches out of churches."[1] He complains especially of a lamentably superficial and formal manner in the relation of experiences for admission to communion. "There are reports, as if in some churches, persons have brought written relations, first to the minister and then to the church, which were not of their own dictating, but devised by others for them. I hope these reports have nothing of truth in them; but if they have, I am sure that such liars to the Holy Ghost have exceedingly provoked the Lord." Harsh as this judgment may seem, and little perhaps as it could be applied directly to individual cases which had actually occurred, yet it is not to be denied that such an innovation was a complete subversion of the Congregationalist principles. Let it go so far that, in place of what these had

[1] Backus, II., p. 24.

required, a mere outward, nay even a counterfeit profession would suffice, and that was repudiated which had originated, and had formed the sum and substance of this particular denomination. The tree would be severed from the root whence it had received life, and the inner sap must dry up of itself.

About the same time, a distinguished minister in Boston, by the name of Willard, one of the advocates of that Third Church, whose formation resulted from the synodial determinations of 1662, but who, in other respects, adhered to primitive principles, thus expressed his views in a discourse entitled "The perils of the times displayed:"[1] "That there is a form of godliness among us is manifest; but the great inquiry is, whether there be not too much of a general denying of the power of it. Whence else is it, that there be such things as these that follow to be observed; that there is such a prevalency of so many immoralities among professors? that there is so little success of the gospel? how few thorough conversions to be observed, how scarce and seldom!—It hath been a frequent observation, that if one generation begins to decline, the next that follows usually grows worse, and so on, until God pours out his spirit again upon them. The decays which we already languish under are sad; and what tokens are on our children, that it is like to be better hereafter? God be thanked that there are some among them that promise well; but alas! how doth vanity abound among them! How do young professors grow weary of the strict profession of their fathers, and become disputants for the things which their progenitors forsook a pleasant land for the avoidance of!"

But there was not merely a continually growing laxity

1 Backus, II. p. 25.

in practice, with regard to the admission of new members. Views respecting admission to the Lord's Supper were publicly advocated which not only contravened the fundamental principles of the Congregationalists at their rise, but even went beyond those of the church which they had abandoned. Solomon Stoddard,[1] a minister in Northampton, Massachusetts, carried out the parallel with the Jewish church so often used, in a very peculiar manner. As all who were under the covenant of circumcision were obliged to keep the Passover, so all that are baptized should come to the table of the Lord; nay, he added "though they know themselves to be in a natural condition." Increase Mather came out in opposition to him. But in his reply, Stoddard went still farther; maintaining not merely that "sanctification is not a necessary qualification to partaking of the Lord's Supper," but even calling this "a converting ordinance." And this view, which might justly be styled the exact opposite of the original principles, gradually gained more and more currency. This aberration from that which formed the characteristic feature, the central point of Congregationalism, was now accompanied by a change in doctrine which completed the decline. But before we pass to the portrayal of these innovations, we must relate the execution of an earlier plan which in the year 1667 had been frustrated by a powerful opposition.

FURTHER ATTEMPT AT APPROXIMATION TO THE PRESBYTERIAN DISCIPLINE IN MASSACHUSETTS AND CONNECTICUT.

We have already spoken of the attempt made by the government of Connecticut[2] to secure a firmer organization of the Congregationalist church-party, through an

[1] Backus, II. pp. 26 and 33. Wisner pp. 41, 58.

[2] P. 195.

approximation to the Presbyterian form of government. But the independence of the several churches was at the same time a principle too strongly rooted in the public mind to allow this effort to succeed. Now, however, to the causes of the gradual change in this respect brought to light by the foregoing development, was added the arrival of individuals of the Presbyterian persuasion from Europe, who attached themselves to the established churches of New England. It was not strange if their view of the subordination of the churches under synods and assemblies should have found favor even with those who had at heart the welfare of their fellow-citizens in respect to religion and church; nay, this more compact outward form might appear to them the very means for arresting the ever-extending ravages of decline. Even if nothing more than an external prop, yet at least it was from the church itself the prop was to be taken which should sustain the tottering fabric. It was while Increase Mather was residing in London as Agent for Massachusetts, that the Presbyterian and Congregationalist ministers of Connecticut had formed a union, and drawn up the 'heads of agreement,' having declared the points in which they differed unessential. But the terms in which they are expressed are very general; and pass over in silence both the subject of special examination of candidates for admission, and that of a lawful power of synods. With this indefiniteness, however, there was unanimity in regard to doctrinal belief; as in Boston also, at a synod held in 1680, the Westminster confession was adopted in all its essential points. These Heads of Agreement now found favor even in New England.

But the matter was not allowed to stop with the decision, that the single churches should have a respectful regard to the judgment of the assemblies of ministers, and should not act in contrariety thereto without manifest reasons out of the word of God. On the 5th of November 1705, several ministers in Massachusetts subscribed to certain propositions for the formation of associations in each county, to which should be committed the licensing of candidates for the ministerial office; and to this should be added a standing council whose sentence should be regarded as final and decisive, yet not without the assent of a majority of the pastors present. But so decided an opposition to the proposals arose in Massachusetts as to render the execution of the measure impracticable; although the views which had thus found expression became, in a milder acceptation, predominant. The occasional meetings of neighboring ministers, which had early been felt as a necessity, and as an advisory and admonitory resort had been constantly recommended, still continued, and sought, by personal influence to supply the want, a want which at that time Increase Mather lamented in strong terms. But they carried the matter farther in Connecticut. Here, in 1707, died Governor Fitz-John Winthrop, who for ten successive years, had been reëlected to the office previously occupied by his father. A law then existed that the Governor should be taken from among the magistrates in nomination;[1] but in contrariety to this rule, Gurdon Saltonstall,[2] a minister of New Lon-

1 In January 1708, this law was repealed, and all freemen of Connecticut were declared eligible to the office.

2 He was one of the Connecticut delegates appointed in the year 1697 to congratulate the Earl de Bellamont, Governor of New York and Massachusetts, who remarked that Saltonstall appeared most like a nobleman of any person he had seen in America. Trumb. I. 417. Backus says of him (II. 35): "He was a great politician, and he exerted all his influence to raise the ministerial power as high as possible."

don, was nominated, and being dismissed from his church in January 1708, entered on his new office. He soon presented to the Legislature the above-named proposals of 1705. But notice being taken of the omission in them of reasons from Scripture, Saltonstall fearing they would be rejected withdrew them. But, on the other hand, the General Assembly at Hartford, May 13th 1708, passed an act which was in substance as follows: This Assembly, from its own observation and the complaint of many others, being made sensible of the defects in church discipline, arising from the want of a more explicit assertion of the rules given for that end in the Holy Scriptures, from which would arise a permanent establishment among ourselves, a good and regular issue in cases subject to ecclesiastical discipline, glory to Christ our head, and edification to his members; do hence ordain and require that the ministers of the several counties in this government, and other delegates of the churches, shall meet together at their respective county towns, there to deliberate on methods and rules for the same, and to elect members for an assembly to be held in Saybrook, at the charge of the public treasury of the colony, when the results of those deliberations should be compared, and a form of ecclesiastical discipline drawn up.

THE SAYBROOK PLATFORM, 1708.

In accordance with this requisition, twelve ministers and four lay delegates from the four counties, came together in Saybrook, on the 9th of September 1708. After an expression of concurrence with the Confession of Faith of 1680, and with the Heads of Agreement, fifteen Articles in respect to church discipline were adopted (no mention being made of the Cambridge Platform) declaring an ecclesiastical subordination in accordance with the principles of the Presbyterians. Articles 1st to 11th treat of the assemblies of ministers and lay delegates; the last four of those which consisted of ministers only; the former were called consociations, the latter, associations. In each county were to be formed one or more of both kinds. All difficult cases of offence which are the subject of church censure, are to come before the consociations and to be decided by the vote of the majority of those present. In connection with this, it is expressly stated that the omission of any church to send delegates shall be no bar to the proceedings of the council, or invalidate their action. Any case brought before a council in an orderly manner, is to be here determined, and the parties concerned are to be satisfied with the same; the consociation seeing to it, that their determination or judgment is duly executed and obeyed, in such a way as shall in their judgment be most suitable and agreeable to the word of God. The pastors and churches who do not submit themselves to such decisions, are to be excluded from fellowship. In difficult cases, a neighboring consociation is to be taken into council. In difficulties between a church and one of its members, the former is to have the privilege, if so desiring, of calling together a consociation; but the right to do this is denied to the latter. The delegates shall hold their office till the occurrence of a new election, that a council may at any time be called together. This is to meet at least once yearly; the moderator at one session to remain in office till the next, in order to be able to summon a council during the time of adjournment. All persons, not appearing after due summons or notification, and without satisfying reasons to offer therefor, shall be judged guilty of scandalous contempt. The associations, which are to meet at least twice yearly for consultation on the duties of their office and on the common interests of the churches, are to consider and decide cases of importance which shall be presented to them by any of their own number or by other ministers; they shall also have the right of examining and recommending candidates for the ministerial work. The ministers thus associated are to take cognizance of any among themselves who are accused of open scandal or heresy, to examine the matter carefully, and if they find just occasion, to direct the calling of the consociation, where such offenders shall be duly proceeded against. The fourteenth article commits to the associations the care of any churches which may be bereaved of their pastors; the fifteenth and last recommends the formation of a general association to consist of delegates from the several county associations, which should meet annually.

These articles were adopted unanimously by the Synod, and in October 1708, were, in connection with the Confession of Faith and Heads of Agreement, declared by the Legislature established by law; with the provision, however, "that no society or church allowed by the laws, which dissented from the united churches here established, should be hindered from the exercise of worship and discipline in their own way, according to their consciences."

It may well excite surprise that this change, expressed in terms so unequivocal, should have encountered no considerable resistance. In the following year, there were formed in the four counties, five consociations and the same number of associations;[1] the General Associations undoubtedly exercised from this time a certain superintendence over ministers and churches. The favorable recep-

1 Two for the county of Hartford.

tion of the conclusions of the Saybrook Synod is chiefly to be explained from the circumstance that they appeared in connection with the Heads of Agreement; and that the required deference to synods was not at variance with the spirit of the Congregationalists. The articles, expressed in terms so explicit, received indeed a modified application in practice. Still it may be said in general, that from this period, the more intimate and settled connection of the Congregationalist churches led to a certain subordinancy, though the strict forms of the Presbyterians did not obtain in full. The associations directed their chief efforts to the oversight of candidates for the ministry. From this it is manifest that the approximation to Presbyterianism was not the result merely of a wish for clerical domination, but was in part dictated by the desire to make secure provision for the wants of the church. Of the interest felt for this object in Connecticut, we have proof in another way. So early as 1698, the inconveniences incident to so great a distance from Cambridge, had suggested the plan of founding a new college. In 1701, the Legislature granted a charter and voted a yearly allowance for its support. Its management, instruction, and religious influence were to have for their object "to promote, in the education of the students, the power and purity of religion, and the best edification of the New England churches." Saybrook was fixed on as the seat of the College; but owing to the continuance of their first chosen Rector with his church at Killingworth in the vicinity of Saybrook, the College was not removed thither till after his death in 1704. Here it remained till 1717; from which time it has existed in New Haven, as Yale College, so called from Elihu Yale, a Director of the East India Company in London, who had bequeathed to it large legacies.

This approximation to the Presbyterians, as it has existed from that time in a continued friendly relation of the two religious parties, received an additional impulse in the beginning of the last century, from the growing activity of the Baptists and Episcopalians in founding new churches. But, though the hostility towards these denominations as also against the Quakers, still continued, it was now become a mere external strife; though complaints were not wanting respecting the oppressive action of the laws, by which the whole body of the inhabitants of a parish, and not merely the actual church-members, were held accountable for the support of the clergy. We notice various controversies of no special moment, and without features of individual interest. The principle above-mentioned, that every parishioner must bear his part in the support of the minister, and, if there was none of his own sect in the place, to that of the prevailing party, was even adopted into the constitution of the State of Massachusetts after the revolution, and was repealed not many years since.[1] In this state also, were maintained yearly assemblies of the clergy, though without the prerogatives conferred by the Saybrook Platform on the Associations in Connecticut.

PROGRESSIVE DECLINE OF PIETY.

In the year 1725, a voice awoke once more in Massachusetts which reminds us of the expressions and the spirit of earlier times. A petition was presented to the Legislature by Cotton Mather, in the name of the assembled General Convention of ministers, praying that, in view of the great

1 Constitution of the Commonwealth of Mass. in the Revised Statutes of the Commonwealth of Mass. Boston: 1836. Part I. Art. 3. and Articles of Amendment, Art. III.

and visible decline of piety in the country, of the laudable example of our predecessors who sought to establish the faith and order of the gospel in the churches by synods, and that now a period of forty-five years has passed since the last convention of this kind, a synod might be called for the remedy of the existing unhappy condition. During the proceedings on the matter in the House of Representatives, the Episcopalians residing in Boston made report of the same in London; whence an order was received to put an immediate end to the affair, as the calling of synods pertained to the king alone. This decision was received by the Representatives, though otherwise still extremely jealous of their rights, without a word of complaint. This silence marks a characteristic of the time.

As the antagonisms in the English church parties had reference chiefly to the constitution of the church, differences in respect to doctrine, were less definitely expressed, and were of a subordinate character; so in the decline of Congregationalism, in New England, we have for a long period, no sign of alteration in the latter respect. Undoubtedly, a declension could not but soon manifest itself even among the clergy. In a constitution like that of the Congregationalists, the reciprocal action of ministers and churches on each other is too immediate, to allow the one to be in a state discordant to that of the other. At first, however, the difference between the present clergy and their predecessors manifested itself, for the most part, only in formality and coldness in the duties of their office. But with the lively intercourse constantly maintained with England, influences from the latter soon made themselves apparent, and Arminianism, which, in the preceding century, had spread from the High Church into the ranks of the Dissenters, now visited North America also. Here, it was precisely from the standpoint of Indifferentism, that it made its appearance. It manifested itself particularly in the view now current, that observance of outward religious ordinances joined with a moral and sober life is all that is needed for Christians. These opinions, in the condition of the church which has been described, found quick and easy entrance; and the spread of unbelief was, in general, much earlier than its decided open manifestation.

In opposition to this state of things, a peculiar phenomenon now presented itself in the religious revivals. They will form the subject of the next and closing chapter of our work. This reaction, it is true, did not wholly counteract the declension; partly, on account of the spurious elements mingled with it; partly, because a period of war and agitation followed, in which the inhabitants of New England believed their very existence at stake. To this was added financial embarrassments, the consequence of excessive emissions of paper-money, from which the colonies were suffering even before the French colonial war and especially during its continuance. From the war itself it seemed that no other result could follow than the subjugation and expulsion of the conquered party; it ended in 1762 with the seizure of all Canada. Scarcely was the foreign foe thus removed out of the way, when the variance with the mother-country rose to such a height as to occasion the war of the Revolution and the separation of the colonies. During the war of Independence, New England itself was for a long period occupied by the enemy. The English, in whose minds rebellion against the government stood in close connection with separation from the State Church, demolished places of worship and destroyed the church-property of Dissenters.[1] Nor must we overlook

1 Wisner relates (p. 108,) that the churches were used as prisons and

the influence of the French who came to North America and were there taken into the relation of friends and kinsmen; those especially who had an active participation in the war were subjected to an influence inimical to positive Christianity. Meanwhile, unbelief expressed itself in a decided form as Unitarianism, and overspread all New England. When a christian life began to reäwaken, churches, church-property, and even the ancient University of Cambridge, were found to be in the hands of Unitarians. A reaction in the present century has again changed the relation; in connection with which the Half-way Covenant has been done away; and the church, now separated wholly from the state, consists only of members received on the original principle of the Congregationalists. The newly awakened life has quickly remoulded public sentiment into enthusiastic sympathy with the Congregationalists, while the influence of the Unitarians has suffered a constant decline.

These relations, as they do not properly belong as yet to the province of history, are not within the scope of our present design. It only remains to exhibit such of their features as constituted, in reference to the church, essentially the closing boundary of the first period.

riding schools, or were torn down for fuel, though there was an abundant supply in the town. Of the nineteen places of worship in New York when the war began, there were but nine fit for use when the British troops left it.

CHAPTER IX.

THE REVIVALS.

REVIVALS IN GENERAL, AND THOSE OF NORTH AMERICA IN PARTICULAR.

THE reaction, which now developed itself in opposition to the ever growing declension of the New England Church, constitutes a peculiar phenomenon. The Revivals did not, it is true, realize the expectations then cherished; indifference to the institutions and the faith of the fathers being predominant in the church, as far down as the beginning of the present century. But the representation of these occurrences is, notwithstanding, a matter of very special interest. They have been repeated in North America in a very striking manner in recent times. They there form one of the main subjects of reports on the state of religion, in the periodical press; and they occupy a very important place in the discussions of theological literature. Different views are indeed entertained in North America, in reference to the methods for developing and conducting revivals. But all the principal parties of the evangelical church are of one mind in regard to their importance; though by some a higher value is attached to them than by others. But with the theologians of North America, these awakenings of a previous century justly rank as, in a certain sense, the type of such manifestations; having been free, in great measure, from the present intermixture of foreign elements. They are, moreover, the better adapted to representation, both as being historically completed, and as having their origin and their explanation in that progressive development of Congregationalism, which we have here traced.

A REVIVAL, that is a simultaneous renewal and advance of the religious life in one or more congregations, is indeed not an unknown occurrence in the cis-atlantic churches. But the form in which it here meets us, appears but rarely in churches which grew, to a greater extent, out of institutions already existing, and whose development has taken a more uniform course. It therefore seems appropriate, in entering on a delineation of these Revivals, to consider the analogy presented in the universal development of christianity, and consequently, among ourselves. A reference to such isolated cases in Europe, would rather itself need this explanation and illustration, than be adapted to furnish it. Revivals in the churches find their nearest parallel in the conversion of individuals. For understanding the latter is needed, on the one side, knowledge of the man's peculiar characteristics, position in life, and previous course of training; but also, on the other side, the perception that something new has here taken place, which cannot be fully explained from the sum of the man's earthly relations. As viewed from this side, the causal condition of conversion lies outside the sphere of his earthly life. Those who would comprehend the entrance of divine grace into the heart of an individual, can only do it by ascertaining the inward state with which this grace connects itself. In this manner we come to a knowledge of the beginning of faith in ourselves and in those around us. Just so, likewise, can we trace the causes of subsequent manifestations, whether they are signs of farther advancement, or of a partial halt, or of retrogression. In the interchange of such knowledge and such experiences lies the importance and the blessing of christian intercourse. But there are cases where these communications are not limited to a narrow circle; where the development of a christian life presents a form adapted to general exhibition. This is the case when it constitutes, either by the attainment of some life-aim inspired by faith, or through the consummation of the earthly life in the Lord, a separate, and, in a certain sense, a perfected whole; when it is manifest that the unity of the single active labors was no other than personal union with the Lord. From the difficulties experienced in preparing such a christian biography, especially in respect to that which, in the proper sense, constitutes its analogy with Revivals, may be seen what we have to contend with in the delineation of the latter. Rare indeed are the cases where all the requisites of such a biography are at command and the sources for the several component features within reach; those single traits which disclose the inner impulse of the life-development, and present it to view as a connected whole. The external relations,—how far social connections, position, and calling in life, account for its prosperous or retarded growth,—these, it is true, are more accessible to the inquirer. But not so easily can it be ascertained, how far the earliest development of character indicated a state susceptible to the Lord's call, or how far it contained adverse and disturbing elements, in which subsequent occasional declensions, or periods of supineness, might find their explanation. Not so easily can we ascertain, whether in the outward activity in the service of the Lord, in that which the eye of man cannot but regard as the fruit of faith, is not concealed something false and selfish; or whether that which to us seems to be self-complacency, carelessness, indifference, is not the expression of eternal peace. The reports of acquaintances and friends are, for such purposes, but an insecure reliance; since it is not acts or words, as such, which are here in question, but the connection of these with the moral sentiment, with the christianity of the heart. Even the portraiture sketched, perhaps at a much later period, by the favored individual himself, though made with rigorous self-examination in simplicity and humility, is yet subject to the abatement of presenting the particulars of early life from the stand-point of a maturer stage. Very seldom does the strictly private diary or genuine confidential correspondence meet the public eye. This deficiency meets us in a very special manner, at the initial period of christian development. Even with those whose awakening to a new life has occurred in a more striking and less gradual manner, there is certainly no disposition in this excitement of their inner being to institute rigid investigations and nice analyses of the change, or to impart such information to others.

When, however, the same phenomena extend over several individuals, we are able to trace farther the causes of the subsequent career; the inward occurrence takes more readily an outward manifestation. Something claiming to be the starting-point of a new life-development, manifesting itself, moreover, in each individual at a point of time fixed with more or less certainty, and under a form to be recognized with more or less distinctness, is a phenomenon witnessed in the christian church, simultaneously extending over numbers of persons. The Holy Spirit indeed lives and works in christian communities and in the Christian Church uninterruptedly to the end of the world. But there are times in which their members withdraw themselves from the influence; times when, ensnared and governed by worldly interests, they have their hearts elsewhere; when they rend the earthly life-development from its connection with the fountain of life. Such times stand before us in harsh lineaments on the page of history. But where the seed-corn has not been killed, but has only died that it may bring forth fruit, there an awakening comes from the Lord through means which affect not only individuals, but churches and denominations. Every epoch of christian Church-history is to be regarded, in a certain sense, as a Revival; since, whether it be in the sphere of the practical or the theoretical, a new state is the result. These awakenings, however, differ among themselves, with the differences of time, of place, culture, manners, the character of churches and denominations; just as the conversion of individuals in respect to their personal traits and relations in life. Where all these relations have developed themselves in the world, in a greater or less estrangement from Christianity, the new life assumes the form of an isolated phenomenon. Such are the awakenings which occur in connection with missions. When, on the contrary, the relations of life, having been to a greater or less degree produced and penetrated by the christian spirit, bear even, as is too often the case, its unrecognized stamp, the quickening manifests itself more as a progressive development from elements already present. As such, we may regard the Reformation, so far as it had for its starting-point the longing already existing in the church for the kingdom of God.

The Revivals in North America, both those which form the subject of our narrative and those of recent date, are revivals of the religious spirit in a practical respect. They are occurrences within the christian congregation, and belong properly to its relation to the Pastor or spiritual guide. In their nature they are limited to such a congregation; although contemporaneous phenomena may have been produced by similar circumstances in neighboring places. We have reports also of such revivals in Colleges and Theological Seminaries, but always in connection with the relation held by the teachers to the students, as spiritual guides.

The preceding chapter exhibits the hostile influence to which these Revivals form a reäction. It was not primarily error in doctrine, or superstition in practice, or gross transgression of law, but lukewarmness and indifference towards the religious institutions that had constituted the palladium of the pilgrim fathers. But the peculiar character of this reäction stands, it is evident, in close connection with the church-constitution of the Congregationalists, and with the course of their development. It was within the congregation, not in the Church as an organized whole, that it took place. The clergy indeed gave the impulse; but they were not, in the proper sense, the depositaries of these movements. If in their first period, the Congregationalists, in spite of their principles, in many respects constituted an ecclesiastical unity (as indeed the events before narrated are connected with the recognition of such a unity) this, since the separation from the State was consummated, had now ceased. The attempt made by means of the Saybrook Platform for securing such a unity and influence of the clergy, had not effected the object. But although, in the cases to come before us, the Revivals had their chief seat in a particular congregation; yet that limitation of the bounds of the congregations which existed in connexion with their independence, suggests also a closer union of the individual members among themselves, forming a circle through which such a religious interest could be more readily propagated and extended. The result of these occurrences was indeed but temporary; their force being crippled by circumstances hereafter to be detailed in particular. But it may perhaps be maintained, in general, that the want of a Church in the proper sense, accounts for the failure of the salutary influence to establish itself on a more solid basis, and to secure a firmer hold.

REVIVAL AT NORTHAMPTON.

We are now concerned particularly with two events which gave expression to the reaction against the decay of the religious life of New England. The more general one, extending over nearly the whole country and particularly over Massachusetts, occurred about the year 1740. It was preceded by a revival inconsiderable in respect to local extent, in the church at Northampton about the year 1735, which is to be regarded not merely as its precursor, but in some respects, as its immediate cause. This occurred under the guidance of Jonathan Edwards, Pastor of the church, one of the most distinguished theologians of North America, from whose hand we have a detailed narrative of its incidents, with special reference to what was peculiar in these occurrences. Occurrences and narrative still rank as models in North America. Standing thus by itself, in respect both to time and place, this Revival invites the attempt to portray, in clear sharp outline, its characteristic features. For this reason, we shall present a copious detail of its phenomena, concluding with the account of the more extended and general Revivals.

The following sketch is taken from an account published in the year 1737, entitled: "A faithful narrative of the surprising work of God in the conversion of many hundred souls in Northampton (Massachusetts) in the year 1735, by Jonathan Edwards." It was again published in New York, 1832, together with his "Thoughts on the Revival of religion in New England in 1742 and the way in which it ought to be acknowledged and promoted." The present editor has prefixed testimonials from several North American Theologians from different religious denominations; among them the following from the President and Professors of the Princeton College, New Jersey: "We know of no works on the subject of Revivals of Religion, at once so scriptural, discriminating, and instructive, as those of the late illustrious President Edwards. At the present day, when this subject so justly engages a large share of the attention of the religious public, we should be glad if a copy of the volume proposed to be republished could be placed in every dwelling in the United States. It exhibits the nature of genuine revivals of religion, the best means of promoting them, the abuses and dangers to which they are liable, and the duty of guarding against these abuses and dangers, with a degree of spiritual discernment and practical wisdom, which have commanded the approbation of the friends of Zion for the greater part of a century." The "Faithful Narrative" is in the form of a letter to Dr. Colman, a minister in Boston, dated November 6th 1736. From the beginning of this letter we learn what had given occasion to it. Tidings of these occurrences had reached London, where they had made a great impression. Watts and Guyse, two Congregationalist ministers, as well as the church of the latter, wishing to receive information respecting them from an eye-witness, applied to the above-named Colman, who requested Edwards to furnish the account. The latter had at first hesitated to give the facts publicity, through fear that they might seem incredible; but he now felt himself, as he says, especially called on to undertake what had been desired. His narrative was then published by Watts and Guyse, accompanied by a preface from themselves as well as from ministers of Boston; it was confirmed, also, by the express testimony of the ministers in the neighborhood of Northampton, as a narrative of what had passed before their own eyes. Watts and Guyse say of it in their Preface: "We are fully convinced of the truth of this narrative, not only from the character of the author, but from the concurrent testimony of many other persons in New England; for this thing was not done in a corner."

"It is, we are informed, a tract of country with twelve or fourteen townships, lying chiefly within the county of Hampshire on the Connecticut river, wherein it has pleased God two years ago to display his free and sovereign grace in the conversion of a great multitude of souls in a short space of time, turning them from a formal, cold and careless profession of Christianity to the lively exercise of every christian grace, and to the powerful practice of our holy religion." The narrative is divided into five chapters. First, after a brief reference to previous circumstances, is given a general sketch of the revival in Northampton. The second chapter contains a detailed description, with very copious reflections, of the particular manner in which the religious quickening developed itself in individual cases. Here is shown, in connection with an exact acquaintance with the state of the church, a deep knowledge of the wants of the human heart universally, and of the manner in which the seed sown springs up in the plant which brings forth fruit; only the different stages of the course of development are not always sufficiently distinguished, nor the transitions made perfectly clear and obvious. To the attempt to present a connected view of the contents of these first two chapters we shall add a brief summary of the three others, which consist of apologetic reflections, the narrative of two particular cases, and an account of the causes which led to a decline.

The town of Northampton, in the county of Hampshire in Massachusetts, lies in the interior of the country remote from connection with the sea. It had, as Edwards tells us, comparatively little intercourse with other parts of the province, which at that time was, in general, sparsely peopled, and without the present means of communication. Founded about the year 1654, it numbered in 1736 some two hundred families, who dwelt more compactly together than was usual in places of its size. To this, perhaps, in connection its greater isolation in other respects, it was owing that impressions of whatever kind spread among them with greater rapidity than elsewhere. Their first minister, Eleazer Mather, a brother of the celebrated Increase Mather, was ordained there in 1669, and died two years after. Mr. Stoddard, his successor, who was the grandfather of our narrator, exercised his office as preacher in Northampton from 1672 to 1729, and was the immediate predecessor of Edwards. With the peculiar views of Stoddard and their disagreement with the principles of Congregationalism, we have already become acquainted. His grandson, who on those questions took ground entirely opposite, testifies to the great zeal with which he discharged his ministerial duties; and Mr. Stoddard himself, in relating the repeated instances of extraordinary religious interest which crowned his labors, was accustomed to say that he had had five harvests. Towards the end of his life, however, a worldliness of spirit prevailed in the town, which maintained its predominance likewise through the first years of Edwards's ministry. In single cases, indeed, there was still manifested an interest in the word of God; but the younger members of the congregation held themselves almost entirely aloof from it, as well as from the restraints of family influence. Thus, in utter contrariety to the custom of the country and of their forefathers, they turned the Sunday into a day of amusement, to great public scandal and the disturbance of family order.

Towards the end of the year 1733, a change commenced in the congregation. Through the admonitions of the pastor, joined with the efforts of heads of families, these scandalous evils were removed and a more lively interest awakened in the worship of God. Things were thus progressing, when there occurred two cases of death, which excited general attention. In April 1734, a young man in the bloom of youth sickened with a violent pleurisy, became immediately delirious and died within two days. Shortly after, followed the death of a young woman. She had been much occupied about the state of her soul, previous to her seizure; but now found herself, at first, in great disquietude. At length she was filled with the consciousness of the saving mercy of God, and died in joyful hope, counselling and exhorting others in a very earnest and affecting manner. The excitement thus produced received an added impulse through the opposition then rising in New England against the doctrine of justification by faith. The spread of such a tendency might easily have had the effect of lulling, or of satisfying, to outward appearance, the germinating religious interest; but, as things now were, it contributed rather to engage the public mind to a still greater degree in the matters of religion, and thereby to counteract the prevailing evil of indifference. Scarcely had a few begun to think earnestly upon their state, than the excitement spread; exhibiting in its manifestations, though with varieties of form in different individuals, an essential general correspondence.

Thus, as was natural, a knowledge of their sinful state was its first result; but to this they were led in a variety of ways. Some who had hitherto been secure and unconcerned in regard to their spiritual condition, were suddenly seized with a sense of their corruption; their consciences were smitten "as if they were pierced through with a dart." In others, these first impressions were more gradual. They began at first to be somewhat more thoughtful and considerate, so as to come to the conclusion that it was best and wisest to delay no longer, but to improve the present opportunity; awakening themselves still farther by earnest reflection, they came at length to a firm and clear conviction of their sinfulness. Others still, who previously had been, to a certain degree, religiously inclined and concerned for the salvation of their souls, were now awakened in a new manner; becoming sensible that their dull and negligent endeavors were not likely to attain their purpose, they were roused to new efforts to enter the kingdom of heaven. This knowledge of one's own state, though indeed it is but the beginning of a new life, and a preparation for passing into it, manifested itself in most cases, at the very outset, as no dead conviction. The immediate effect was twofold. On the one hand, evil practices and sinful habits of life were seen to be forsaken; long-standing quarrels and slanders, mischievous intermeddling with the affairs of others, and the various manifestations of levity ceased; and while new sacredness was attached to the Sabbath, each day was regarded as a day of the Lord. On the other hand, was witnessed an application to the means through which deliverance from the former state might be hoped for, reading of the Bible, prayer, reflection, the ordinances of the church, and conferences for mutual benefit. Their cry was: What must I do to be saved?

Progress, in such times of religious excitement, is identical with practical earnestness in the settlement of this question. One may indeed become conscious that he has committed sin and is a sinner; but this concern may be soon quieted or may pass away, if the conviction is not added that men's sins are their destruction. Assent to this truth is indispensable; but its utterance from the whole heart, free from all reserve and qualification, is at the price of bitter humiliation. Submission to this conviction is hard to the proud heart; progress in it and deliverance from it difficult for the despairing heart. The conflicts and hindrances experienced in connection with the revival at Northampton arose chiefly from the latter source. Thus, it soon became general (though under various forms of expression), for individuals to declare themselves sensible that while in sin they were on the way to destruction. This was accompanied by a state of extraordinary anxiety and disquiet. Some expressed themselves as so affected by the consciousness of their sin and guilt that they were unable to sleep at night; others, that on lying down, the thought of sleeping in this condition was so frightful, that they were scarcely free from terror even when asleep, and on awakening, fear, heaviness and distress were still abiding on their spirits. Yet sometimes these persons supposed themselves to be wholly without feeling, forsaken by the Spirit of God, and given over to hardness of heart. Thus with a well-grounded anxiety, arising from the consciousness of sin, was mingled an unnecessary distress and melancholy, which, as Edwards remarks, exposed those who were thus affected, to dangerous temptation, and hindered their progress in the good way. "One knows not," he adds, "how to deal with such; they turn everything that is said to them the wrong way, and to their own disadvantage; next to the actual corruption of the human heart, there seems to be nothing so dangerous to men in the way of temptation, as a melancholy humor." This was particularly manifest in connection with their inward conflicts. The feeling of their ruined state rose in some individuals to such a height, that soul and body could scarcely endure it, nay, they were near sinking under their misery; yet still declaring themselves amazed at their own insensibility and sottishness in such an extraordinary time. It was evident that this feeling, if not in some way relieved, must lead to utter despair. It was a frequent expression of some, under the conviction of their sinfulness, that they seemed to themselves to differ from all others, and being the worst and vilest of all, could never hope to obtain mercy. Many, indeed, whose convictions had taken this melancholy turn, were seized with a strong feeling of envy towards those among their associates and acquaintances who had been truly converted; at other times, their hearts rose against God in their despair, and murmured at his dealings with others, and particularly with themselves.

When conviction of the need of redemption has taken possession of the heart with such completeness and power, there could supervene no pause; it would be fatal. But the efforts put forth for help, would first lead one to try his own strength. The attempts made to reach, through this, the goal so desired and longed for, are, it is true, connected with a still defective knowledge of one's own sinfulness; and Edwards indeed speaks of the tendency still often manifested to fix the attention exclusively on single and outward transgressions. Self-confidence is, moreover, properly a temptation whose source is pride of heart; but it always mingles itself also in a certain manner, though perhaps in a slighter degree, with the feeling of despair. The peculiar way in which these legal efforts appeared, at Northampton, as the transition-struggle into true conviction of personal inability, shows that also in this stage of development such temptations predominated. Edwards depicts these efforts, as they presented themselves in general, in a form more or less painful, longer or shorter in duration, in the following words:

"Very often under first awakenings, when they are brought to reflect on the sin of their past lives, and have something of a terrifying sense of God's anger, they set themselves to walk more strictly, and confess their sins, and perform many religious duties, with a secret hope of appeasing God's anger, and making up for the sins they have committed; and oftentimes, at first setting out, their affections are moved, and they are full of tears in their confessions and prayers, which they are ready to make much of, as though they were some atonement, and had power to move correspondent affections in God too; and hence they are for a while big with expectation of what God will do for them, and conceive that they grow better apace, and shall soon be thoroughly converted. But these affections are but short-lived, they quickly find that they fail, and then they think themselves to be grown worse again; they do not find such a prospect of being converted as they thought; instead of being nearer, they seem to be farther off; their hearts they think are grown harder, and by this means, their fears of perishing greatly increase. But though they are disappointed, they renew their attempts again and again; and still as their attempts are multiplied, so are their disappointments; all fail, they see no token of having inclined God's heart to them, they do not see that he hears their prayers at all, as they expected he would; and sometimes there have been great temptations arising hence to leave off seeking, and to yield up the case. But as they are still more terrified with the fears of perishing, and their former hopes of prevailing on God to be merciful to them in a great measure fail, sometimes their religious affections have turned into heart-risings against God, because that he would not pity them, and seems to have little regard to their distress and piteous cries, and to all the pains they take. They think of the mercy that God has shown to others, how soon, and how easily others have obtained comfort, and those too that were worse than they, and have not labored so much as they have done, and sometimes they have even had dreadful blasphemous thoughts in these circumstances.

"But when they reflect on these wicked workings of heart against God, if their convictions are continued and the Spirit of God is not provoked utterly to forsake them, they have more distressing apprehensions of the anger of God towards those whose hearts work after such a sinful manner about him; and it may be have great fears that they have committed the unpardonable sin, or that God will surely never show mercy to them that are such vipers, and are often tempted to leave off in despair.

"But then perhaps, by something they read or hear of the infinite mercy of God and all-sufficiency of Christ for the chief of sinners, they have some encouragement and hope renewed; but they think that as yet they are not fit to come to Christ, they are so wicked that Christ will never accept them; and then it may be, they set themselves upon a new course of fruitless endeavors in their own strength to make themselves better, and still meet with new disappointments; they are earnest to inquire what they shall do. They do not know but there is something else to be done, in order to their obtaining converting grace, that they have never done yet. It may be they hope they are something better than they were; but then the pleasing dream all vanishes again. If they are told that they trust too much to their own strength and righteousness, they cannot unlearn this practice all at once, and find not yet the appearance of any good, but all looks as dark as midnight to them. Thus they wander about from mountain to hill, seeking rest and finding none; when they are beat out of one refuge, they fly to another, till they are, as it were, broken, debilitated, and subdued with legal humblings; in which God gives them a conviction of their own utter helplessness and insufficiency, and discovers the true remedy in a clearer knowledge of Christ and his gospel."

Thus have we portrayed in the author's own words, the process by which conviction of sinfulness, and of the destructive nature of sin, was developed into the sense of personal insufficiency and helplessness. It would naturally be expected, that now the eye would be turned in quest of the promises of God's mercy. But our narrator here adds a detailed exhibition of the generally prevailing views respecting God's holiness and justice; thus assigning the turning-point in the conflict to the time when the real enemy began to reign. It was from the very stand-point of legal effort, that the inquiring spirit now gave itself up in a singular manner to speculation on the penal justice of God. So entirely did this occupy the soul as to leave no room for any other mental operation. The belief of being given over to eternal destruction, and the grounds of this conviction, were stated under a variety of forms. Edwards says: "Some viewed God as sovereign, and that he might receive others and reject them; some expressed themselves as convinced that God might justly bestow mercy on every person in the town, and on every person in the world, and damn themselves to all eternity; some, that God may justly have no regard to all the pains they have taken, and all the prayers they have made; some that they see, if they should seek, and take the utmost pains all their lives, God might justly cast them into hell at last, because all their labors, prayers and tears, cannot make an atonement for the least sin, nor merit any blessing at the hands of God. Some have declared themselves to be in the hands of God, that he can and may dispose of them just as he pleases; some that God may glorify himself in their damnation, and they wonder that God has suffered them to live so long, and has not cast them into hell long ago."

Even if we separate the meaning of these words from their peculiar phraseology, there yet seems to be here the intermingling of some foreign and disturbing element; at least, they are not the expression of progress, but still belong wholly to the legal stand-point. It is only from this stand-point that one, truly conscious of deserving the penalty of destruction for his own guilt, can, on a comparison of himself with others, recognize the divine justice in their exemption from it. He who has found by experience, that the goal is not to be reached by the most strenuous efforts of his own, looks away, in the feeling of his helplessness, towards the mercy of God, and where he sees this shown to others, he rejoices in the token that here the very thing has happened for which he himself hopes. In a christian community, experience of the insufficiency of means, employed in dependence on one's own strength, cannot be conceived of as unaccompanied by a reasonable hope in the help of God; and this help must present itself to the mind, as that wherein it is God's will to glorify himself.

Now Edwards maintains that "every minister, in such circumstances, will find himself under a necessity greatly to insist upon it that God is under no manner of obligation to show any mercy to any natural man whose heart is not turned to God; and that a man can challenge nothing, either in absolute justice or by free promise, from anything he does before he has believed in Jesus Christ, or has true repentance begun in him." If indeed no doctrine of Scripture can be alleged in opposition to these grounds of fear, so presented, it may yet well be doubted whether the application of them made in the following passage could be really salutary: "I have found," says Edwards, "that no discourses were more remarkably blessed, than those in which the doctrine of God's absolute sovereignty with regard to the salvation of sinners, and his just liberty with regard to answering the prayers or succeeding the pains of mere natural men, continuing such, have been insisted on. I have never found so much immediate saving fruit, in any measure, of any discourses I have offered to my congregation, as some from those words, Rom. 3: 19, 'That every mouth may be stopped;' endeavoring to show from thence that it would be just with God forever to reject and cast off mere natural men." But the persons thus addressed, although they had not, in their spiritual conflict, wholly risen above the stand-point of legal endeavors, were no longer to be designated as mere natural men; yet, since they had not already experienced in their hearts the word of forgiveness, they must, each in particular, account themselves among the rejected. Hence such expressions as the following, which Edwards, however, contemplates as the fruit of a high exercise of grace, in saving repentance, and evangelical humiliation: "They found a sort of complacency of soul in the attribute of God's justice, as displayed in his threatenings of eternal damnation to sinners. Sometimes at the discovery of it, they can hardly forbear crying out, ''T is just! ''T is just!' Some express themselves that they see the glory of God would shine bright in their own condemnation; and they are ready to think that if they are damned, they could take part with God against themselves, and would glorify his justice therein." Some expressed to our narrator "a feeling of willingness to be damned." To this he adds, however, that "these persons had, it must be owned, no clear and distinct ideas of damnation, nor does any word of the Bible require such a self-denial as this." Could we even regard it as an exalted sense of their unworthiness to be partakers of God's grace; yet in this tendency of the feelings there ever lies, in connection with the essential contradiction in the mode of expression, great danger, if not of absolute despair, yet of abandonment to the severest assaults of despondency. Still, at this time, chiefly through the labors of a pastor well acquainted with the condition and wants of the human soul, progress of the most important character succeeded to these legal apprehensions and strivings. We shall now, having thus far shown the process in which old things passed away, proceed to exhibit that, in which all became new.

As there is but one ground for real disquietude of soul, sin; so also there is but one ground of peace, namely, the grace of God in Christ. This it was, which after all these conflicts manifested itself in Northampton, and herein was the change thus effected also one and the same. But varied were the forms in which the Lord revealed himself to the perturbed spirits, varied their accounts of what they had experienced. To both these points we will now give our consideration.

In exact accordance with the individual character, this or that particular attribute of God, of Christ, rose up before the soul which had been penetrated with the sense of its own helplessness. Now it was the thought of God's grace and mercy in general, now of his infinite power to save men and lead them in the way of salvation, now of the divine truth and faithfulness in reference to particular promises. With some, the divinity of Christ as the Son of God, chiefly engaged the thoughts; with others, his reconciling death. Many dwelt chiefly on the obedience or the love of the Saviour, or on the excellence of the way of salvation by Christ, and its correspondence to all their wants. This change was,for the most part, placed in explicit connection with the Holy Scriptures, in some cases with entire passages and a succession of promises, in some, likewise, with a particular word or a single promise; while in others the calm began without direct connection, by reading or meditation, with any particular portion or expression of Scripture.

In respect to the accounts given by the persons so affected,—it was, in most cases, the specific thought of Christ, which in this transition gave joy to the soul. With some, however, he was the object of the mind in a more implied manner, and they spoke particularly of their sense of the sufficiency of God's grace for them and for the whole world. From a careful weighing of their expressions and after searching interrogation, it became clear that the revelation of God's grace in the Gospel formed the ground of their encouragement and hope; that it was indeed the mercy of God through Christ which had been discovered to them, and that it was this on which they relied, not upon anything in themselves. Although they had felt the divine call without thinking explicitly of

Christ, yet afterwards, they were taught by their own experiences that it was, nevertheless, the call made by God to sinners through his Son. One peculiarity is especially noticeable. Very many, after such an effectual working of the Lord upon them, had no idea that such a thing had occurred, but still remained in expectation of something farther, of which they could themselves give no account. In their view, the customary expressions used to describe conversion, and the gracious operations of the Holy Spirit, were not appropriate to their state. Such terms as spiritual sight of Christ, faith in Christ, poverty of spirit, trust in God, submission to God, seemed not to produce in them corresponding ideas. Edwards remarks that this imperfect conception of their own state had an essential connection with their former false conceptions of the operations of God's grace, which, indeed, cannot be perceived or understood by the natural man. But to this our narrator justly adds, that they were too much filled with the superabundance of these new and joyful emotions to institute such examinations in regard to themselves. The fact that reflection in respect to their state did not predominate in the accounts given by the converts of their first steps of progress in the way of peace, affords indeed a striking proof that these phenomena belonged to their own living experience, and were no deception. And, as the new life had not manifested itself to the awakened precisely according to their preconceived notions, so they were, in general, still less able to fix the time when the first tokens appeared that the gracious impressions had become effectual. With many, the enlightening was of a more gradual character, and by such, as Edwards very beautifully remarks, the first dawning which precedes the full light was often wholly overlooked.

The path, from the starting point of the christian life to its final goal, is not here on earth an entirely smooth one. Even where the consciousness of divine assistance has been added to the experience of its power, there intervenes a time of conflict and temptation. Thus also in Northampton, there appeared in individual cases a resistance, more or less strong, to a progressive development of the awakenings, manifesting itself partly in renewed disquietude, partly in a returning indifference. The distress occasioned by this new interruption of a steady course of progress must needs be more severe than that previously felt, in proportion as it was connected with the remembrance of what had been already experienced. Here now Edwards believed himself called on to assist the work by directing attention to what had been already attained. Where, for instance, the declarations and the whole temper, of one thus suffering from renewed doubts, justified the firm conviction of his converted state, Edwards did not hesitate to express such a conviction. He compares persons in this condition, to "seed in the spring suppressed under a hard clod of earth;" as this is quickened by the warm beams of the sun, so has the hope presented to the doubting chased away that despondency which enveloped and concealed the inner spiritual life. The indifference, which manifested itself here and there, was counteracted by turning the eye towards those who were hastening onward in the new state. In a certain condition of mind, knowledge of the progress of others in the kingdom of God, may, as we have already seen, awaken a spirit of wicked envy, and lead to sullen obduracy; for the present stage reference to what had been attained by some, was held by Edwards, certainly on just grounds, to be an efficient means of quickening others. But he adds the cautious remark: "I have often signified to my people how unable man is to know another's heart, and how unsafe it is depending on the judgment of ministers or others; and I have abundantly insisted on it with them, that a manifestation of sincerity in works brought forth, is better than any manifestation they can make of it in words alone, and that, without this, all pretences to spiritual experiences are vain."

The principal means for counteracting these interruptions, as well as of forwarding the work begun, were found in the study of the Scriptures and the truths of the Gospel. At this point we will add some remarks of our narrator, before proceeding to a description of the final stage of these religious awakenings. As did the commencement, so the progress of this change stood in a connection more or less explicit, with sentences of Scripture. Comforting and instructive passages presented themselves to the minds of the anxious, often in a manner which was wholly inexplicable. For the most part, indeed, it was while led by God into such states of feeling and to such reflections as were in harmony with the texts of Scripture, that they came, as it were on a sudden, to their remembrance. But often, as Edwards thinks, an immediate influence of the Spirit of God must be presupposed, in order to explain the recollection of passages so remarkably adapted to the special case; though the use of the memory as the medium is, indeed, not to be excluded.

The effect of this comfort and instruction from the word of God, as well as of that derived from preaching, was a living conviction of the truth of what was taught in the Gospel. Here too was manifested a difference in the mode of experience, particularly in a twofold direction. In some, it was more like an instantaneous conviction, seizing possession of the entire man. "They were," so they declared, "as far from doubting the divinity of the Gospel, as they were from doubting whether there be a sun, when their eyes are open in the midst of a clear hemisphere and the strong blaze of his light overcomes all objections against his being." On being questioned, they were able to assign no other reason for their convictions than that "they saw them to be true;" but from more particular inquiry it became evident that these truths had indeed been the object of intuitive perception and immediate experience. They were not able indeed to retain such a clear discovery of them at all times in equal measure. When, for a season, their living spiritual feeling suffered a decrease, the medium of conviction seemed to them to have withdrawn itself; but, if their assurance had been genuine, it again revived "like fire that lay hid in ashes." In others, on the contrary, it was more through attention to some single prominent doctrines of the Scriptures, whose grounds of evidence became clear to them partly from the teachings of the pulpit, partly from their own meditations, that full conviction was attained. These were indeed already known to them; but they now came with a new and before unexperienced power. "Before, they had heard it was so, and they allowed it to be so; but now they see it to be so indeed. Things now look exceeding plain to them, and they wonder that they did not see them before. They are so greatly taken with their new discovery, and things appear so plain and rational to them, that they are at first ready to think they can convince others, and are apt to engage in talk with almost every one they meet, to this end; and when they are disappointed, are ready to wonder that their reasonings make no more impression." But these persons also, who had attained to conviction by a more gradual process, were still liable, oftentimes, to be again disturbed by doubt. Some of this class were disquieted in respect to the nature of the work in them, on account of its having taken place in so natural a manner; erroneously supposing that the divine purpose cannot be attained by a method which seems purely human. It is worthy of notice that the truths which had been so often heard and read, now presented themselves to the mind as something entirely new. Some found, they said, in the familiar pages of the Bible, "new chapters, new psalms, new histories." It was they who were changed; within themselves all had become new.

In the state of calmness which succeeded those agonies and terrors, Christ became the object towards which the the soul was turned, and the inward work was subjected, by those who had experienced it, to the strictest scrutiny by the word of God. This alike guarded them against errors and secured their progress in the right way. Nor was the peace now withheld which the Lord promises to his own. They hardly knew how to paint the joy which had taken up its abode in their hearts. They described themselves as swallowed up in longing after God and Christ, as ravished with the delightful contemplation of the glory and wonderful grace of God, and of the excellency and dying love of Jesus Christ. Even younger members of the congregation expressed themselves in the same manner, and declared their willingness to forsake father and mother and all things in the world, in order to be with Christ. In some, the bodily strength could hardly sustain the inward experience; nay, it seemed as if the body must dissolve, if that fulness of manifestation should be any more increased.

Certainly, one would not venture to measure the language of christian exaltation in such circumstances, by the standard of expression belonging to a quiet and ordinary tone of feeling; it is by other signs that the product of

God's spirit is to be distinguished from self-seeking fanaticism. Free from the airs of assumption, self-deception, and self-conceit, these persons were characterized by a spirit of meekness, and unassuming humility, mingled with distrust of their own power, and a lowly estimate of their own capacities. None were so deeply convinced of their need of being taught, none so ready and eager to receive instruction. Free from self-exaltation in respect to men, they bowed with continual and unfeigned humility before God, ascribing that which was done in them in no way to their own strength and righteousness, but solely to the quickening power derived from Christ. They declared, also, that what they sometimes experienced in especially favored moments, it was beyond their power to express in words; that all the pains and trouble they had taken in seeking salvation was not to be once compared with their present joy and satisfaction; and that in contrast with these all earthly pleasures seem mean and worthless. Yet they did not feel themselves disturbed or troubled by a look towards earth; on the contrary, all around them received a new charm through their inward joy. "All things abroad, the sun, moon and stars, the clouds and sky, the heavens and earth, appeared, as it were, with a cast of divine glory and sweetness upon them." And as the contemplation of outward nature harmonized with and exalted their affections, even so was it with the thought of redemption. Here, the former conflict in their souls, if it had not terminated, had as it were receded into the background. The chief object of their joy was not so much the consciousness of being saved from sin and punishment, as that of being partakers of divine grace, confidence in Christ as their guide to future glory. There seemed to be in their hearts but one complaint; the complaint that with all their desire, all their longing to praise God, they could not do it worthily, even when, in contemplation of the creation around them and the redemption within them, they were filled with peace and joy and perfect satisfaction.

Besides these effects, which, being more or less wrought within, hardly reveal themselves in their peculiar and entire significance to the eye of the beholder, there were not wanting visible good fruits brought forth by the good tree. Mutual affection united those who had become sharers in such glorious manifestations, and many expressed the love they felt towards all mankind, even towards those who had hitherto been least friendly to themselves. "Never was so much done in confessing injuries and making up differences, as in this year." This love was mingled also with a heartfelt desire for the salvation of others. But with a living activity for this end, on the part of those so highly favored, they yet recognized the distinction between that which was essential and common to all, salvation in Christ, and that which was special and varied, the way thither and the outward expression. Keeping their hearts open, moreover, to the truth that the leadings of God in this respect are manifold, they were not disposed to make their own experiences a standard for others, but refrained from censoriousness and strove to increase in charity, as in the manifestation of faith. At the same time, there grew up also a very endearing relation between the church and its pastor; diligent attendance at the house of God, living sympathy for the preaching of the gospel, and strict observance of the Sabbath were united with eager study of the Bible, particularly of the New Testament, the Psalms, and the Prophecy of Isaiah. And this use of the means of grace, this occupation in religious things, seemed not like a duty and a task, but a satisfaction and a joy.

We have yet to add, in respect to the outward spread and extension of these phenomena, that the influence was shared by the immediate vicinity at an early period. The accounts of what was occurring in Northampton drew thither many strangers, and in such cases, as well as in that of accidental visitors, the feeling of astonishment often ended in personal participation. These persons, returning to their own congregations, awakened there the same excitement, though perhaps in a lower degree. But, as a general thing, its spread was limited to the immediate neighborhood of Northampton, or at farthest, to the county of Hampshire. Nor does there seem to have been any very close connection among these movements, except that the report of similar occurrences in other places heightened and promoted the progress of the work in Northampton itself. Here the change extended itself to all ranks, conditions and ages; while not only those who had passed the term of middle life, but even little children gave the most striking proofs of a vitalizing religious influence. A large part of the inhabitants of Northampton had never become members of the church in full fellowship. Edwards reports, that before one celebration of the sacrament[1] about one hundred were admitted, eighty of them at one time, on the open, explicit profession of Christianity. From subsequent events it indeed appears, that it was not a profession in the strict sense of the covenant of the first Congregationalists, although, certainly, Edwards was already unfavorable to the peculiar views of his grandfather.

After quiet mature reflection and careful severe discrimination, it was Edwards's opinion that the number of those

[1] It was celebrated in this church once in eight weeks.

who had been savingly converted through the influence of this awakening was not far from three hundred. The number of communicants embraced nearly the entire body of adults, being six hundred and twenty persons, out of two hundred families.

Before proceeding to a representation of the decline of this religious interest, and the transition to a state of quiet, Edwards communicates, in the third and fourth divisions of his letter, some apologetic observations together with a narrative of two individual cases. The relations given by some church-members, of what they had seen in moments of exaltation, seemed to furnish ground for the oft-repeated imputation of enthusiasm. Edwards says: "There have indeed been some few instances of impressions on persons' imaginations, that have been something mysterious to me, and I have been at a loss about them; for though it has been exceeding evident to me, by many things that appeared in them, both then (when they related them) and afterwards, that they had indeed a great sense of the spiritual excellency of divine things accompanying them; yet I have not been able well to satisfy myself, whether their imaginary ideas have been more than could naturally arise from their spiritual sense of things. However, I have used the utmost caution in such cases; great care has been taken both in public and in private, to teach persons the difference between what is spiritual and what is merely imaginary. I have often warned persons not to lay the stress of their hope on any ideas of any outward glory, or any external thing whatsoever; and have met with no opposition in such instructions." It happened that some persons associated what was passing with such living reality in their minds, with corresponding images; as for example, with the inward sense of what they had attained through Christ, they received the impression of an image of the crucified Saviour. But this, as Edwards justly remarks, is no cause of wonder to those who have observed how strong excitement, in regard even to temporal matters, will excite lively ideas and manifold pictures in the mind. In regard to a second objection, that these religious experiences formed so exclusively the subject of conversation in Northampton at this time, nothing more is to be said than that it lay in the very nature of the circumstances. An excitement like this, interesting at the same time all the inhabitants of a place alike, would make itself the subject of discourse when they met. It is indeed not to be expected that the communications will in all cases be made in an equally discreet manner, or will always produce good results; but in general, Edwards saw the most beneficial results from these narrations of personal experience.

There is something peculiar in the choice of examples given in the fourth chapter; it seems to have been guided by the desire, certainly a commendable one, that the published account of what had been experienced in an individual case should not, by any chance, fall into the hands of the person himself. A young woman, Abigail Hutchinson by name, having had her attention awakened by the first of the deaths before-mentioned, was exceedingly disturbed in mind; but after a violent inward conflict soon attained to the consciousness of inward peace. During an agonizing sickness, she manifested a spirit of entire submission. A few months after this change, she died of actual starvation, her neck being so swollen that she could take no nourishment; yet as long as she could speak, she expressed by words her joyful state of mind, and by signs and gestures manifested the same through her long protracted death-struggles to the very end. The second example was designed to exhibit the participation of children, even of the tenderest age, in the general religious interest. Edwards presents the case of a child of four years, concerning which the London editor justly remarks, that the language of children loses its peculiar charm for one who does not himself see and hear. In this case, even the language seems to have undergone a certain change and remoulding, so that her thoughts on the salvation of the soul, and the feeling of anxiety for others, in this respect seem rather like expressions belonging to a mature age. It cannot be denied that the very earliest age is susceptible of a religious influence, and that this may also be communicated, as it were involuntarily, from the childish stand-point. But favorable as a time like that under consideration might be to such a development, it is precisely at such a time that it is most difficult, if not impossible, to distinguish what has really been wrought in the soul from the effect of mere outward imitation.

To that time of spiritual excitement succeeded of necessity a period of greater calm, which, on the whole, was not without tokens of the richest fruit. Nevertheless, a growing coldness made itself apparent, in part under the form of opposition to the phenomena here described. The exciting cause is worthy of notice, being attributable to that tendency to melancholy humor, or morbid self-inspection before adverted to. The solicitude to penetrate into the depths of one's own spirit does indeed impress on the individual the conviction of his own state, and break down the proud heart; but it obstructs his access to the only true help, and furnishes a nourishment to the dejected heart which leads to despair. In the midst of the time of most vivid religious interest, a person under overwhelming distress of mind made the attempt to commit suicide. It was without effect, and he afterwards sincerely repented for having yielded so far to the temptations of his own heart. But about a year after the first tokens of the awakening made their appearance, another person succeeded in the terrible design. He was a man of more than ordinary intellectual gifts, strictly moral in his course of life, outwardly religious, skilful in business, and very highly respected in the town; but partaking of a strong family tendency to melancholy, by which his mother also had lost her life. During the whole year he had been earnestly concerned about the state of his soul, and although there was in his experience much of a hopeful and cheering character, he did not venture to entertain any such hope for himself. He consequently grew disheartened, and his melancholy gained such power over him that he became incapable of receiving counsel or listening to reason. Whole nights he remained awake meditating terrors, so that he scarcely slept at all for a long time together. At length it was noticed that he was scarcely capable of managing his ordinary business; and at the coroner's inquest, he was judged to have been in a state of delirium. After this occurrence, many complained of being affected with similar temptations. Just at this time certain fanatics made their appearance, who busied themselves, in part, with persuading persons in that melancholy and anxious condition that they could be helped by repeating over certain consolatory forms of prayer; in part, with preaching that the last times promised in the Scriptures had now come. One man who had made himself especially conspicuous in this way, afterwards confessed the error into which he had fallen, and lamented the injury done thereby; but the legitimate consequences of egotistic fanaticism followed, in a growing spirit of worldliness and coldness. To this was superadded the dissipating influence of various matters, which just at that time occupied in a special manner the attention of the people of Northampton; among others, a visit from the governor of the colony, the public meetings held in reference to the treaty of peace with the Indians, and the controversy in a neighboring town respecting the choice of a minister. Still, however, the blessed influence of these manifestations had not disappeared; as it still lived for individuals, so also did it reveal itself in the susceptibility of the neighboring region and of all New England for a similar quickening.

THE GREAT REVIVAL.

Although the revival of the year 1735 extended only to the immediate vicinity of Northampton, and again declined in the town itself, it had awakened the utmost attention through all New England, as already seen in the interest which it excited in London and in the notices of it by Watts and Guyse. It recalled the times of the first settlement of the colonies; the degeneracy of the present state was clearly seen and deeply felt. This manifested itself most conspicuously in Boston, the scene of labor to so many remarkable men. In the year 1739, George Whitefield, the celebrated founder of Methodism, made his second visit to America. The colony of Georgia, which had been settled a few years before, principally engaged his energies; but his powerful and effective preaching was heard also on his travels through Carolina, Virginia, Maryland, Philadelphia and New York. The report of his distinguished gifts and wonderful success, procured him an invitation to Boston. On the 14th of September 1740, he landed at Newport in Rhode Island, where he remained three days. The invitation had not proceeded merely from private citizens; as he approached Boston, he was received by the son of the Governor, with several clergymen and many of the principal inhabitants, who conducted him to a dwelling expressly prepared for his reception. During his two months stay, he not only preached in Boston, but travelled through New England, and made a visit to Edwards. He then returned to Boston, and directed his course through Hartford and New Haven to the more southern colonies. The result of this visit surpassed all expectation. The same spirit which had been witnessed in Northampton spread through the whole country, and its manifestations were characterized no less by the active zeal of the ministers than by the sympathy of the churches. Voices from every quarter of New England extolled the new work, as the revival of the primitive religious spirit. Out of a multitude of testimonials to the eloquence of Whitefield, and to his zeal in the cause of the Lord, we select the following words from a clergyman's letter: "Among the good effects of his preaching on the churches, it is especially worthy of remark, that the word preached by us now seems more precious and acts with greater power." An aged preacher, the successor of John Eliot, exclaimed: "The old days of New England are revived!" Whitefield, who had preached his farewell discourse in Boston to an audience of twenty thousand persons, and who could not but wish to contribute all in his power to the continuance and promotion of the work, on his return to New Jersey persuaded Gilbert Tennant, a distinguished minister in that colony, to go to New England. He was received with joy, and the blessing which attended his preaching in the year 1741 was generally acknowledged.

This labor of itinerant preachers was evidently something out of the ordinary course, but seems justified by the manifest coldness and indifference of many ministers at that time, and by the general recognition of the call to such a work. Especially was this true of Whitefield; of whom also it is recorded, that his aim in preaching was not a display of his personal gifts of eloquence, but simply and above all things, to show forth the truth of the gospel itself. It was on this that thoughtful men grounded their hope of a safe and permanent impression. In consequence of the continued religious interest, and of the destitution made known in various directions, perhaps encouraged also by Whitefield's appeal to Tennant and the successful labors of the latter, many clergymen now thought they found in the revival of their own religious feelings the proper call and the complete qualification for traversing New England as evangelists. Although successful in awakening a living interest in single localities, although it was in the exercise of true zeal in the cause of God, free from spiritual pride, that they felt themselves impelled to this course; yet in the misconception of their position lay from the first an occasion for the abuses and disorders which followed, as well as for the development of an opposing party. Many, for instance, took it upon themselves to preach among the churches without waiting for any outward call, and thus the most favorable result might be nothing more than personal attachment to themselves. But these revivals among the Congregationalists of New England, which are to be contemplated as religious movements on ground already occupied by vital Christianity, must strengthen to the utmost the relation of pastor and people, if they would remain true to their peculiar character, and be attended by enduring results. The experimental knowledge of Christ by faith is indeed a call to preach the gospel; but the example of another instrument of the Lord, differently gifted and differently called from ourselves, is not a reason for forsaking our appropriate and appointed sphere.

DISTURBING AND HOSTILE INFLUENCES.

The appearance of itinerant preachers was indeed hailed in many places with great joy, and was regarded as a token of God's special favor to these awakenings. Opposition to it first manifested itself in Connecticut, where a rigid organization and method had obtained since the adoption of the Saybrook Platform. So early as November 1741, a general consociation, assembled at Guilford, declared it disorderly for any minister to enter the parish of another, for the purpose of preaching and administering the sacraments, without or against the consent of the latter. In the year 1742, specific regulations in regard to this matter were drafted and laid before the Legislature, by whom they were made legal enactments. According to these, any preacher who should enter uninvited a parish not under his charge, or should take part in an association which intrudes on the limits of another by the licensing or ordination of a candidate, shall be excluded from the benefit of any laws made for the support of the ministry. And every layman, under like circumstances, should pay a fine of one hundred pounds and give security for his good behavior. And any foreigner, whether minister or not, should be dealt with as a vagrant, and be sent from constable to constable, out of the bounds of the colony.[1] At the ground of these proceedings there was, unfortunately for the interests of this work, not merely a prejudice against

[1] Under this law, no less a person than Samuel Finley, afterwards President of Princeton College, was arrested and carried out of the colony as a vagrant. — Tr.

the special phase, but a decided aversion to everything which might disturb the quiet course of established forms. If in Massachusetts the religious decline manifested itself more as indifference, in Connecticut it was rather the rigidity of torpor. The opposition, proceeding from this quarter, which refused to recognize what was true and vital in these manifestations, produced its natural result, excess on the other side. Many ministers felt themselves justified, by the extraordinary interest in hearing the word which still continued among the people, to abandon their churches in order to preach in various places; and the same was done by many laymen. The prospect of becoming martyrs to the cause seems not to have been without its charm in these cases. Among those who espoused this side, James Davenport, a highly gifted minister, a grandson of the celebrated John Davenport, took the most decided ground and exerted the most pernicious influence. Leaving his church on Long Island, he repaired to Connecticut, where he felt it his special duty to bear testimony against unconverted ministers. After experiencing some persecutions here, he came to Boston; but his preaching and expressions were of such a character that most of the ministers united, July 1st 1742, in signing the following declaration: "He appears to us to be truly pious, and we hope God has used him as an instrument of good to many souls; yet we judge it our duty to bear testimony against the following particulars. 1. His being acted much by sudden impulses. 2. His judging some ministers in Long Island and New England to be unconverted; and thinking himself called of God to demand of his brethren, from place to place, an account of their regenerate state, when, or in what manner the Holy Spirit wrought upon and renewed them. 3. His going with his friends, singing through the streets and highways, to and from the houses of worship, on Lord's days and other days. 4. His encouraging private brethren to pray and exhort in assemblies gathered for that purpose. We judge it therefore our present duty not to invite him into our places of worship, as otherwise we might readily have done." This, however, did not hinder Davenport, while in Boston, from undertaking to examine each of the ministers in private and then report publicly against them, denouncing some as unconverted and calling on the people to separate from them. In this manner he traversed the country; but, on his return to Boston in August 1742, he was imprisoned and brought to court for trial on a charge of slandering the ministers. The jury, however, judged him to be *non compos mentis*, and on that ground acquitted him. Thence he returned to Long Island, but again came to New London in Connecticut, where, in connection with some others, he ran into extremes[1] still more surprising. Through these proceedings, especially through the preaching of laymen wholly uncalled to the work, great scandal came upon the cause. The ministers of Massachusetts, who had experienced in their congregations the manifold blessings of the time, recorded their testimony against these errors at their annual meeting on the 25th of May 1743. But in order to give more effect to their action, all the brethren who were favorably inclined to the work itself were requested either to appear personally at a meeting to be held in July, there to express their minds on the subject, or to send in their thoughts in writing. Sixty-eight minis-

[1] Having first burnt a considerable number of books which they considered erroneous, they were about to destroy a quantity of fine clothing and ornaments, under the pretence of putting an end to idolatry; but this was stopped by a man who remarked to Davenport: "If all my idols are to be burnt, you will be the first."

ters met and signed a letter testifying, as a matter of their own knowledge, that an incredible number of persons had been awakened, after a true acquaintance with their state as sinners, to a new life through faith in Christ; and they expressed their decided disapproval of the charge made by some, that all these phenomena were nothing but enthusiasm, delusion, and disorder. At the same time, they lamented the tares which had been sown among the wheat; specifying as such the tendency, manifested here and there, to make inward impressions the criterion of conduct without due regard to the written word, but more especially the invasion of the regular ministerial office, and the distrust awakened between ministers and people. Similar declarations were sent in by forty-three other preachers. But this expression, though so generally approved, and discriminating so clearly between the nature of the thing and its abuses, was not followed by the expected results. Decided opposers took the field, and the revivals themselves began to decline. Edwards had shortly before published his celebrated "Thoughts on Revivals." To counteract this work, the Rev. Dr. Chauncey, who was generally regarded as the chief promoter of the Arminian and Unitarian tendency, now made a journey through the colonies of New England, New York, and New Jersey, collecting materials for a virulent reply to Edwards, which he published in 1743. It found special favor with the higher classes. It seems also not to have been without influence on the proceedings in Connecticut, where the above-mentioned acts were now actually put in practice, in the persecution of those who were striving to rekindle the spirit which was already on the wane. On the one side, the adventitious element had gained too wide a hold; while on the other, in the assault thus made on the fundamental doctrines of Scripture, indifference found the opiate and the cloak for which it asked. Davenport came to a just sense of his conduct, and having drawn up a confession of his errors, lamenting what he had said and done, sent his retraction to a minister in Boston for publication. But it was too late for the removal of the prejudices which had been imbibed. Enemies had too well used the opportunity for bringing the work itself into suspicion, to allow of its now being retrieved by its friends. How greatly all had changed is most clearly seen in the cool, nay, to some extent, the hostile reception experienced by Whitefield on his renewed visit in the year 1745. Not only was he assailed by individual ministers and associations; but the colleges of Cambridge and New Haven, the former of which had extolled the blessed influence of his labors at his first coming, now entered the lists against him, with special animosity. With the declining fellowship for the revivals vanished also the revived interest in religion. It is indeed a peculiar indication of the state of disunion which followed, that when Edwards, some years after, declared himself decidedly against regarding the Lord's Supper as a converting ordinance, he encountered such opposition in his church as obliged him to quit the place where he had been so favored an instrument of the Lord; and the consociation before which the controversy with the church was tried, declared their adhesion to Stoddard's view. To what a degree political interest swallowed up all others in New England during the succeeding period, and the desolating ravages of unbelief within the church kept pace with those of the war without, we have already mentioned.

The genuine religious element, out of which had grown the colonization and primitive constitution of New England, has again presented itself to view, in recent times. The professed disciples of the Lord in that land, now look back with joy upon the labors and the influence of their progenitors. The most recent revival of the religious spirit has been connected with phenomena similar to those described in this chapter; but they have not been confined to one church-party merely, and on that very account vary in form and significance among themselves. For exhibiting them, a characterization of the evangelical churches of North America is needed, as well as an exposition of the relation, now fully established, of a total separation of Church and State. Such being the case, they belong to the department of ecclesiastical statistics, and are foreign to the object of this work, whose aim it was to exhibit the progressive development of the New England church-constitution, and the phenomena with which the change in that constitution was accompanied.

APPENDIXES.

APPENDIX I.

ROBINSON'S LETTER TO THE LEYDEN EMIGRANTS, JULY 27, 1620.

LOVING CHRISTIAN FRIENDS,

I do heartily and in the Lord salute you, as being those with whom I am present in my best affections, and most earnest longings after you, though I be constrained for a while to be bodily absent from you: I say constrained; God knowing how willingly, and much rather than otherwise, I would have borne my part with you in the first brunt, were I not by strong necessity held back for the present. Make account of me in the meantime as a man divided in myself, with great pain (and as natural bonds set aside) having my better part with you; and although I doubt not, but in your godly wisdoms you both foresee and resolve upon that which concerneth your present state and condition, both severally and jointly, yet have I thought it but my duty to add some further spur of provocation unto them who run already, if not because you need it, yet because I owe it in love and duty.

And first, as we are daily to renew our repentance with our God, especially for our sins known, and generally for our unknown trespasses; so doth the Lord call us in a singular manner, upon occasions of such difficulty and danger as lieth upon you, to both a narrow search and careful reformation in his sight, lest he calling to remembrance our sins forgotten by us, or unrepented of, take advantage against us, and in judgment leave us to be swallowed up in one danger or another; whereas, on the contrary, sin being taken away by earnest repentance, and the pardon thereof from the Lord sealed up to a man's conscience by his spirit, great shall be his security and peace in all dangers, sweet his comforts in all distresses, with happy deliverance from all evil, whether in life or death. Now next after this heavenly peace with God and our own consciences, we are carefully to provide for peace with all men, what in us lieth, especially with our associates; and for that, watchfulness must be had, that we neither at all ourselves do give, no, nor easily take offence being given by others. *Wo be to the world for offences*, for although it be necessary, considering the malice of Satan and man's corruption, *that offences come*, yet wo unto the man, or woman either, *by whom the offence cometh*, saith Christ, Matt. xviii. 7. And if offences in the unseasonable use of things, in themselves indifferent, be more to be feared than death itself, as the apostle teacheth, 1 Cor. ix. 15, how much more in things simply evil, in which neither the honor of God nor love of man is thought worthy to be regarded? Neither yet is it sufficient that we keep ourselves, by the grace of God, from giving offences, except withal we be armed against the taking of them, when they are given by others; for how imperfect and lame is the work of grace in that person, who wants charity to *cover a multitude of offences?* as the scripture speaks. Neither are you to be exhorted to this grace only upon the common grounds of Christianity, which are, that persons ready to take offence, either want charity to cover offences, or duly to weigh human frailties; or, lastly, are gross though close hypocrites, as Christ our Lord teacheth, Matt. vii. 1–3; as indeed in my own experience, few or none have been found which sooner give offence, than such as easily take it; neither have they ever proved sound and profitable members in societies, who have nourished this *touchy humor*. But besides these, there are divers motives provoking you above others to great care and conscience in this way; as first, there are many of you strangers to the persons, so to the infirmities of one another, and so stand in need of more watchfulness this way, lest when such things fall out in men and women as you expected not, you be inordinately affected with them, which doth require at your hands much wisdom and charity for the covering and preventing of incident offences that way. And lastly, your intended course of civil community will minister continual occasion of offence, and will be as fuel for that fire, except you diligently watch it with *brotherly forbearance*. And if taking offence causelessly or easily of men's doings be so carefully to be avoided; how much more heed is to be taken that we take not offence at God himself? Which yet we certainly do, so oft as we do murmur at his providences in our crosses, or bear impatiently such afflictions wherewith he is pleased to visit us. Store up therefore patience against the evil day; without which we take offence at the Lord himself in his just works. A fourth thing there is carefully to be provided for, viz., that with your common employments, you join common affections, truly bent upon the general good, avoiding as a deadly plague of *your* both common and special comforts, all retiredness of mind for proper advantage; and all singularly affected every manner of way, let every man repress in himself, and the whole body in each person, as so many rebels against the common good, all *private respects of men's selves*, not sorting with the general convenience. And as men are careful not to have a new house shaken with any violence, before it be well settled, and the parts firmly knit; so be you, I beseech you, my brethren, much more careful that the house of God, which you are and are to be, be shaken with unnecessary novelties, or other oppositions, at the first settling thereof.

Lastly, whereas you are to become a body politic, using amongst yourselves civil government, and are not furnished with special eminency above the rest, to be chosen by you into office of government, let your wisdom and godliness appear, not only in choosing such persons as do *entirely* love, and will promote the common good; but also in *yielding* unto them all due honor and obedience in their lawful administrations, not beholding in them the ordinariness of their persons, but God's ordinance for *your good;* not being like the foolish multitude, who more honor the *gay coat*, than either the virtuous mind of the man, or the glorious ordinance of the Lord; but you know better things, and that the image of the Lord's power and authority, which the magistrate beareth, is honorable, in how mean person soever; and this duty you may the more willingly, and ought the more conscionably to perform, because you are, at least for the present, to have them for your ordinary governors, which yourselves shall make choice of for that work. Sundry other things of importance I could put you in mind of, and of those before-mentioned, in more words; but I will not so far wrong your godly minds, as to think you heedless of these things, there being also divers among you so well able both to admonish themselves and others of what concerneth them. These few things therefore, and the same in few words, I do earnestly commend to your care and conscience, joining therein with my daily incessant prayers unto the Lord, that he who has made the heavens and the earth, and sea, and all rivers of waters, and whose providence is over all his works, especially over all his dear children for good, would so guide and guard you in your ways, as inwardly by his spirit, so outwardly by the hand of his power, as that both you, and we also for and with you, may have after matter of praising his name all the days of your and our lives. Fare you well in him in whom you trust, and in whom I rest, an unfeigned well-wisher to your happy success in this hopeful voyage.

JOHN ROBINSON.

APPENDIX II.

THE AUTHORITIES USED IN THIS WORK.

As already mentioned, (p. 118), New England found historians at a very early period. Cotton Mather has treated this subject most at length, and with careful use of his predecessors.

MAGNALIA CHRISTI AMERICANA, or the Ecclesiastical History of New England, from its first planting in the year 1620 unto the year of our Lord 1698, by Cotton Mather, Past. of the North Church in Boston. London 1702. Fol. (republished at Hartford 1820. 2 vols. 8vo.)

The author, whose family on the paternal side has often been mentioned in the foregoing work, was a descendant of the Pilgrims on the mother's side also; being the great grandson of John Cotton, minister at Boston. His work shows great learning and extensive acquaintance with books, but is arranged in the oddest method; abounds with the most unexpected and irrelevant episodes, and his apologetic stand-point is not maintained without prejudice and partiality. What with citations from writers ancient and modern, he often can scarcely make his way to the subject itself; whole pages have frequently no more matter, strictly speaking, than could be expressed in as many lines. Still, the courage of the wearied reader is sustained by the wit and humor, which are displayed even in the titles and superscriptions. The work is divided into seven books. First Book; ANTIQUITIES, (reporting: The design where-*on*, the manner where-*in*, and people where-*by*, the several Colonies of New England were planted,) in seven chapters. Chap. 1. *Venisti tandem?* The early discoveries of America. Chap. 2. *Primordia.* The settlement of New Plymouth. Chap. 3. *Conamur Tenues Grandia.* Farther history of New Plymouth. Chap. 4. *Paulo Majora!* The settlement of Massachusetts. Chap. 5. *Peregrini Deo Curae.* Progress of the new colony. Chap. 6. *Qui trans mare currunt.* Settlements in Connecticut, New Haven, Hampshire, Maine. Chap. 7. *Hecatompolis*, or a field which the Lord hath blessed. A catalogue of the ministers. With a Supplement: "*The Bostonian Ebenezer;* some Historical Remarks on the state of Boston;" and a map, showing the earlier division of New England. The Second Book is entitled: ECCLESIARUM CLYPEI; and contains biographical sketches of the most distinguished early Governors, as well as a catalogue of the Assistants, whom he calls in one place Patres Conscripti, in another, בַּעֲלֵי נֶפֶשׁ id est Viri Animati. Third Book; POLYBIUS, or the Lives of forty-seven Divines. Fourth Book: SAL GENTIUM, or the History of Harvard College, and biographies of eleven eminent persons, who were educated in the University. Fifth Book: ACTS AND MONUMENTS. This is the most important portion of the work, containing the conclusions in full of the Massachusetts Synods, with very interesting extracts from controversial writings. Sixth Book: THAUMATURGUS. The narration of wonderful deliverances at sea (ch. 1. *Christus supra aquas*), and in tempests (ch. 3. *Ceraunius*), is followed by accounts of conversions, of criminal trials, of Missions among the Indians, and finally by stories of demons and witches. Seventh Book: ECCLESIARUM PRŒLIA. (Ch. 1. *Mille nocendi artes.* Of the trials of the New England churches in general. Ch. 2. *Little Foxes.* Roger Williams, and political enemies. Ch. 3. *Hydra decapitata.* The Antinomians and the first Synod of 1637. Ch. 4. *Ignes fatui.* The Quakers, and, very briefly, the Anabaptists. Ch. 5. *Wolves in sheep's clothing.* Imposters, who pretended to be ministers. Ch. 6. *Arma virosque cano.* Wars with the Indians.) — In the numerous biographical sketches, the author's materials often run short, and the deficiency is supplied in a very peculiar fashion. Thus, he knows nothing of Adam Blackman, except that he exercised his ministry in two places, and was very simple and intelligible in his mode of preaching. He begins therefore with a reference to Niger, the teacher at Antioch (Acts 13: 1), expresses the opinion that it could not be said of our Blackman: *hic niger est, hunc tu Romane caveto;* he being rather a Nazarite, purer than snow, whiter than milk. Thereupon he passes to Melancthon, and closes with Beza's epitaph upon him. No one is dismissed without his epitaph, sometimes longer, sometimes shorter. *Avolavit!* suffices for the Rev. Mr. Partridge.

We subjoin the following words of the Abbot Steinmetz in reference to the Magnalia, which occur in his Preface to the Faithful Narrative of the glorious work of God in Northampton; Magdeburg and Leipzig 1738. "It is only to be lamented, that the book is made too prolix by the exuberance of ornaments, which the fertile genius and immense reading of the author threw into his hands. I have therefore readily embraced the proposal to extract the substance of the work, and, if the Lord should accept it as useful for his kingdom, to give it to the press in our language." (This plan has not been as yet carried into execution.) But whatever exceptions may be taken to Mather's exhibition of historical facts, and however much he may have been used by his successors, the numerous legal documents as well as the synodical decisions in full, which are found no where but in his work, render it one of the highest importance.

The foregoing work forms the basis of:

The History of New England to the year of our Lord 1700, by Daniel Neal. 2 vols. 2 ed. London 1747 (1st ed. 1719) 8vo.

Neal, also the author of the History of the Puritans, was an English Dissenter. His chief source was Mather's Magnalia; but he made use of many other works and fugitive writings, and has furnished a very full statistical representation, as well as a statement in alphabetical order of the laws in force in New England. The historical narration is chronologically arranged, and is on the whole unprejudiced and impartial. With a sympathy for the Congregationalists natural in a Dissenter, he has nevertheless examined and used the accounts of those opposed to them. (See above, p. 118.)

From an entirely different stand-point, we have:

A History of New England, with particular reference

TO THE DENOMINATION OF CHRISTIANS CALLED BAPTISTS; by Isaac Backus, Past. of the First Baptist Church in Middleburgh. 2 vols. Boston and Providence 1777 and 1784.

The first volume extends to the year 1690, and is enriched with numerous extracts from the writings of distinguished men, as Robinson, Cotton, Williams. In his account of the treatment of the Baptists, the author takes strong polemic ground against the ruling party and the theocratic constitution in New England; thus supplementing Mather and even Neal. In the second part (down to 1784) are contained many documents relative to the declension in the religious and church life; in this connection is expressed, as might be expected, decided disapproval of the proceedings in Connecticut in 1708.

Owing to the connection of Church and State, much in the representation we have given, especially for the first period, is touched by the political historians. Thus in:

HUTCHINSON'S HISTORY OF MASSACHUSETTS TO THE YEAR 1750. 2 vols. 3 ed. Salem 1765. 8vo. (1st ed. 1764).

The author was Governor of Massachusetts at the breaking out of the Revolution, and was in possession of a very rich collection of original legal documents, which, however, were in great part destroyed during a riot in Boston. The style of representation is very plain; as is also that of the following work, by a clergyman:

BENJAMIN TRUMBULL'S COMPLETE HISTORY OF CONNECTICUT. 2 vols. Hartford 1797. 8 vo.

The first volume, the one used in the foregoing work, extends to the year 1713. It contains also the history of New Haven, and devotes two chapters particularly to the history of the Church. Among other documents we find here the Saybrook Platform, complete.

FRANCIS BAYLIES' HISTORICAL MEMOIR OF NEW PLYMOUTH. 1830. 4 vols. 8vo.

This work extends to the union of New Plymouth with Massachusetts, and is very particular in its details.

Caleb H. Snow's History of Boston from its origin to the present period. 2 ed. Boston 1828.

More in the form of annals; full for a later period.

A Collection of original papers relative to the History of the Colony of Massachusetts Bay. Boston 1769.

Very interesting letters, and important legal documents from the earliest period, chronologically arranged. In the copy in the Berlin Library, a portion is wanting at the end; it extends to November 1655.

For the same period:

J. Winthrop's Journal. Hartford 1790.

This diary of the distinguished first Governor of Massachusetts furnishes a very graphic view of the earlier relations. It extends, however, only to 1644.

The following works have for their stand-point the total separation of Church and State now prevailing in North America.

Memoir of Roger Williams, the Founder of the State of Rhode Island. By James D. Knowles. Boston 1834.

The author, who is a Baptist, regards Williams as the father of those principles, in reference to the relation of Church and State, now established in North America. He is decidedly unfavorable to the Theocracy. Many of his investigations indicate the careful study of richly instructive sources; still we cannot reckon on an impartial judgment, from one who remarks in reference to the occurrences at Munster in 1535: "It seems to have been a just revolt, and a struggle for liberty; but it failed, and the leaders have been stigmatized as fanatics, and as guilty of every species of crime. The story has been told by their oppressors and enemies, and is entitled to very little credit."

The results of very thorough investigation are embodied in:

The History of the Old South Church in Boston, in four sermons by Benjamin B. Wisner, Pastor of the Church. Boston 1830.

This work has been particularly used in Chapter VII. of our history; it has reference chiefly to the relations of the early period. The author exhibits a very clear conception of the essential nature of the Congregationalist Theocracy, though regarding the total separation of Church and State as the salvation of the church.

From the same point of view, still more strongly taken, we have: L' UNION DE L' EGLISE ET DE L' ETAT DANS LA NOUVELLE ANGLETERRE, CONSIDEREE DANS SES EFFETS SUR LA RELIGION AUX ETATS-UNIS. Par un Americain. Paris 1837.

From want of access to the sources, the author's data are insufficient, and indeed incorrect. Much as he extols the Puritans for their piety and morality, the greatness of soul in which they undertook to found their theocracy seems not to be recognized; and the most recent revival of evangelical christianity is treated as a wholly negative result of the completed separation between Church and State.

APPENDIX III.

CHRONOLOGICAL VIEW.

	England.	Expeditions—Settlements—Charters.	Domestic Events.	Indians.
1602	The Independents in the north of England.	Capt. Gosnold in Massachusetts Bay.		
1603	James I.			
1606		Patents for North and South Virginia.		
1608		Settlement on the Sagadahoc, Maine.		
1614		Capt. John Smith. New England.		
1620		Patent for the Plymouth Colony; New Plymouth.		
1623		Bradford's Patent; transferred by him to the Gen'l Court.		
1625	Charles I.		The Colony of New Plymouth separates from the Company.	
1629		Patent for Massachusetts Bay.	Ralph Smith in New Plymouth.	
		Salem and Charlestown.	The Salem Church. The broth's Brown.	
1630		Expedition under John Winthrop. Boston.	Transfer of the Gov't for Massachusetts Bay.	
1633		Newtown (later, Cambridge).		
1634			Controversies with Roger Williams.	
1636		Providence on Narraganset Bay; Hartford, and oth. places on the Connecticut.	Sir Henry Vane in Boston.	
1637	Emigration forbidden.	New Haven. Setlem'ts in N. Hampshire and Maine.	Antinomian Controversies; the first Synod.	Pequot War.

	England.	Expeditions —Settlements — Charters.	Domestic Events.	Indians.
1638			Harvard College founded.	
1640			New Hampshire united with Massachusetts.	
1641	Civil War.			Mayhew.
1643		Patent for Rhode Island and Providence Plantations.	Confederation of the four United Colonies of N. England.	
1646				Eliot.
1647			Agitations in Massachusetts.	
1648	Westmins'r Confession.		Cambridge Synod. (PLATFORM).	
1649	Charles I. executed.			
1651			The Anabaptists in Massachusetts.	
1653	Oliver Cromwell.			
1656			The first Quakers in Boston.	
1657			Religious Agitations; Synods in Connecticut.	
1658	Savoy Confession; Richard Cromwell.			
1660	Charles II.		Excut'n of Quakers.	
1662	Act of Uniformity.		Boston Synod in ref. to Baptism.	
1663		Confirmation of the Charter of Rhode Island.		
1664		Connecticut and N. Haven Charter.	Royal Commissioners in N. England. Attempt of the Baptists to found a Church in Boston.	
1668			Third Church in Boston.	
1676				K. Philip's War.
1679			N. Hamp. separated from Massachus'ts. REFORMING SYNOD.	
1684		Colonies deprived of their Charters.		
1685		James II.	Increase Mather in England.	

	England.	Expeditions—Settlements—Charters.	Domestic Events.	Indians.
1688	Wm. and Mary.			
1689			Revolution in Boston.	
1692	HEADS OF AGREEMENT.	New Charter.	Witch Trials.	Border Wars.
1702	Anne.			
1704			College at Saybrook (afterwards Yale College).	
1708			Saybrook Platform	
1714	George I.			
1725			Proposal for a Synod in Boston.	
1727	George II.			
1735			Awakenings in Northampton.	
1740			The Great Awakenings.	

INDEX.

GOULD & LINCOLN,

PUBLISHERS AND BOOKSELLERS,

59 WASHINGTON STREET, BOSTON.

CHARLES D. GOULD. JOSHUA LINCOLN.

☞ G. & L. would call attention to their extensive list of publications, embracing valuable works in THEOLOGY, SCIENCE, LITERATURE AND ART, TEXT BOOKS FOR SCHOOLS AND COLLEGES and MISCELLANEOUS, etc., in large variety, the productions of some of the ablest writers, and most scientific men of the age, among which will be found those of Chambers, Hugh Miller, Agassiz, Gould, Guyot, Marcou, Bayne, Rogers, Dr. Harris, Dr. Wayland, Dr. Williams, Dr. Ripley, Dr. Kitto, Dr. Krummacher, Dr. Tweedie, Dr. Choules, Dr. Sprague, Newcomb, Banvard, "Walter Aimwell," Bungener, Miall, Archdeacon Hare, and others of like standing and popularity; and to this list they are constantly adding. Among their late publications are the following, viz.:—

Knowledge is Power. The Productive Forces of Modern Society, and the Results of Labor, Capital, and Skill. By KNIGHT. Illustrated. Am. Edi. Revised, with additions. By D. A. WELLS. 12mo. Cloth, $1.25.

Emphatically a book for the people, containing an immense amount of important information, which everybody ought to possess.

Annual of Scientific Discovery in Science and Art, exhibiting the most important Discoveries and Improvements in Mechanics, Useful Arts, Natural Philosophy, Chemistry, Astronomy, Meteorology, Zoology, Botany, Mineralogy, Geology, Geography, Antiquities, &c. Edited by D. A. WELLS, A. M. With a Portrait of Prof. Wyman. 12mo. Cloth, $1.25.

VOLUMES OF THE SAME WORK for 1850, 1851, 1852, 1853, 1854, 1855, 1856. With Portraits. $1.25 per volume.

Chambers' Cyclopædia OF ENGLISH LITERATURE. The choicest productions of English Authors, from the earliest to the present time. Connected by a Biographical History. 2 octavo vols. of 700 pages each. 300 elegant Illustrations. Cloth, $5.

Open where you will, you will find matter for profit and delight. The selections are gems,—"*A whole English Library fused into one Cheap Book!*"

Chambers' Miscellany. With Illustrations. Ten vols. Cloth, $7.50.

Chambers' Home Book. A Choice Selection of Interesting and Instructive Reading, for the Old and Young. 6 vols. 16mo. Cloth, $3.

Cyclopædia of Anecdotes. A Choice Selection of Anecdotes of the various forms of Literature and the Arts, and of the most celebrated Literary Characters and Artists By KAZLITT ARVINE, A. M. With Illustrations. 725 pages, octavo. Cloth, $3.

The choicest collection of anecdotes ever published. It contains 3040 anecdotes, 350 fine illustrations, and such is the wonderful variety, that it will be found an almost inexhaustible fund of interest for every class of readers.

Works by Hugh Miller:

Testimony of the Rocks.
Footprints of the Creator.
Old Red Sand tone.
My First Impressions of England and its People.
My Schools and Schoolmates.

Life of James Montgomery. Abridged from the recent London seven vol. ed. By Mrs. H. C. KNIGHT, author of "Lady Huntington and her Friends." Illustrated. 12mo. Cloth, $1.25.

Essays; in Biography and Criticism. By PETER BAYNE, author of the "Christian Life." 12mo. Cloth, $1.25.

Text Books:

WAYLAND'S *Moral Science and Political Economy.* The same, *abridged.*
BLAKE'S *Philosophy and Astronomy.*
BAILEY'S *Young Ladies' Class-Book.*
DILLAWAY'S *Roman Antiquities.*
PALEY'S *Theology.*
AGASSIZ' and GOULD'S *Zoölogy.*
LOOMIS' *Geology.*
HAVEN'S *Mental Philosophy.*
GUYOT'S *Earth and Man*, and *Mural Maps.*
BARTON'S *Grammar*, and *Exercises in Composition.*

Thesaurus OF ENGLISH WORDS AND PHRASES. So classified as to facilitate the expression of ideas, and to assist in literary composition. By PETER MARK ROGET. Revised and Edited, with a List of Foreign Words defined in English, by BARNAS SEARS, D. D., Pres. of Brown Univ. 12mo. Cloth, $1.50.

Facilitates a writer in seizing upon just the right word for his purpose.

Visits to European Celebrities. By W. B. SPRAGUE, D. D. 12mo. Cl., $1.00.

A series of graphic and life-like Personal Sketches of the most Distinguished Men and Women of Europe.

Cruise of the North Star. The Excursion made to England, Russia, Denmark, France, Spain, Italy, Malta, Turkey, Madeira, etc. By Rev. J. O. CHOULES, D. D. Illustrations, etc. 12mo. Cloth, gilt, $1.50.

The Natural History OF THE HUMAN SPECIES: Its Typical Forms and Primeval Distribution. By CHAS. HAMILTON SMITH. With an Introduction containing an abstract of the views of writers of repute. By SAMUEL KNEELAND, Jr., M. D. With Illustrations. 12mo. Cloth, $1.25.

The Camel: His Organization, Habits and Uses, considered with reference to his introduction into the United States. By GEORGE P. MARSH, late U. S. Minister at Constantinople. 12mo. Cloth, 63 cts.

This book treats of a subject of great interest, especially at the present time. It furnishes the only complete and reliable account of the Camel in the language.

VALUABLE WORKS.

Diary and Correspondence OF THE LATE AMOS LAWRENCE. Edited by his son, WM. R. LAWRENCE, M. D. Octavo, cloth, $1.25; also, royal 12mo. ed., cl., $1.00.

Kitto's Popular Cyclopædia OF BIBLICAL LITERATURE. 500 illustrations. One vol., octavo. 812 pages. Cloth, $3.

Intended for ministers, theological students, parents, Sabbath-school teachers, and the great body of the religious public.

Analytical Concordance of the Holy SCRIPTURES; or, The Bible presented under Classified Heads or Topics. By JOHN EADIE, D. D. Octavo, 836 pp. $3.

Dr. Williams' Works.

Lectures on the Lord's Prayer — Religious Progress — Miscellanies.

☞ Dr. Williams is a profound scholar and a brilliant writer. — *New York Evangelist.*

Modern Atheism. Considered under its forms of Pantheism, Materialism, Secularism, Development and Natural Laws. By JAMES BUCHANAN, D. D., LL. D. 12mo. Cloth, $1.25.

The Hallig: or the Sheepfold in the Waters. A Tale of Humble Life on the Coast of Schleswig. From the German, by Mrs. GEORGE P. MARSH. 12mo. Cl., $1.

The Suffering Saviour. By Dr. KRUMMACHER. 12mo. Cloth, $1.25.

Heaven. By JAMES WM. KIMBALL. 12mo.

Christian's Daily Treasury. Religious Exercise for every Day in the Year. By Rev. E. TEMPLE. 12mo. Cloth, $1.

Wayland's Sermons. Delivered in the Chapel of Brown Univ. 12mo. Cl., $1.00.

Entertaining and Instructive Works FOR THE YOUNG. Elegantly illustrated. 16mo. Cloth, gilt backs.

The American Statesman. Life and Character of Daniel Webster. — *Young Americans Abroad;* or Vacation in Europe. — *The Island Home;* or the Young Cast-aways. — *Pleasant Pages for Young People.* — *The Guiding Star.* — *The Poor Boy and Merchant Prince.*

THE AIMWELL STORIES. Resembling and quite equal to the "Rollo Stories." — *Christian Register.* By WALTER AIMWELL. *Oscar;* or the Boy who had his own way. — *Clinton;* or Boy-Life in the Country. — *Ella;* or Turning over a New Leaf. — *Whistler;* or The Manly Boy. — *Marcus;* or the Boy Tamer.

WORKS BY Rev. HARVEY NEWCOMB. *How to be a Lady.* — *How to be a Man.* — *Anecdotes for Boys.* — *Anecdotes for Girls.*

BANVARD'S SERIES OF AMERICAN HISTORIES. *Plymouth and the Pilgrims.* — *Romance of American History.* — *Novelties of the New World, and Tragic Scenes in the History of Maryland and the old French War.*

God Revealed in Nature and in CHRIST. By Rev. JAMES B. WALKER, Author of "The Philosophy of the Plan of Salvation." 12mo. Cloth, $1.

Philosophy of the Plan of Salvation. New enlarged edition. 12mo. Cloth, 75 c.

Christian Life; SOCIAL AND INDIVIDUAL. By PETER BAYNE. 12mo. Cloth, $1.25.

All agree in pronouncing it one of the most admirable works of the age.

Yahveh Christ; or the Memorial Name. By ALEX. MACWHORTER. With an Introductory Letter, by NATH'L W. TAYLOR, D. D., in Yale Theol. Sem. 16mo. Cloth, 60 c.

The Signet Ring, AND ITS HEAVENLY MOTTO. From the German. 16mo. Cl., 31 c.

The Marriage Ring; or How to Make Home Happy. 18mo. Cloth, gilt, 75 c.

Mothers of the Wise and Good. By JABEZ BURNS, D. D. 16mo, Cloth, 75 c.

☞ A sketch of the mothers of many of the most eminent men of the world.

My Mother; or Recollections of Maternal Influence. 12mo. Cloth, 75c.

The Excellent Woman, with an Introduction, by Rev. W. B. SPRAGUE, D. D. Splendid Illustrations. 12mo. Cloth, $1.

The Progress of Baptist Principles IN THE LAST HUNDRED YEARS. By T. F. CURTIS, Prof. of Theology in the Lewisburg University. 12mo. Cloth, $1.25.

Dr. Harris' Works.

The Great Teacher. — The Great Commission. — The Pre-Adamite Earth. — Man Primeval. — Patriarchy. — Posthumous Works, 4 volumes.

The Better Land; OR THE BELIEVER'S JOURNEY AND FUTURE HOME. By Rev. A. C. THOMPSON. 12mo. Cloth, 85 c.

Kitto's History of Palestine, from the Patriarchal Age to the Present Time. With 200 Illustrations. 12mo. Cloth, $1.25.

An admirable work for the Family, the Sabbath and week-day School Library.

The Priest and the Huguenot; or, PERSECUTION IN THE AGE OF LOUIS XV. From the French of L. F. BUNGENER. Two vols., 12mo. Cloth, $2.25.

This is not only a work of thrilling interest, but is a masterly Protestant production.

The Psalmist. A Collection of Hymns for the Use of Baptist Churches. By BARON STOW and S. F. SMITH. With a SUPPLEMENT, containing an Additional Selection of Hymns, by RICHARD FULLER, D. D., and J. B. JETER, D. D. Published in various sizes, and styles of binding.

This is unquestionably the best collection of Hymns in the English language.

☞ In addition to works published by themselves, they keep an extensive assortment of works in all departments of trade, which they supply at publishers' prices. ☞ They particularly invite the attention of Booksellers, Travelling Agents, Teachers, School Committees, Librarians, Clergymen, and professional men generally (to whom a liberal discount is uniformly made), to their extensive stock. ☞ To persons wishing copies of Text-books, for examination, they will be forwarded, per mail or otherwise, on the reception of *one half* the price of the work desired. ☞ Orders from any part of the country attended to with faithfulness and dispatch.

RECENT PUBLICATIONS.

THE EVIDENCES OF CHRISTIANITY, as exhibited in the writings of its apologists, down to Augustine, by W. J. BOLTON, of Gonville and Caius College, Cambridge. 12mo, cloth. 80 cents.

The essay contained in this volume received the Hulsean prize (about $500) in England. The author is a professor in Gonville and Caius College, Cambridge, and evidently a very learned student of the patristic writings and the whole circle of ecclesiastical history. He has presented to the world in this essay an admirable compendium of the arguments for the truth of Christianity advanced in the works of the Apologetic Fathers during the third, fourth, and fifth centuries of the Christian era. These arguments are classified as being deduced from antecedent probability, from antiquity, from prophecy, from miracles, from the reasonableness of doctrine, from superior morality, and from the success of the Gospel. — *N. Y. Commercial.*

This is a work of deep research, and of great value to the theological student. — *Transcript.*

We had occasion, some time since, to notice this work, when we expressed a high estimate of its merits. We can only say that, in looking through it a second time, our appreciation of both the learning and the ingenuity which it discovers is heightened rather than diminished We thankfully accept such an effort as this of a profound and highly-cultivated mind. — *Puritan Recorder.*

The work bears the marks of great research, and must command the attention and confidence of the Christian world. — *Mercantile Journal.*

THE BETTER LAND; or, Thoughts on Heaven. By A. C. THOMPSON, Pastor of the Eliot Church, Roxbury. 12mo, cloth. $1.00. *Just published.*

THE MISSION OF THE COMFORTER; with copious Notes. By JULIUS CHARLES HARE. Notes translated for the American edition. 12mo, cl. $1.25.

We hardly remember any treatise which is so well calculated to be useful in general circulation among ministers, and the more educated laity, than this, which is rich in spirituality, strong and sound in theology, comprehensive in thought, vigorous and beautiful in imagination, and affluent in learning. — *Congregationalist.*

We have seldom read a book with greater interest. — *N. Y. Evangelist.*

The volume is one of rare value, and will be welcomed as an eloquent and Scriptural exposition of some of the fundamental doctrines of our faith. — *New York Recorder.*

THE VICTORY OF FAITH. By JULIUS CHARLES HARE, author of "The Mission of the Comforter," etc. 12mo, cloth. *In press.*

FIRST LINES OF CHRISTIAN THEOLOGY. In the form of a Syllabus, prepared for the use of Students, with subsequent Additions and Elucidations. By Rev. JOHN PYE SMITH. Edited from the author's manuscripts, with Additional Notes and References, etc. 1 vol. Royal octavo. $5.00.

☞ A most important work for ministers and theological students.

THE RELIGIONS OF THE WORLD, and their relations to Christianity. By FREDERICK DENISON MAURICE, A. M., Professor of Divinity in King's College, London. 16mo, cloth. 60 cents.

The effort we deem masterly, and, in any event, must prove highly interesting by the comparisons which it institutes with the false and the true. His investigations into the Hindoo and Budhist mythologies will itself repay the reader's trouble. — *Methodist Quarterly.*

GUIDO AND JULIUS. THE DOCTRINE OF SIN AND THE PROPITIATOR; or, the True Consecration of the Doubter. Exhibited in the Correspondence of two Friends. By FREDERIS AUGUSTUT O. THOLUCH, D. D. Translated from the German, by JONATHAN EDWARDS RYLAND. With an Introduction by JOHN PYE SMITH, D. D. 16mo, cloth. 60 cents.

☞ It might naturally be expected that a work by authors so distinguished in the literary and religious world would prove one of great interest and value. This expectation will not be disappointed. It is pre-eminently a book for the times — full of interest, and of great power.

WORKS JUST PUBLISHED.

THE BETTER LAND; or, THE BELIEVER'S JOURNEY AND FUTURE HOME. By REV. A. C. THOMPSON. 12mo, cloth. 85 cents.

CONTENTS. — The Pilgrimage — Clusters of Eschol — Waymarks — Glimpses of the Land — The Passage — The Recognition of Friends — The Heavenly Banquet — Children in Heaven — Society of Angels — Society of the Saviour — Heavenly Honor and Riches — No Tears in Heaven — Holiness of Heaven — Activity in Heaven — Resurrection Body — Perpetuity of Bliss in Heaven.

A most charming and instructive book for all now journeying to the "Better Land."

THE SCHOOL OF CHRIST; or, CHRISTIANITY VIEWED IN ITS LEADING ASPECTS. By REV. A. L. R. FOOTE, author of "Incidents in the Life of Our Saviour," &c. 16mo, cloth, 50 cts.

MEMORIES OF A GRANDMOTHER. By a Lady of Massachusetts. 16mo cloth. 50 cents.

"My path lies in a valley which I have sought to adorn with flowers. Shadows from the hills cover it, but I make my own sunshine."

The little volume is gracefully and beautifully written. — *Journal.*

Not unworthy the genius of a Dickens. — *Transcript.*

HOURS WITH EUROPEAN CELEBRITIES. By the REV. WILLIAM B. SPRAGUE, D. D. 12mo, cloth. $1.00. SECOND EDITION.

The author of this work visited Europe in 1828 and in 1836, under circumstances which afforded him an opportunity of making the acquaintance, by personal interviews, of a large number of the most distinguished men and women of that continent; and in his preface he says, "It was my uniform custom, after every such interview, to take copious memoranda of the conversation, including an account of the individual's appearance and manners; in short, defining, as well as I could, the whole impression which his physical, intellectual and moral man had made upon me." From the memoranda thus made, the material for the present instructive and exceedingly interesting volume is derived. Besides these "pen and ink" sketches, the work contains the novel attraction of a fac-simile of the signature of each of the persons introduced.

THE AIMWELL STORIES.

A series of volumes illustrative of youthful character, and combining instruction with amusement. By WALTER AIMWELL, author of "The Boy's Own Guide," "The Boy's Book of Morals and Manners," &c. With numerous Illustrations.

The first three volumes of the series, now ready, are —

OSCAR; or, THE BOY WHO HAD HIS OWN WAY. 16mo, cloth, gilt. 63 cents.

CLINTON; or, BOY-LIFE IN THE COUNTRY. 16mo, cloth, gilt. 63 cents.

ELLA; or, TURNING OVER A NEW LEAF. 16mo, cloth, gilt. 63 cents.

☞ Each volume will be complete and independent of itself, but the series will be connected by a partial identity of character, localities, &c.

THE PLURALITY OF WORLDS. A NEW EDITION. With a SUPPLEMENTARY DIALOGUE, in which the author's reviewers are reviewed. 12mo, cloth. $1

This masterly production, which has excited so much interest in this country and in Europe, will now have an increased attraction in the addition of the Supplement, in which the author's reviewers are triumphantly reviewed.

☞ The Supplement will be furnished separate to those who have the original work.

INFLUENCE OF THE HISTORY OF SCIENCE UPON INTELLECTUAL EDUCATION. By WILLIAM WHEWELL, D. D., of Trinity College, Cambridge Eng., and the alleged author of "Plurality of Worlds." 16mo, cloth. 25 cts

THE LANDING AT CAPE ANNE, or, THE CHARTER OF THE FIRST PERMANENT COLONY ON THE TERRITORY OF THE MASSACHUSETTS COMPANY. Now discovered and first published from the ORIGINAL MANUSCRIPT, with an inquiry into its authority, and a HISTORY OF THE COLONY, 1624–1628. Roger Conant Governor. By JOHN WINGATE THORNTON. 8vo, cloth. $1.50.

This is a curious and exceedingly valuable historical document.

A volume of great interest and importance — *Evening Traveller.*

IMPORTANT NEW WORKS.

THE CHRISTIAN LIFE: Social and Individual. By PETER BAYNE, A. M. 12mo. Cloth. $1.25.

Contents.—PART I. STATEMENT. I. The Individual Life. II. The Social Life. PART II. EXPOSITION AND ILLUSTRATION. *Book I. Christianity the Basis of Social Life.* I. First Principles. II. Howard; and the rise of Philanthropy. III. Wilberforce; and the development of Philanthropy. IV. Budgett; the Christian Freeman. V. The social problem of the age, and one or two hints towards its solution. *Book II. Christianity the Basis of Individual Character.* I. Introductory: a few Words on Modern Doubt. II. John Foster. III. Thomas Arnold. IV. Thomas Chalmers. PART III. OUTLOOK. I. The Positive Philosophy. II. Pantheistic Spiritualism. III. General Conclusion.

PARTICULAR attention is invited to this work. In Scotland, its publication, during the last winter, produced a great sensation. Hugh Miller made it the subject of an elaborate review in his paper, the Edinburgh *Witness*, and gave his readers to understand that it was an extraordinary work. The "*News of the Churches*," the monthly organ of the Scottish Free Church, was equally emphatic in its praise, pronouncing it "the religious book of the season." Strikingly original in plan and brilliant in execution, it far surpasses the expectations raised by the somewhat familiar title. It is, in truth, a bold onslaught (and the first of the kind) upon the Pantheism of Carlyle, Fichte, etc., by an ardent admirer of Carlyle; and at the same time an exhibition of the Christian Life, in its inner principle, and as illustrated in the lives of Howard Wilberforce, Budgett, Foster, Chalmers, etc. The brilliancy and vigor of the author's style are remarkable

PATRIARCHY; or, the Family, its Constitution and Proba By JOHN HARRIS, D. D., President of "New College," London, and author of "The Great Teacher" "Mammon," "Pre-Adamite Earth," "Man Primeval," etc. 12mo. Cloth. $1.25. ☞ **A new work of great interest.**

This is the third and last of a series, by the same author, entitled "Contributions to Theological Science." The plan of this series is highly original, and has been most successfully executed. Of the two first in the series, "Pre-Adamite Earth" and "Man Primeval," we have already issued four and five editions, and the demand still continues. The immense sale of all Dr. Harris's works attest their intrinsic worth. This volume contains most important information and instruction touching the family—its nature and order, parental instruction, parental authority and government, parental responsibility, &c. It contains, in fact, such a fund of valuable information as no pastor, or head of a family, can afford to dispense with.

GOD REVEALED IN NATURE AND IN CHRIST: Including a Refutation of the Development Theory contained in the "Vestiges of the Natural History of Creation." By the Author of "THE PHILOSOPHY OF THE PLAN OF SALVATION." 12mo. Cloth. $1.00.

THE author of that remarkable book, "The Philosophy of the Plan of Salvation," ha devoted several years of incessant labor to the preparation of this work. Without being specifically controversial, its aim is to overthrow several of the popular errors of the day, by establishing the antagonist truth upon an impregnable basis of reason and logic. In opposition to the doctrine of a mere subjective revelation, now so plausibly inculcated by certain eminent writers, it demonstrates the necessity of an external, objective revelation. Especially, it furnishes a new, and as it is conceived, a conclusive argument against the "*development theory*" so ingeniously maintained in the "Vestiges of the Natural History of Creation." As this author does not publish except when he has something to say, there is good reason to anticipate that the work will be one of unusual interest and value. His former book has met with the most signal success in both hemispheres, having passed through numerous editions in England and Scotland, and been translated into four of the European languages besides It is also about to be translated into the Hindoostanee tongue. (m)

IMPORTANT WORKS.

ANALYTICAL CONCORDANCE OF THE HOLY SCRIPTURES;

or, The Bible presented under Distinct and Classified Heads or Topics. By JOHN EADIE, D. D., LL. D., Author of "Biblical Cyclopædia," "Dictionary of the Bible," &c., &c. One volume, royal octavo, 836 pp. Cloth, $3.00; sheep, $3.50. *Just published.*

The publishers would call the special attention of clergymen and others to some of the peculiar features of this great work.

1. It is a concordance of *subjects*, not of *words*. In this it differs from the common concordance, which, of course, it does not supersede. Both are necessary to the Biblical student.

2. It embraces all the topics, both secular and religious, which are naturally suggested by the entire contents of the Bible. In this it differs from Scripture Manuals and Topical Text-books, which are confined to religious or doctrinal topics.

3. It contains *the whole of the Bible without abridgment*, differing in no respect from the Bible in common use, except in the classification of its contents.

4. It contains a synopsis, separate from the concordance, presenting within the compass of a few pages a bird's-eye view of the whole contents.

5. It contains a table of contents, embracing nearly two thousand heads, arranged in alphabetical order.

6. It is much superior to the only other work in the language prepared on the same general plan, and is offered to the public at much less cost.

The purchaser gets not only a *Concordance*, but also a *Bible*, in this volume. The superior convenience arising out of this fact, — saving, as it does, the necessity of having two books at hand and of making two references, instead of one, — will be readily apparent.

The general subjects (under each of which there are a vast number of sub-divisions) are arranged as follows, viz.:

Agriculture,	Genealogy,	Ministers of Religion,	Sacrifice,
Animals,	God,	Miracles,	Scriptures,
Architecture,	Heaven,	Occupations,	Speech,
Army, Arms,	Idolatry, Idols,	Ordinances,	Spirits,
Body,	Jesus Christ,	Parables and Emblems,	Tabernacle and Temple,
Canaan,	Jews,	Persecution,	Vineyard and Orchard,
Covenant,	Laws,	Praise and Prayer,	Visions and Dreams,
Diet and Dress,	Magistrates,	Prophecy,	War,
Disease and Death,	Man,	Providence,	Water.
Earth,	Marriage,	Redemption,	
Family,	Metals and Minerals,	Sabbaths and Holy Days,	

That such a work as this is of exceeding great convenience is matter of obvious remark. But it is much more than that; it is also an instructive work. It is adapted not only to assist the student in prosecuting the investigation of preconceived ideas, but also to impart ideas which the most careful reading of the Bible in its ordinary arrangement might not suggest. Let him take up any one of the subjects — "Agriculture," for example — and see if such be not the case. This feature places the work in a higher grade than that of the common Concordance. It shows it to be, so to speak, a work of more mind.

No Biblical student would willingly dispense with this Concordance when once possessed. It is adapted to the necessities of all classes, — clergymen and theological students; Sabbath-school superintendents and teachers; authors engaged in the composition of religious and even secular works; and, in fine, common readers of the Bible, intent only on their own improvement.

A COMMENTARY ON THE ORIGINAL TEXT OF THE ACTS

OF THE APOSTLES. By Horatio B. Hackett, D. D., Professor of Biblical Literature and Interpretation, in the Newton Theological Institution. ☞ A new, revised, and enlarged edition. Octavo, cloth. *In Press.*

☞ This most important and very popular work, has been throughly revised (some parts being entirely rewritten), and considerably enlarged by the introduction of important new matter, the result of the Author's continued, laborious investigations since the publication of the first edition, aided by the more recent published criticisms on this portion of the Divine Word, by other distinguished Biblical Scholars, in this country and in Europe.

IMPORTANT NEW WORKS.

THE TESTIMONY OF THE ROCKS: or, Geology in its Bearings on the two Theologies, Natural and Revealed. By HUGH MILLER. "Thou shalt be in league with the stones of the field." — *Job.* With numerous elegant illustrations. 12mo, cloth, $1.25.

The completion of this important work employed the last hours of the lamented author, and may be considered his greatest and in fact his life work.

MACAULAY ON SCOTLAND. A Critique. By HUGH MILLER, Author of "Footprints of the Creator," &c. 16mo, flexible cloth, 25c.

When we read Macaulay's last volumes, we said that they wanted nothing but the fiction to make an epic poem; and now it seems that they are not wanting even in that. — PURITAN RECORDER.

He meets the historian at the fountain head, tracks him through the old pamphlets and newspapers on which he relied, and demonstrates that his own authorities are against him. — BOSTON TRANSCRIPT.

THE GREYSON LETTERS. Selections from the Correspondence of R. E. H. GREYSON, Esq. Edited by HENRY ROGERS, Author of "The Eclipse of Faith." 12mo, cloth, $1.25.

"Mr. Greyson and Mr. Rogers are one and the same person. The whole work is from his pen; and every letter is radiant with the genius of the author of the 'Eclipse of Faith.'" It discusses a wide range of subjects in the most attractive manner. It abounds in the keenest wit and humor, satire and logic. It fairly entitles Mr. Rogers to rank with Sydney Smith and Charles Lamb as a wit and humorist, and with Bishop Butler as a reasoner.

If Mr. Rogers lives to accomplish our expectations, we feel little doubt that his name will share, with those of Butler and Pascal, in the gratitude and veneration of posterity. — LONDON QUARTERLY.

Full of acute observation, of subtle analysis, of accurate logic, fine description, apt quotation, pithy remark, and amusing anecdote. . . . A book, not for one hour, but for all hours; not for one mood, but for every mood, to think over, to dream over, to laugh over. — BOSTON JOURNAL.

A truly good book, containing wise, true and original reflections, and written in an attractive style. — Hon. GEO. S. HILLARD, LL. D., in *Boston Courier.*

Mr. Rogers has few equals as a critic, moral philosopher, and defender of truth. . . . This volume is full of entertainment, and full of food for thought, to feed on. — PHILADELPHIA PRESBYTERIAN.

The Letters are intellectual gems, radiant with beauty and the lights of genius, happily intermingling the grave and the gay. — CHRISTIAN OBSERVER.

ESSAYS IN BIOGRAPHY AND CRITICISM. By PETER BAYNE, M. A., Author of "The Christian Life, Social and Individual." Arranged in TWO SERIES, OR PARTS. 12mo, cloth, each, $1.25.

This work is prepared by the author exclusively for his American publishers. It includes eighteen articles, viz.:

FIRST SERIES: — Thomas De Quincy. — Tennyson and his Teachers. — Mrs. Barrett Browning. — Recent Aspects of British Art. — John Ruskin. — Hugh Miller. — The Modern Novel; Dickens, &c. — Ellis, Acton, and Currer Bell. — Charles Kingsley.

SECOND SERIES: — S. T. Coleridge. — T. B. Macaulay. — Alison. — Wellington. — Napoleon. — Plato. — Characteristics of Christian Civilization. — Education in the Nineteenth Century. — The Pulpit and the Press.

LIFE AND CHARACTER OF JAMES MONTGOMERY. Abridged from the recent London, seven volume edition. By MRS. H. C. KNIGHT, Author of "Lady Huntington and her Friends," &c. With a fine likeness and an elegant illustrated title page on steel. 12mo, cloth, $1.25.

This is an original biography prepared from the abundant, but ill-digested materials contained in the seven octavo volumes of the London edition. The great bulk of that work, together with the heavy style of its literary execution, must necessarily prevent its republication in this country. At the same time, the Christian public in America will expect some memoir of a poet whose hymns and sacred melodies have been the delight of every household. This work, it is confidently hoped, will fully satisfy the public [illegible]. It is prepared by one who has already won distinguished laurels in this department of literature. (x)

GOULD AND LINCOLN,

59 WASHINGTON STREET, BOSTON,

Would call particular attention to the following valuable works described in their Catalogue of Publications, viz.:

Hugh Miller's Works.

Bayne's Works. Walker's Works. Miall's Works. Bungener's Work.

Annual of Scientific Discovery. Knight's Knowledge is Power.

Krummacher's Suffering Saviour,

Banvard's American Histories. The Aimwell Stories.

Newcomb's Works. Tweedie's Works. Chambers's Works. Harris' Works.

Kitto's Cyclopædia of Biblical Literature.

Mrs. Knight's Life of Montgomery. Kitto's History of Palestin

Wheewell's Work. Wayland's Works. Agassiz's Works.

William's Works. Guyot's Works.

Thompson's Better Land. Kimball's Heaven. Valuable Works on Missions.

Haven's Mental Philosophy. Buchanan's Modern Atheism.

Cruden's Condensed Concordance. Eadie's Analytical Concordance.

The Psalmist: a Collection of Hymns.

Valuable School Books. Works for Sabbath Schools.

Memoir of Amos Lawrence.

Poetical Works of Milton, Cowper, Scott. Elegant Miniature Volumes.

Arvine's Cyclopædia of Anecdotes.

Ripley's Notes on Gospels, Acts, and Romans.

Sprague's European Celebrities. Marsh's Camel and the Hallig.

Roget's Thesaurus of English Words.

Hackett's Notes on Acts. M'Whorter's Yahveh Christ.

Siebold and Stannius's Comparative Anatomy. Marco's Geological Map, U. S.

Religious and Miscellaneous Works.

Works in the various Departments of Literature, Science and Art.

www.ingramcontent.com/pod-product-compliance
Lightning Source LLC
LaVergne TN
LVHW020236110826
845151LV00003B/938

* 9 7 8 1 4 2 5 5 3 0 3 8 9 *